B-1-4

THE FIRST HUNDRED YEARS OF

WAGNER'S TRISTAN

THE FIRST HUNDRED YEARS OF

WAGNER'S

TRISTAN

BY ELLIOTT ZUCKERMAN

COLUMBIA UNIVERSITY PRESS
NEW YORK AND LONDON
1964

Elliott Zuckerman is a Tutor at St. John's College.

To My Mother

PREFACE

In the last year of his sanity, Nietzsche wrote about the "dangerous fascination" of Wagner's *Tristan and Isolde*. According to *Ecce Homo*, the most profound critic of Wagner's music was still looking for a work "of an equally shivery and sweet infinity"; and he observed that "the world is poor for those who have never been sick enough for this 'voluptuousness of hell.'" Nietzsche's confession suggested the subject of this book. It occurred to me to look for other instances of an infatuation with the music of *Tristan*, among people who are also worthy of interest for other reasons. Not every one I investigated exhibited, as Nietzsche did, the need to pass judgment on his response. But in almost every case there were biographical as well as artistic indications of *Tristan's* power —and there was sufficient evidence to warrant the composition of a history of what I came to call, for short, "Tristanism."

How Wagner went about writing *Tristan* and launching it is the subject of chapters I and II; how listeners have responded to it is the subject of the rest of the book. In the first chapter I have looked into the sources of the extraordinary effectiveness of the music, and said some things about the Tristan legend. Chapter II takes *Tristan* to its first performance, and tells how the work affected the people associated with its early history: this chapter is an essay in comparative biography. Chapter III outlines the classic case of Tristanism—that of Nietzsche. The remaining chapters extend into social history and comparative literature, music criticism and music theory. Chapter IV is about Symbolist poets and French composers, and chapter V about novelists—particularly D. H. Lawrence, Gabriele D'Annunzio, and Thomas Mann. The final chapter brings *Tristan* well into the twentieth century, with an account of its enshrinement by analysts and enthusiasts, and by the theorists of atonalism.

In each chapter my aim was to be selective rather than all-inclusive. But it was necessary, for contrast and elucidation, to enter into the history of Wagnerism. This was done most thoroughly in chapter IV, about Paris, which seemed to provide the material for the clearest contrast between the power of the *Tristan* music and the influence of doctrinaire Wagnerism, particularly of the literary sort. As a consequence the chapter presents a fairly complete brief history of French Wagnerism from about 1850 to the turn of the century.

I have received many helpful suggestions from the people who read these chapters in their first completed form. I wish to record my thanks to Professor Peter Gay, Professor Walter Sokel, Professor Fritz Stern, and Professor Lionel Trilling. My thanks are particularly due to Professor Jacques Barzun, who approved the early outlines of this work and gave me the benefit of his command of fact and style. I am also indebted for assistance to Dr. Eva Brann; to Miss Beate Ruhm von Oppen for help in matters of German history and musical taste; to Miss Elisabeth L. Shoemaker for her intelligent editorial scrutiny; to Miss Judith Sterne, who graciously assisted in correcting the proofs; and to Professor John Rosenberg, who read the manuscript and indicated many ways of increasing interest and clarity.

I must add the names of those whose encouragement sustained me while I wrote this book. They are Mrs. Gustave Siegel, Madame Vera Maurina Press, Dr. Frederick Sobel, Mr. Ralph Zuckerman, Robert and Millicent Pinckert, John and Barbara Rosenberg, and Miss Judith Sterne. First among them was my mother, Mrs. William Cohen. During the most difficult stages the fine work of my friend Robert Kabak, and his devotion to it, provided an example that spurred me on.

My debt, in the early chapters of this book, to the *Life of Richard Wagner* by Ernest Newman should be evident to anyone who knows that thorough and reasonable work. No recent writing about Wagner's life could afford not to lean heavily on those four volumes which set the record straight about so many matters, and proved that works about Wagner can be reverent without being idolatrous.

March, 1964   ELLIOTT ZUCKERMAN

ACKNOWLEDGMENTS

Grateful acknowledgment is made to the following for permission to quote from the book or books indicated:

Doubleday and Co., Inc., for the quotations from the translation by Francis Golffing of Nietzsche's *The Birth of Tragedy and The Genealogy of Morals* (Anchor Books), copyright 1956.

Harcourt, Brace and World, Inc., for the quotation from *The Waste Land* by T. S. Eliot, from *Collected Poems 1909-62*, copyright 1936 by Harcourt, Brace and World, Inc.; copyright 1963, 1964 by T. S. Eliot.

Alfred A. Knopf, Inc., for the quotations from *Essays of Three Decades, Stories of Three Decades, A Sketch of My Life*, and *Buddenbrooks*, by Thomas Mann, all translated by H. T. Lowe-Porter; for the quotations from *The Life of Richard Wagner* and *The Wagner Operas* by Ernest Newman; for the quotations from *The Letters of Hans von Bülow to Richard Wagner, et al.*, edited by Richard Count du Moulin Eckart; and for the quotation of the letter of Thomas Mann in *Metapolitics* by Peter Viereck (reprinted Capricorn Books).

W. W. Norton and Co., Inc., for the quotations from the *Memoirs of Malwida von Meysenbug: Rebel in Bombazine*, edited by Mildred Adams from the translation by Elsa von Meysenbug Lyons.

The Oxford University Press, for the quotation from *French Music, from the Death of Berlioz to the Death of Fauré*, by Martin Cooper.

The Philosophical Library, for the quotations from Nietzsche's *Unpublished Letters*, translated by Kurt F. Leidecker.

Laurence Pollinger Limited and the Estate of the Late Mrs. Frieda Lawrence, for the quotations from *The Trespasser* by D. H. Lawrence, published by William Heinemann, Ltd.

The Public Trustee and The Society of Authors, for the extract from "Bayreuth and Back" by Bernard Shaw, reprinted in *How to Become a Musical Critic*, edited by Dan. H. Laurence (Hill and Wang, 1961).

CONTENTS

chapter I

SCHOPENHAUER, THE MYTH, AND

THE MUSIC (1854-1859)

The World as Will

In the autumn of 1854 the poet Georg Herwegh recommended the philosophy of Schopenhauer to Richard Wagner. Nothing Herwegh did was more important. Although Wagner did not easily acknowledge indebtedness, he repeatedly admitted that reading Schopenhauer changed the course of his life.[1] After studying *The World as Will and Idea* he revised his theories and reconsidered the meaning of his largest work, of which one third of the music had already been written. The new ideas also contributed to the remarkable expansion of his musical powers that occurred in the middle of his career. Schopenhauer seemed to justify Wagner's gloomiest moods and to encourage his most extravagant displays of emotion. In his later music dramas Wagner imposed these moods and emotions on European culture.

Three years earlier, in a diffuse and idiosyncratic volume of prose, Wagner had expounded his theory of the synthesis of music, poetry, and drama in a Total Work of Art. Now he modified that theory in accordance with Schopenhauer's view that music is the most powerful and expressive of the arts. Moreover, Wagner's misunderstanding of Schopenhauer's pessimism confirmed changes in the resolution of the *Ring,* which had been sketched out in a spirit of revolutionary optimism after 1848, and was to be finished twenty-four years later in a splendid medley of renunciation and self-destruction. But the modification of the great tetralogy is overshadowed by a more direct result of Schopenhauer's influence. For Wagner's further study of the philosophy led to the day in July, 1857, when he abandoned the young Siegfried under a linden tree in Fafnir's forest and took up the composition of *Tristan und Isolde*.[2]

Schopenhauer's masterpiece was at that time by no means the required reading for European intellectuals that it was to become by the end of the century. Published in 1819, it was not reprinted until 1844. The professors of philosophy ignored it—willfully so, according to the embittered and anti-Hegelian author.[3] Not until 1853 was it brought to the attention of the literary world, in an article on "Iconoclasm in German Philosophy" in *The Westminster Review*.[4] The community of political exiles in Zurich, which included Herwegh and Wagner, was among those aroused by the revival of interest in romantic pessimism. The new cult required a third edition of the work in 1859, shortly before Schopenhauer's death. The cult, however, could not have been widespread, for in 1865 it had not yet reached the young Nietzsche, who came across Schopenhauer's essays accidentally while browsing in a secondhand book shop. And as late as the eighties the poets of French symbolism looked upon Schopenhauer as their fresh discovery.[5]

Wagner astonished his circle in Zurich by the speed with which he seemed to assimilate the new philosophy.[6] Soon Schopenhauer was added to the *Ring* and the request for money as a recurrent subject in his long letters to his friends; and Wagner began to lecture on the World as Will to the social gatherings of princesses and musicians who, for the main entertainment of the evening, had to hear the text of entire acts of the tetralogy read to them aloud.[7] Like Nietzsche a decade later, Wagner was particularly impressed by Schopenhauer's noble conception of music; and one would suppose that Wagner's self-pity was corroborated by Schopenhauer's observation that geniuses must endure the maximum of suffering.

But what drew him to reread the philosophy—and to study the difficult post-Kantian metaphysics on which Schopenhauer had based his appealing aesthetics—were the ideas about renunciation and negation of the will. Such ideas Wagner found particularly captivating because he himself had anticipated them in the poems of *The Flying Dutchman, Tannhäuser,* and *Lohengrin.*

Despite the implications of these operas, Wagner's explicit philosophy had been positivist and optimistic. The world could be improved through some kind of social regeneration—and Wagner was in exile because in 1849, with Röckel and Bakunin, he had participated in one of the attempts to effect the revolution. Now he could reasonably abandon this "Hellenic optimism," which had inspired the original poem and plot of *Siegfrieds Tod,* in favor of a pessimistic philosophy which clearly expounded what his artistic intuition had been telling him all along.[8] Soon after he read Schopenhauer he was openly disparaging Feuerbach, to whom he had once gratefully dedicated his essay on "The Art-work of the Future."* The dusk of the Gods found its justification, and the budding conception of *Tristan* was nourished by well-reasoned arguments for the denial of the will to live.

"The final negation of the desire for life," Wagner wrote to Liszt, "is Schopenhauer's chief idea." It is, Wagner admits, a terribly stern idea, but it offers the only salvation possible. He hastens to add that the idea is not new to him: indeed, it cannot be conceived by anyone in whose mind it does not already exist. But not until he read Schopenhauer did he find the idea expounded clearly. He then gives Liszt an example of the newfound clarity:

When I look back on the storms of my heart, and on the terrible convulsions with which, against its will, it has clung to the hope of life—when, indeed, these storms have swelled, as they often still do, to hurricane proportions—I have now found a *quietus* that at last helps me to sleep in wakeful nights. This is the heart-felt and intense longing

* *Das Kunstwerk der Zukunft* (1850). "Art-work" for *Kunstwerk* and "Total-art-work" for *Gesamtkunstwerk* are admittedly unidiomatic, but they have become familiar through the standard English translations of Wagner's prose works, and have almost the status of technical terms. "Work of art" and "total work of art" do not sound Wagnerian enough.

for death, for complete unconsciousness, total non-existence, the disappearance of all dreams—the only final salvation.[9]

Wagner's private meditations on Schopenhauer seem like studies for the text of *Tristan* without the rhyme; and it is fitting that the letter which includes this prose-poem about Nirvana also contains Wagner's first reference to his plans to write his musical memorial to death in love. Despite his protestations, in no sense of the word was Wagner's "will" to be denied. Bernard Shaw notes how in consecutive letters to the same correspondent Wagner could preach the renunciation of the will to live and, with equal enthusiasm, describe his undertaking of "a most beneficial course of hydropathy."[10] Four monumental music-dramas and the construction of an operatic empire still lay ahead of this seeker after a *quietus*. And these projects would require renunciation on the part of almost everybody connected with them *except* himself.

"Opera and Drama" Revised

In his major theoretical work, *Opera and Drama*, published in 1851, Wagner had expounded the presumably new and later famous theory of the *Gesamtkunstwerk*.[11] Poetry, music, drama, and spectacle were to be aesthetically synthesized, and Wagner went so far as to deny the validity of any of them as an independent form of art. Each art fully reveals its best qualities only when it is cooperatively subordinate to the total purpose—like the citizen in an organic state.

Schopenhauer's view of art rejects such a synthesis. Music should not be subordinated to the other arts, because it is superior to them: while they merely represent the world of phenomena, music directly expresses the world as Will. In fact Schopenhauer explicitly condemned what he considered the barbaric habit in opera of joining music too closely to words and action. If music can express the inner nature of the will itself, it ought not to be required to imitate appearances.[12]

Not until his later years did Wagner formulate an entirely new theory of art-synthesis based upon Schopenhauer's aesthetics. His essay on Beethoven appeared in 1870, at the time when a reverent visitor to Wagner's home had begun to formulate the most far-reaching interpretation of Schopenhauer's ideas about art, *The Birth of Tragedy;* and the Beethoven essay reveals that by then the old Wagner was as thoroughly Schopenhauerian as the young Wagnerite. But well before that time Wagner had begun to adopt the view that music, as he wrote to Liszt as early as 1855, was "the artistic proto-image of the world itself."[13] And he attempted to incorporate the view even into those essays in which the thesis of *Opera and Drama* is ostensibly maintained.*

In 1861 Wagner took the occasion of the publication of a French prose translation of four of his dramas (including *Tristan*) to write a preface intended as a restatement of his aesthetic ideas. The quotation marks of the title of the preface—"Music of the Future"—were supposed to indicate that Wagner was annoyed by the errors and prejudices which had been associated with his avant-garde theory ever since the publication of "The Art-work of the Future" in 1850, and which the new essay was designed to dispel.[14] But the essay is not an accurate restatement of the theories that were now more than a decade old. Wagner even admits that he has not re-read the works he has been asked to summarize. He is no longer, he says, in the proper frame of mind for "threading through that labyrinth of theoretical speculation"[15]—a change of mood, it may be noted, that came too late to save the friends to whom, in the winter of 1851, he had read the entire text of *Opera and Drama*, in the course of twelve evenings.†

Wagner was nevertheless committed to defending his old theory of art-synthesis. At the same time, he had come to accept Schopenhauer's welcome arguments for the uniqueness of music. The prob-

---

* This is demonstrated by Jack M. Stein, in *Richard Wagner and the Synthesis of the Arts* (Detroit, Wayne State University Press, 1960). Stein shows that Wagner's later works must be judged according to the aesthetics of the later theoretical essays, and not—as has usually been the case—according to the theories of *Opera and Drama.*

† Wagner did not read the proofs of *Oper und Drama.* Later on he tried to inflict on Nietzsche the proofreading of *Mein Leben*—nearly a thousand pages, type-set by an Italian ignorant of German.

lem was to find a theoretical justification for adding words and action to a form of art whose superior expressiveness required no supplement. Why, in short, write musical dramas when the symphony, as Beethoven composed it, was already the most dramatic music? According to Wagner's interpretation of Schopenhauer, it is possible that the direct revelations of pure music can confuse the human understanding. This is because they express movements in a world that is beyond (or, to be more strictly Schopenhauerian, "within") the world of logical relation and causality. Here is where the drama and its ancillaries can help. The poet-dramatist depicts an action that convinces in the more ordinary manner. This lifelike action arouses in the beholder a sympathetic interest, which can in turn raise him to an ecstatic state where he finds the supra-logical revelations of the music intelligible.[16] As Nietzsche later codified a similar relationship, the "Apollonian" drama functions as intermediary between the audience and the otherwise incomprehensible or unbearable "Dionysian" music.

In Wagner's essay, as in *The Birth of Tragedy*, the poet-dramatist is seen as providing the connection with the phenomenal world that makes the music intelligible to the listener. Now *Opera and Drama* had already stressed the importance of the poet-dramatist's role, to the degree of insisting on the efficacy of every consonant and every gesture; and it was well known how severely Wagner had attacked the composers who set their melodic formulas to tailor-made librettos written by subservient librettists. The most polemical of Wagner's prose works had, in fact, been directed against a prevailing operatic tradition that was too exclusively musical—although the musicality was, in Wagner's opinion, vocal and decorative rather than dramatic. In each successive theoretical work Wagner departed further from the extreme position of *Opera and Drama*, in the direction of allotting to music a greater part in the famous synthesis; and the signicant advantage of the new formulation in "The Music of the Future" was that it allowed the composer to exercise his powers with a minimum of restraint.

In an imaginary dialogue between the operatic collaborators,

Wagner has the Poet tell the Composer that he may "plunge fear-lessly into the full tide of the sea of music":

Hand in hand with me you can never lose touch with what is most comprehensible to everyone; for because of me you stand on the solid ground of the dramatic action, and that action at the moment of its presentation on the stage is the most directly understandable of all poems.

"Expand your melody boldly," the Poet goes on to say, "so that it pours like a ceaseless stream" over the entire work. "In it say what I refrain from saying because only you can say it, and silently I will utter everything because it is my hand that guides you."[17]

Before this was written Wagner the Poet had allowed Wagner the Composer to take the musical plunge. Music had already "poured like a ceaseless stream"—into the second and third acts of *Tristan*. The water metaphors are *Tristan* metaphors. Nietzsche similarly associated the Dionysian music of *Tristan* with diving, swimming, and drowning; and from *The Birth of Tragedy* to D'Annunzio's *Triumph of Death*, in the songs of Swinburne and the stories of Thomas Mann, Wagner's chromaticism has connoted the ocean. But we do not need the verification of maritime imagery to know that in "The Music of the Future" Wagner had in mind the music he had most recently finished. It was when composing *Tristan* that Wagner had at last found himself able to move with complete freedom, rather like the student who, having studied strict counterpoint, is allowed to compose a free fugue. At that time, Wagner tells us, he forgot all his theories: he had the sense that with *Tristan* he had far surpassed any system. And it was then that he discovered that there is no greater delight for the artist than the entirely *un*critical frame of mind he experiences while creating.[18] When the critical faculties returned, the new theoretical essay had to justify the unforeseen dominance of the music. Wagner now had to allow unrestricted freedom to the composer who had earlier been restrained within a highly disciplined relationship. The older and widely known ideas of the *Gesamtkunstwerk* had been imperfectly but recognizably exemplified in the first two parts of the *Ring*. In most of *Tristan*, on the other hand, the music had done its work independently of the other arts.

Born of the Spirit of Music

Wagner always wrote and sometimes published his poems before he began to compose the music. But as early as 1844 (before the completion of *Tannhäuser*) he had told a correspondent that when he sat down to write a verse or a plot he was "already intoxicated by the musical aroma" of his subject.[19] There is little indication that he began the poems of the earlier operas with anything more than this general sense of what the music would be like. And the main text of the *Ring* was written during a long period, after *Lohengrin*, in which his musical powers had been put aside for ripening. But in the case of *Tristan* there is every sign that the music began to assert its chromatic will even before Wagner had drawn up a dramatic scenario.[20]

Nine months before he drafted the poem, he told the Princess Marie Wittgenstein that Tristan was intruding on Siegfried "in the shape of a melodic thread which . . . kept on spinning itself, so that I could have spent the whole day developing it." The few bars he wrote down have been identified as a first version of an important theme in the love-duet.[21] A week later Wagner informed Otto Wesendonk that he could no longer get into the mood for *Siegfried:* his musical sensibility was already reaching "far beyond that, into a realm more consonant with my mood—the realm of melancholy."[22] Later on he could refer to parts of *Tristan* as "*only music as yet.*"[23] And after the text had been completed and the sketch of the score begun, letter upon letter indicates that the music, as Schopenhauer might have predicted, kept revealing to him the deepest implications of the poem.

Ernest Newman adduces additional evidence to demonstrate that "if ever there was an opera born of the spirit of music itself it is *Tristan and Isolde*."[24] For Newman, as for Nietzsche, *Tristan* was an example of tragedy that is born *aus dem Geiste der Musik*. Another Wagnerite goes so far as to argue that music itself is the subject of *Tristan*—"music as identified with love, woman, night, and the yearning for death."[25] The corollary of these conclusions is, as Newman tells the readers of his summary of *Tristan*, that "the bulk of the opera would make an organic whole if played through by the orchestra without the voices."[26] Long before, Schopenhauer had observed that the best operatic music "has a wholly independent, separate, and as it were abstract existence by itself, to which the incidents and characters of the piece are foreign, and which follows its own unchangeable rules; it can therefore be completely effective even without the text."[27] No doubt Schopenhauer had in mind the melodies of his favorite Rossini, which he considered separable from the most ludicrous farce to which they might have been attached. But his observation now seems more immediately applicable to the work in which Wagner was most unrestrained in his determination no longer to use the orchestra, as he thought it had been used in Italian opera, "like a monstrous guitar."[28]

There is good argument, then, in favor of the "symphonic syntheses" of *Tristan* we used to hear before the days of complete opera recordings; or the performances, still to be heard, of the Prelude-and-*Liebestod*—originally arranged, it should be noted, by Wagner himself. In a purely orchestral Night of Love we do not have to see the soloists, or strain to hear the syllables of their metaphysical soliloquies. "To all intents and purposes," an unsympathetic critic once decided, *Tristan* is "a symphonic poem to which voice parts have been not too skilfully added."[29] If it is not strictly true that the voice parts were superimposed—the verses, at least, were there from the start—they do seem to be carried along by the orchestral wave, and sometimes to sink into it. Apart, perhaps, from the narratives and dialogues of the first act, *Tristan* is a vast symphonic poem. Moreover, it is not the sort of symphonic poem that illustrates a program. The literalness and subservience to a story that were the requirements of some post-Wagnerian tone poems may, to be sure, be traceable to Wagner, but they are early Wagnerian, not Tristanesque. The formulas of Richard Strauss derive from the pre-*Tristan* style of the *Ring* (while his hopping diatonic tunes derive from the work which followed *Tristan, Die Meistersinger*). There is another kind of symphonic poem the aim of which is not illustration but dramatization. Such, at any rate, was the intention of Liszt, and with the best of Liszt's orchestral dramas the attached programs are supererogatory commentaries on music that is self-sufficient. *Tristan*, composed at the end of the decade in which Liszt invented his new form, has properly been described as "the most eloquent vindication of the Lisztian ideals."[30]

Wagner got to know the symphonic poems of Liszt at the time when *Tristan* was incubating. "They are the only music which occupies me at present," he told Liszt in the summer of 1856. "Every day I read through one score or another, and each time I feel as if I had dived down into some crystal water."[31] After the warmer water of *Tristan* had begun to flow, Wagner was annoyed whenever it was observed that he had been influenced by Liszt— an almost certain confirmation that the observation was true. Liszt at least escaped the public abuse which was Wagner's reward for Meyerbeer, Mendelssohn, and other "Jewish" composers unlucky enough to have provided parts of the Wagnerian language. "Of course, there are things we are quite willing to admit among ourselves," Wagner complained to Hans von Bülow, after a young Wagnerite had published an article unapproved by the Master, "such as, for example, that since I got to know Liszt's compositions, I have become a very different sort of harmonist from what I was formerly. But when friend Pohl blabs this secret to all the world, right at the head of a short article discussing the Prelude to *Tristan and Isolde*, it is, to say the least, indiscreet."[32]

The music of *Tristan*, however, betrays the secret without the help of Richard Pohl's indiscretion. Nor did Wagner hide the debt to Liszt when he observed that *Tristan* was "more thoroughly musical" than his earlier works, and that in it he had "poured himself out in music" as if he had been "writing a symphony."[33]

For his most thoroughly musical work, Wagner had composed a poem which was, as he put it, "altogether built for music."[34] The prosody shows a departure from the austere principles of *Opera and Drama* in order to give the music predominance. Rhyme, for example, which had been banished from the *Ring* in favor of insistent alliteration, reappears in *Tristan*. The emphasis on vowel sounds that rhyme provides is especially useful in the long lyrical sections where the words are little more than singable syllables: it is significant that there are more than twice as many rhymes in the symphonic second act as in the first act, which is chiefly narrative.[35] The alliteration that is carried over from the *Ring* seems less harsh and gutteral than it does in that clanging world of dwarfs and giants; it gives way to an assonance which does not interrupt the musical line with staccato consonants, but allows the words to merge into a continuous sound. Words can convey little meaning when they are prolonged as they are in Brangaene's warning song, or distorted as they are at the climax of the love-duet, where they are further disguised by canonic imitation. But in both cases the orchestra is sounding its richest harmonies.

The first act, to be sure, still contains textbook examples of that literal paralleling of words and music which is characteristic of *Das Rheingold* and *Die Walküre*. In Isolde's Narrative, for example, Tristan's name is sung to a descending fifth, shortly after his pseudonym "Tantris" has been sung to the same interval ascending.[36] The contrast between the two phrases in which the names appear is reinforced by rhyme, alliteration, modulation, and tone color. Thus half the battery of the Wagnerian arsenal is called into duty to draw attention to a naive anagram.* Such literalness is far less frequent in acts two and three. Once the love potion has been

---

* Apparently the audience of the medieval romancers enjoyed the wordplay as much as Wagner's audience is expected to enjoy its musical embellishment. "They sound so similar," observes Gottfried von Strassburg's Isolde, as she tries the two names on her tongue; "There is surely some mystery here?" Later she explains the solution to her mother: "I . . . found that the letters needed for either were exactly the same. For, whichever way I read it, it contained only 'Tantris' or 'Tristan,' and both were comprised in either. Now, mother, divide this name Tantris into a 'tan' and a 'tris,' and say the 'tris' before the 'tan,' and you will say 'Tristan.' Say the 'tan' before the 'tris,' and you will say 'Tantris' again!" "Bless me!" said Isolde's mother. "However did you come to think of that?" Translation by A. T. Hatto (Baltimore, Penguin Books, 1960), pp. 174, 181.

drunk, the characteristic *Tristan*-music drowns such details. Indeed, throughout a great part of Tristan's monologue in the third act the voice is quite properly lost in the mass of orchestral sound.

The complex interweaving of leitmotifs in this turbulent monologue best illustrates the difference between the total-art-works of the *Opera and Drama* period and most of *Tristan*. In the earlier works of the *Ring* the motifs representing the various characters and objects are unambiguous—of the sort that suggested to Saint-Saëns the analogy of visitors presenting their calling-cards in person.[37] But few of the leitmotifs that are interwoven into the symphonic texture of *Tristan* are identifiable with particular things or simple emotions. Instead they represent interrelated psychological states which have been proven unlabelable by a century of argument among writers of thematic guides. Most of the motifs in the second and third acts originate in the orchestra and are therefore not even associable—as are so many in the *Ring*—with words of the vocal line. *Tristan* is least open to the criticism that in Wagner everything happens twice over, the orchestra mechanically repeating every detail of the action on stage. Much of the propelling action of *Tristan* occurs exclusively in the orchestra, which, in fulfillment of the highest aesthetic role assigned to music by Schopenhauer, expresses the otherwise inarticulable emotions of the characters.*

"Spectacle dans un Fauteuil avec Orchestre"

To fulfill Schopenhauer's ideal in a new work had not been Wagner's avowed reason for putting aside the grandiose complications of the *Ring* in the summer of 1857. He did, in letters, admit to his "boundless longing to revel in music," and speak of raising a monument to Love. But his public excuse was that he planned to write a "practical" opera for an "ordinary theater."[38] The small theater

---

* One could imagine a nineteenth-century Gluck saying that *Tristan* was excessively musical. Gluck had complained of too many arias, pointless repeats, and virtuoso display. His successor would condemn instead the excesses of "endless melody" and relentlessly repeated harmonic progressions. It should be noted that Gluck himself, in his best music, no more closely adhered to his theory that made music the handmaiden of poetry than Wagner, in *Tristan*, followed the dictates of *Opera and Drama*.

at Strasbourg was chosen for the debut, until the producer and theater-historian, Eduard Devrient, happy to learn that Wagner had at last cut his canvas to a reasonable size, and bringing news of the good will of the grand duke of Baden, switched Wagner's hopes to Karlsruhe. Yet *Tristan* was not produced until six years after its completion, having been abandoned as unproducible by half a dozen opera companies.

The new work did in some ways turn out to be more practical than the uncompleted tetralogy; it required fewer leading singers —one in each of the five standard voice ranges—and no special scenic effects: no action that took place under water, no magic fire, and no dragons. But shortly after its inception *Tristan* began to take on the accretions of Buddhism and Novalis, and the ruminations about Night, Day, Love, and Death, which turned the simple libretto into a philosophical document. These additions extended the text of the major roles to a length that frightened away all singers except, eventually, two who were unusually idealistic and hard-working. And at no time in the course of its composition was *Tristan* modest in its musical dimensions. Thus the "practicality" of the opera consisted merely in making more demands on the talents of the singers than on those of the engineers.[39]

In comparison with the complex goings on at Valhalla and Nibelheim, or the elaborate farce in the streets of Nuremberg, the plot of *Tristan* is bare. It requires a summary of three short paragraphs, and most of that is taken up with an account (repeated twice in the course of the opera) of what happened before the action begins.* So much more room, then, for the long monologues and the very long duet which take up almost four of the five hours of performance. Into the long stretches of static situation which lay between the rare moments of stage action, Wagner could pour his philosophical paradoxes—and his overrich harmonies. The simple plot—Saint-Saëns called it a "spectacle dans un fauteuil avec orchestre"—left ample space for musical reveling.[40]

Wagner's source for the legend was a modern German rendering

---

*Wagner did not agree with Gottfried von Strassburg that "there is no need to serve [the listener] with the same account twice running" (Hatto translation, p. 88).

of the most beautiful medieval version, that of Gottfried von Strassburg. Gottfried had used as his scaffolding the version of Thomas of Britain, but he rejected many of what he considered to be the more naïve details that had accreted to the traditional legend, and embellished it instead with the language of erotic mysticism.[41] Some of Gottfried's favorite themes found their way into the music-drama. He delighted, for example, in descriptions of the hunt—the same hunt whose horn-sounds are diffused in the music of Wagner's second act. Music itself is a theme of Gottfried's poem: the young Tristan, an accomplished harpist, had once tutored the lady Isolde in the playing of stringed instruments. Wagner makes the most use, however, of Gottfried's repeated observations about the glances and gazes of lovers. "Where lovers gaze into each other's eyes," Gottfried observed, "they feed love's fire apace"; and it is because they cannot refrain from "ensnaring each other's eyes with tender glances" that Tristan and Isolde are recognized as lovers at King Mark's court.[42] Wagner's Isolde tells in her autobiographical narration how she had refrained from killing the sick Tristan because of the way he looked into her eyes. The motif which accompanies her account—it is repeated, of course, when the lovers have drunk the potion and gaze at each other—is interwoven with motifs of anguish and desire at the climax of the Prelude.

The medieval poems were spun out to great length by means of magical interventions and unexpected turns of fate. On occasion the lovers seem inconsistently to be carried away by the enthusiastic cleverness with which they devise the schemes and counterplots which prolong the narrative. In the interest of dramatic simplicity, Wagner had to condense the plot, into what he called "three main situations of drastic intent."[43] He reduced the group of conspirators against Tristan to one man, and he cut out entirely the "other" Isolde (of the White Hands). All the subplots and extra narratives were eliminated, leaving him with the barest and most believable elements of the legend.

Even the one magical element Wagner must retain—the drinking of the love potion—is rationalized. In Gottfried's poem the lovers, casually thirsty, drink the potion by mistake. There is no death potion, and, although Isolde hates Tristan, no indication that she plans to kill him (or herself) on the way to Cornwall. Nor can it be assumed that she is already in love with Tristan, and wants him to marry her. According to Gottfried, it is her mother's intervention, her ladylike delicacy, and then Brangaene's advice, that prevent her from killing Tristan when she recognizes him as the slayer of Morold; she also wants to save herself from marrying an unpleasant steward.[44] There is no suggestion that she was deterred by a twelfth-century equivalent of subconscious love. Wagner's Isolde, on the other hand, reveals unmistakably (for the leitmotifs keep making the point) that her hatred for Tristan is really love; and Tristan himself, in what may be called his third-act self-analysis, comes to the tragic recognition that he "brewed the love-potion himself."* Brangaene's substitution allows them to acknowledge a suicidal attraction that they had long felt and disguised. For Wagner the potion is not the agent of a magical enchantment, but the symbol of a passion that is psychologically inevitable.[45]

Gottfried had addressed his poem to the "edele herzen"—an elite of lofty spirits who could understand a love experience that was expressed mystically.[46] Wagner wrote for an Audience of the Future—by 1872 the audience had been found—who would think of themselves as enlightened, and whose enlightenment demanded literal explicitness. He had also persuaded himself that he was reviving the traditions of Attic drama. For these reasons he is careful to endow his characters with up-to-date motivations, whatever strange symbolic actions they may have to go through, and however single-minded they may be. Wagner is post-romantic: his characters would perhaps seem less out of place in the middle plays of Ibsen than in the operas of Weber—or in the medieval legends the characters derive from. Romances were Wagner's sources, but

---

* "Ich selbst, ich hab' ihn gebrau't!" This modern conception is foreign to Gottfried.

he eliminated from them what was superficially irrational or irrelevantly picturesque.[47] When reading Wolfram von Eschenbach
(for *Parsifal*) Wagner was annoyed because the profundity of the
poem was so often reduced into what he thought were "insubstantial fantasies."[48] He was equally disappointed with the art of
Gottfried. Wagner's plots remain legendary, but never fanciful,
and his characters are mythical without being either charming or
absurd (although the singers may unwittingly convey these qualities). The enchantments and transformations, the parallel narratives
and recurrent images of the medieval tales seem capricious and in-
explicable. Similar devices in Wagner have the opposite effect, for
there are musical clues to the meaning of every symbol. The
medieval poet may be said to display "fancy" and "imagination"—
the romantic terms that could never suitably describe the faculties
of will and calculation whereby Wagner projected his ego into an
oversized and slowed-down medieval setting. If there is a sameness
about Wagner's characters, if most of them seem to be motivated
by similar aggressive impulses, it is because they are extensions of
his own personality, objectified passions in the display of his
megalomania.

In his book about the Tristan legend, Denis de Rougemont discusses the unrealistic, dreamlike quality of the romances, and tries
to account for the puzzling contradictions that lie at every turn of
the story.[49] Their function, he concludes, is to extend the narrative
—the forward motion of the story having been far more important
to the medieval poet and his audience than any concern for consistency in the psychology of the lovers or among the various codes
of chivalry that were conveniently invoked.[50] The narrative had to
be extended in order to excite and intensify the feelings that were
attendant upon the separation of the lovers. Each time Tristan and
Iseult were parted their longing—and the audience's sympathy
with it—increased; and if it happened that there was nothing in
the immediate circumstances to obstruct or separate the lovers,
then apparently any pretext could have been acceptably invented.
In the countless retellings of the legend, from neoclassical tragedies

to novels of adultery and French films, the point and pleasure of the story which seems to have captivated the sensibility of European man has, according to Rougemont, always been in the sympathy felt for the unfulfilled longing of star-crossed lovers.

Wagner sacrificed the extended narrative on which the medieval poems depended, and at the same time managed to intensify the meaning of the myth. What the romances did by means of narrative he did in the orchestra. The longing that Rougemont considers the soul of the myth can be conveyed—as many audiences ignorant of German and uninterested in the details of the stage action have discovered—without Wagner's poetry and story, even without the singers, simply in orchestral transcription. The longing of the lovers is merely objectified in the poem and plot: it is expressed directly in the music. Although Rougemont does not use the Schopenhauerian formulation, he comes to the same conclusion when he observes that in Wagner the myth has been charged with its fullest virulence: "Music alone," according to Rougemont, "could utter the unutterable, and music forced the final secret of Tristan."[51]

Harmony

It was Wagner's new power as a harmonist that enabled him to utter the unutterable. As a melodist and rhythmist he had always been deficient: in his later works his melodic and rhythmic weaknesses may be expertly hidden but they are never overcome. Nietzsche knew this when he insisted that "unending melody" was not melody at all and that Wagner's music never "danced." Wagner's undeniable harmonic powers, on the other hand, burst into full force in *Tristan*—the work to which Nietzsche never ceased responding. Modulation and harmonic coloration account for *Tristan's* characteristic effectiveness.*

The famous First Chord proclaims this fact. When played on the piano, this single harmonic cluster—it is a matter of debate

* Verdi's *Otello* comes naturally to mind as a foil to *Tristan*: so rich in melody and piquant in rhythm, it epitomizes the "Mediterranean" music which Nietzsche recommends as the antidote to Wagnerism, choosing, *faute de mieux*, Bizet's *Carmen* as his example.

whether it ought to be called a chord—can summon up the sound of *Tristan*.* No tune or leitmotif could evoke the work's predominant mood so economically and no rhythmic trope could do it at all.[52] Not much that is essential to the effect of *Tristan* is lost in harmonic reduction of the score. In the *Liebestod*, for example, the snatches of melodic line that are sung by Isolde or carried on in the upper instruments are merely outlines of the harmony, or rows of notes dictated by the harmonic movement. Apart from the syncopation in the passage leading up to the famous climax, there is hardly a rhythmic device worth mentioning. But modulations or at least transitions of key occur in almost every bar, disguising the four-squareness of the fundamental movement, and providing the effects of unrest and motion forward that represent Isolde's transfiguration. Many of the transitions are in the form of the deceptive cadence—the device which, throughout *Tristan*, Wagner utilizes for joining short sequences into a continuous texture. The carrying over of notes from a preceding or subsequent chord adds to the effect, which in this case can be described by the technical names for these devices: suspension and anticipation. Schopenhauer has described the suspension: "It is a dissonance delaying the final consonance that is with certainty awaited: in this way the longing for it is strengthened, and its appearance affords the greater satisfaction." He notes that the device is clearly analogous to the satisfaction of the will which is enhanced through delay.[53]

For Schopenhauer, however, it is *melody* that represents the striving will. "The highest grade of the objectification of the will" can be recognized only in "the high, singing principal voice leading the whole and progressing with unrestrained freedom."[54] To be sure, the melody has its origin in the harmonic bass—and Schopenhauer endorsed the theory that the major triad has its origin in the natural system of overtones. But music is humanized, as it were, in proportion as the upper voices predominate. The deep bass, according to Schopenhauer, moves ponderously, representing the

* In German it is called the "Tristan-Akkord," a name which bypasses the argument about what the theoretical designation ought to be. *Tristan* is significantly the only work of music that has given its name to a dissonance.

crudest mass of inorganic nature: "Its rising and falling occur only in large intervals, in thirds, fourths, fifths, never by *one* tone, unless it be a bass transposed by double counterpoint."[55] Melody alone has a significant and intentional stepwise connectiveness. The constant digressions from and return to the keynote and its consonant intervals correspond to the transition in man from wish to satisfaction and from satisfaction to a new wish. Schopenhauer's musical world was classical opera; his descriptions evoke the sublime diatonic melodies of Gluck and Mozart, and the composer he mentions by name in this passage is Rossini. It may not be reliably reported that he found the chromatic music of Wagner dissonant and directionless; but if he did indeed hear the music, this might well have been his response. For not the movement of melody notes within a harmony, but the movement of entire chords from one harmony to another, is Wagner's expressive means. "I am now inclined," he wrote, after *Tristan* had been finished, "to call my subtlest and profoundest art the 'art of transition'"; and he declares that his masterpiece of subtle transitions is the second act of his latest work.[56] These transitions often rest on a bass which, in defiance of Schopenhauer's sense of harmony, moves chromatically. In the love-duet, for example, there are twenty-two measures (from Tristan's words "Tristan du"; repeated in the *Liebestod* in eleven measures, from the words "Wonne klagend") during which the bass moves down the chromatic scale through two octaves. And the prominent motif that is associated with the words *Todgeweihtes Haupt* consists of two triads a half step apart. In Schopenhauer's classical tonality this is not a tonal relationship at all, and he would probably have found the remarkable shift in color arbitrarily sudden. If the unexpected movement into a remote key is, as Schopenhauer hyperbolically maintains, like death,[57] then the second and third acts of *Tristan* represent (as they should) a continuous dying.

Wagner speaks of the leitmotifs in act three of *Tristan* as "restlessly emerging, developing, separating, then again reuniting, growing, diminishing, finally clashing, embracing and well-nigh engulfing one another."[58] In contrast with this turbulence,

Schopenhauer's economical movement of the melody from consonance to dissonance seems to belong to a calmer and quieter world. In his exaggerated representation of the striving will—in this case, the restless memories and hopes, guilt feelings and desires, of Tristan's feverish self-analysis—Wagner had to do with chromatically altered harmonies what Schopenhauer describes as being done in a diatonic tune.

For their fullest expression, Wagner observed, the motifs of *Tristan* required not only "the most complete harmonization" but also "a most independent orchestral treatment."[59] But it is the harmonization, not the orchestration, that affects us. Instrumentation was, he admitted, the "last enjoyment" of his inventiveness.[60] Expert as his orchestration is, it merely adds extra tinting to the vivid hues already inherent in the harmonies. The master of instrumentation does not seem to have conceived his music orchestrally. It might be replied to his criticism of the "guitar-like" accompaniment of the Italian band that he himself used the orchestra as though it were a louder and more richly colored variant of that most mechanical of music boxes, the piano. In the letters of the *Tristan* years, one can trace the transportation of the composer's favorite piano from Zurich to Venice to Lucerne. "I have my Erard now," he writes to Liszt, from Venice. "It stands in a great echoing hall which serves me for a study. It is there that *Tristan* is to be finished this winter."[61] And he could not undertake the orchestration of the second act until "this wondrous soft, sweet melancholy instrument" had wooed him, as he put it, right back to music.[62] As a consequence of such inspiration his scores are effective in piano transcription in a way that is impossible for the scores of composers—Berlioz comes to mind, and Sibelius— whose original instrument, so to speak, was the orchestra. It is not characteristic of Wagner's orchestration that single instruments are used solo for purposes of particular coloration: the typical Wagnerian sound is a rich *tutti* that seems to be independent of its individual components. His orchestra is like a public amplification of the Erard echoing in a high-ceilinged Venetian palace.

Wagner did not invent a new harmonic language. He compiled it out of the vocabulary of more original composers, such as Liszt and Berlioz, and out of the stock in trade of romantic chromaticism. But never before had a borrowed language been employed so relentlessly. One can perhaps encounter in Chopin places where one is allowed to linger on a dominant seventh chord, without requiring its resolution. On the first page of *Tristan* none of the dominant sevenths is resolved, and in the context of extreme chromaticism we accept as a consonance what was once the most kinetic of chords.[63] The ceaseless intensity of *Tristan* brought something new to music. Effects that other composers had used sparingly because of the exigencies of form or the dictates of good taste were now piled on and unsparingly reiterated. It should be remembered that the uniqueness of music, according to Schopenhauer, lay not only in its direct representation of the will, but in its direct action upon it—that is to say, upon "the feelings, passions, and emotions of the hearer."[64] Nevertheless the end of aesthetic experience for Schopenhauer was a calm contemplation of existence: we are moved but at the same time happily detached from the excitement in what moves us. The listener to the music of *Tristan*, on the other hand, must surrender to the experience at the expense of being uncomfortably involved in its excitement. *Tristan* is intentionally overeffective. The listener is supposed to be overwhelmed. Wagner's harmonic lushness is not merely productive of aesthetic delight: it is pathogenic, and the disease is hyperaesthesia.

Wagner's earlier works had also, to be sure, required the "surrender" of the audience. According to the principles of *Opera and Drama* the audience had been attacked by an arsenal of all the arts—and Wagner had no more regard for the integrity of the individual arts than he had for that of his friends, or the members of the audience: anyone can be seduced. In the late fifties, however, when he left the *Ring* and took up *Tristan*, he discovered that he could express his desire to dominate by almost exclusively musical means.

The Unhealthiest Eros

Tristan and Isolde never consummate their union. Of the two
sexual climaxes that are unmistakably depicted in the orchestra,
one is interrupted by the entry of Kurvenal on an unnamable dis-
cord, and the other occurs after Tristan has been dead for twenty
minutes. The subject of *Tristan* is unconsummated passion. The
legend tells of passion as desire and passion as suffering—and of
what Rougemont calls the "dark and unmentionable fact" that
passion is associated with death.[65] Without the *Liebestod* the story
has no point.

Gottfried had set his poem in a world where only death could
free lovers from the anguish of sensual passion. In verses[66] that
seem to anticipate the paradoxical poetry of Wagner's second act,
he introduces his readers to "ein ander werlt":

> diu samet in eine herzen treit
> ir süeze sur, ir liebez leit,
> ir herzeliep, ir senede not,
> ir liebig leben, ir leiden tot,
> ir lieben tot, ir leidez leben.*

In the thematic prelude of Gottfried's account, Rivalin and Blancheflor, Tristan's parents, die of love. When Tristan is exiled in the
land of Isolde of the White Hands, he regrets that he cannot die at
once, and composes love songs that end in this refrain:

> Isot ma douce, Isot mamie,
> en vus ma mort, en vus ma vie![67]

In like manner the abandoned Isolde "would gladly die, if I could
—but he who keeps my life will not let me."[68] So intimately connected are love and death for the lovers that Gottfried allows them
to joke about the connection. When Brangaene tells them that the
draught they have drunk contains their death, Tristan observes that
he has been poisoned most sweetly. "This death suits me well!" he

---

* "It is another world that I mean, which bears in one heart at the same time
bitter-sweetness and the misery of love, its heart's love and its yearning misery,
its life of love, its death of misery, its death in love, its life in sorrow."

replies. "If my adorable Isolde were to go on being the death of me in this fashion I would woo death everlasting."[69]

This un-Wagnerian Tristan has already slept with his Isolde. Consummation was the immediate consequence of drinking the potion—a precipitance which required the substitution of the still virginal Brangaene in the wedding bed of King Mark. Gottfried's lovers continue to consummate their love—"no less than eight times in as many days" during one later episode[70]—and much of the central part of the story is given over to accounts of the ruses and lies they use in order to get together. Death may be their only ultimate fulfillment, but "who else," asks Gottfried (with half the story still untold) "could have severed them from the ill they shared but Union, the knot that joined their senses?"[71]

The medieval Isolde is the mistress of Tristan and the wife of Mark. Wagner's Isolde is neither. It is possible, of course, to find in the text vestigial indications that the lovers have met illegally before their Night of Love. But Wagner's simplification of the legend requires us to think of this night as not only archetypal but unique. And here Tristan and Isolde merely sing together, at a time when we can be fairly certain that she has not yet shared the bed of the King of Cornwall.[72] Oddly enough, Wagner seems to have purified the medieval narrative for Victorian morality. Like other bowdlerizings, Wagner's plot—quite apart from the music— places an uncomfortable emphasis on the offense that is not committed.[73] For Wagner the proper idea of love-in-death excluded as inartistic the achievement of any earthly union. Nietzsche once remarked that Wagner's heroines, once they have been divested of their heroic husks, are almost indistinguishable from Emma Bovary;[74] and it is true that Isolde, like Madame Bovary (and Lady Chatterley), cannot marry her lover. But Isolde cannot even be an adulteress. Not even extramarital intercourse would be sufficient for lovers who are fatally driven toward a magnificent and desirable self-annihilating disaster. Wagner's myth does not merely signify that love and marriage are incompatible; it insists that great

love is incompatible with any sort of tangible or temporal satisfaction.

The lovers, in short, are in love not with each other but with
love itself. Their quest is not for transitory fulfillment but for the
obstacles that prolong passion—ultimately for the final obstacle,
death, which is paradoxically the only permanent fulfillment.[75] The
poets of the romance can convey this sense of prolonged desire and
suffering by stretching out the narrative between the episodes of
consummation. Wagner does so by extending to great length a
situation in which the lovers will be interrupted at a climax (most
of Act II) and a situation in which they are painfully separated
(most of Act III) and by filling out the superficially static situations with music that expresses obsessive desire and obsessive suffering. Hence *Tristan* apotheosizes the unhealthiest Eros—the
boundless desire for a suicidal union with the Infinite, objectified in
a human love impossible of fulfillment.[76]

It is still a debated question through what paths this Eros entered
the Christian tradition and was assimilated into Christian mysticism.
Rougemont traces it to heretical, especially Catharist, sects of Eastern origin.[77] Whether or not this thesis is correct, it is interesting that
Wagner anticipated it when he filled out his own conception of
the legend with quasi-oriental notions. He sensed an affinity between
the eroticism of Gottfried's romance, the "Indian" pessimism of
Schopenhauer, and the oriental antithesis, popularized by the German romantic poets, of false transitory Day and true eternal
Night.[78]

When he conceived *Tristan*, Wagner also sketched out the plot
of a drama—*Die Sieger*—about the last journey of the Buddha.
The drama appears to have been about the efforts of a favorite
disciple to induce the Master to admit a woman into the community of saints. In the end everyone, including Woman, is re-
deemed and transfigured.[79] But "Nirvana," as Wagner told Mathilde
Wesendonk, "changes for me quickly into *Tristan*"; and the only
indication we have of the *Sieger* music is this representation of the

Buddhist theory of the world's creation: "A breath blurs the clarity of the heavens:

It grows, condenses, and solidifies, until finally the whole world confronts me again in all its impenetrable bulk."[80] No doubt some of the Buddhist motifs eventually found their way into *Parsifal*, which was conceived at the same time. Wagner had, in fact, contemplated bringing into the third act of *Tristan* the hero of what turned out to be his final drama of renunciation and redemption. "Parzifal," according to Hans von Wolzogen's report of a conversation with Wagner, "questing for the Grail, was to come in the course of his pilgrimage to Kareol, and there find Tristan lying on his death-bed, love-racked and despairing. Thus the longing one was brought face to face with the renouncing one, the self-curser with the man atoning for his own guilt, the one suffering unto death from love with the one bringing redemption through pity."[81]

Although the "renouncing one" was, on second thought, saved for a drama of his own, not written until twenty years later, the twin conception of *Tristan* and *Parsifal* is evident in the musical affinity between the works. Wagner saw fit to equip his final music-drama with Dresden amens and pseudomedieval chantings. That sort of religiosity is absent in *Tristan*. Not the ceremonial but the chromatic music of *Parsifal* reveals the connection between the works. Indeed, two thirds of *Parsifal* invokes the extreme chromaticism of *Tristan*, freely indulged in again after the predominantly diatonic *Meistersinger* and the completion of the *Ring*.

The music of Amfortas—whom Wagner considered the central figure of *Parsifal*— is related to the music of Tristan's great monologue. Long before the sufferings of Amfortas were set to music, Wagner had identified him with Tristan of the third act, ill from his wound and unable to die, moving from "the most unheard-of suffering" to "the most turbulent exaltation."[82] The festering wounds of the two sinners are represented by similar anguished modulations. Wagner also spoke of the kinship between the "ascending chromaticism" of *Tristan* and the "descending chromaticism" of *Parsifal* —the latter almost certainly referring to the sinking ninth chords of Amfortas' agony. "Amfortas is my Tristan of the third act, at his unthinkable culmination."[83]

Wagner often maintained that composers of symphonies had failed to plumb the depths of harmonic possibilities because there was no compelling reason for them to do so. This could be taken as an acknowledgment that he himself had to be compelled by some extramusical stimulus. Tristan and Amfortas, the heroes wounded by passion, appear to have provided it. Anguish and longing, guilt-ridden desire and the yearning for redemption—what he called the "fearful agony of love"[84]—suggested to Wagner his richest and most complex chromaticism.*

Wagnerism and Tristanism

The composition of *Tristan*, the conception of *Parsifal*, and the sketching of a Buddhist opera indicate how far Wagner had, by the late fifties, moved away from the ideals of 1848. He had undergone a change similar to that of his heroine Brunnhilde, who (as Nietzsche put it) had originally been supposed to retire from the *Ring* with a song in honor of free love, while consoling the world with the hope of a socialistic Utopia; but ultimately found herself versifying the fourth book of *The World as Will and Idea*."[85] "Renunciation of the world" included the temporary abandonment of all efforts to improve it; and intermittently Wagner even gave up manipulating it for personal advantage. For a brief time he actually withdrew from politics and people—to Venice, where he scored the second act of *Tristan*, read Köppen's history of Buddhism, and wrote a romantic diary in the form of letters to Mathilde

---

* Tristan's final ecstasy also moved Wagner to make his only memorable departure from standard musical meter. When Tristan knows that Isolde has arrived, and tears the bandages from his wounds, the music alternates between triple and quadruple time, and there are a few remarkable measures of 5/4.

Wesendonk. During a few weeks of that time he saw no one, living in a "solitude of soul"[86] in which the only things that mattered were "silence and sleep."* In other weeks he composed "as if I meant to work on nothing else for the rest of my life," as he told Mathilde in letters addressed to her from Tristan to Isolde, or from Ananda (the abstinent lover of *The Victors*) to his saintly Sawitri.[87]

When Wagner had been a revolutionary, opera had not been a sufficient vehicle for his ideas, and he wrote tracts. Now, even before he left for Venice, it was not enough to glorify withdrawal from the world in *Tristan*: he had to preach it to his friends. In *Mein Leben* he records his first meeting with Malwida von Meysenbug, an idealistic lady who later became one of the most influential of the female Wagnerites who brightened the Master's life with serious devotion. When Wagner met her—in London, in 1855—Malwida had been caring for the children of the Russian exile, Alexander Herzen.† She had been an enthusiastic reader of "The Art-work of the Future" and Wagner found her "full of the desires and projects for the future perfection of the human race" which he had expressed in that essay. But Wagner had, as we know, recently turned away from those ideas, "under the influence of Schopenhauer," as he puts it, "and a profound realization of the intense tragedy of life and the emptiness of its phenomena." Annoyed by her outmoded ideas, he expounded Schopenhauer to the lady who had, incidentally, in her Frankfurt youth watched the eccentric philosopher walking his dog. She was converted, studied the new philosophy earnestly, and when she met Wagner again, five years later, in Paris, confessed that her former optimism had been shallow.[88]

In her memoirs—they are called the *Memoirs of an Idealist*, and will be quoted from time to time in the course of this narrative—Malwida describes that first meeting with Wagner as one of the

---

* Political matters almost did intrude. The chief of police of Vienna put pressure on the Venetian police to keep the former revolutionary under close surveillance. But the Venetian police councilor turned out unexpectedly to be a Wagnerite.

† Some years before, Herzen's wife had gone off with Wagner's Zurich neighbor, Georg Herwegh.

most impressive evenings of her life. She had not heard a note of Wagner's music, but in his prose works she had recognized what she thought of as Germany's future, and she found such poetry as the text of *Tannhäuser* to be full of deep ethical meaning. During the conversation she had been particularly struck by the phrase "negation of the will to live"; it was an idea, she says, which "attracted me with inspiring awe, as though it must be the key to the gate . . . behind which the light of final perfection would appear to me."[89] Later, in Paris, she was present when the pianist Klindworth played through *Tristan*, with Wagner singing the roles. She realized then that Wagner could count on her support unto death, because his genius would be one of the few flashes of brilliance which would make her life worth living:

I could only compare these works with Shakespeare's, but here one has also the music which enfolds the mighty course of tragic action in its transfiguring cloud. . . . Now I understood the man whose powerful daemon forced him to create such great and marvelous things. From that time on I knew that nothing would make me lose confidence in him, that I would understand him even in his dark moods, in the violent outbreaks of his sensitive nature, in the peculiarities which would lead most people to throw stones at him.[90]

"Ah! these Germans, particularly Germans of the female sex, and particularly those who are afflicted with the virgin innocence of old maids!" This is how Herzen expressed himself after experiencing the more high-minded moods of this lady, who had devoted her life to the spiritual education of his motherless daughter.[91] Wagner recognized in Malwida's innocence a cue for the presentation of his financial difficulties. He spoke to her "as to a friend of long standing," and the flattering intimacy prompted in her various reflections on how geniuses, who cannot concede to the uncomprehending masses, ought, on the heights of ideals, to be free of impecuniousness. "In practical life," Malwida observed, Wagner "had that helplessness of genius which is so touching because it is combined with a deep naïveté and a lack of understanding of conditions of ordinary life."[92]

By that time—it was during the preparations for the Paris *Tann-häuser* in 1861—Wagner had returned to the active world, whose conditions he would once again prove himself to have understood very well. His return ought to have been evident to his philosophical disciple when he asked her to serve as go-between for a loan from a rich English widow.[93] The *Tristan* period was followed by Wagner's sojourns in Paris and Munich—periods of intense social and political involvement; and the next work was the extrovert *Die Meistersinger*, with its nationalistic message. Then came the completion of the *Ring*, and the building of the Festival Theater in which it could be seen. The stay in Venice, in 1859, had been a rare moment of retreat in a long life of activity. But this brief renunciation of politics and society left its impression on *Tristan*. And it is curiously reflected in the history of the response to that work.

For the history of the influence of *Tristan* can be studied apart from the history of social and literary Wagnerism. The avowed Wagnerism that flourished in the years between the earliest success of Bayreuth and the First World War had, for the most part, the worst characteristics of a cult. As often as not, the cult was based on misconceptions. The theory of art-synthesis was declared to be new despite the writings of Gluck and Grétry, and the Music of the Future was thought of as the acme of modernism long after it had become old-fashioned. To find some definite political commitment in the confused allegory of the complete *Ring* one had to ignore at least part of it. In his careless and contradictory writings Wagner promoted everything from racism to vegetarianism; but to make out of any of them a convincing cause one had to draw on the glosses and inventions of other Wagnerians. There were, to be sure, many Wagnerites who studied the revered works of the Master, but their knowledge of Wagner's theories appears to have required little direct experience of his music. And the devotion of handbook-readers need not have been musically confirmed by anything more than the occasional enjoyment of concert numbers.

The as yet unwritten history of Wagnerism would have to account for the pernicious political and racial ideas, the influential aesthetic programs, and the social fads and snobberies which have invoked for their support half-truths about Wagner's music and whole lies from his prose. It would be a history of doctrines and movements: Symbolism, Naturalism, Aestheticism; anti-Semitism, Nazism, the Cult of Bayreuth. Within that history *Tristan* would have to be set apart. The political Wagnerites neglected the music-drama that was least suited to the propagation of programs about the Superman, the Revolution, evolutionary socialism, or the Race. Nor was there a special fondness for *Tristan* among the doctrinaire "literary" Wagnerites. For the primacy of the music tended to refute their favorite aesthetic doctrine.

In contrast to Wagnerism, what I have chosen to call "Tristanism" begins with a direct response to the music. It is private rather than public, the result of a personal infatuation rather than an ideological commitment. Its history is not social but biographical. The Wagnerite must learn theories and cultivate habits. The Tristanite only has to be overwhelmed. He could, to be sure, go on to verbalize his experience in impressionistic prose-poetry, as Gabriele D'Annunzio did, or the American essayist James Huneker. Or he could, as a theorist, devote his energies to analysis of the music. A composer could find the music of *Tristan* obtrusively recurring in his own. This happened to Emmanuel Chabrier and Ernest Chausson, later to Arnold Schoenberg, and in some degree to almost every composer who worked between 1880 and 1910. And an infatuation with the music could lead to a pondering of the myth. In some of the stories of Thomas Mann, for example, the legend is ironically retold, enacted by characters for whom the music is unwholesome as well as overpowering. In this respect Mann was recapitulating the experience of Nietzsche, who found the music fascinating but at the same time more dangerous than any form of ideological Wagnerism.

Even before the music of *Tristan* was made public, it had begun to have an immoderate effect on people's behavior and their careers.

How this happened will be described in the next chapter. Among the people affected were the woman who is supposed to have inspired the work, the couple who created the major roles, and the conductor of the first performance. Chief among them was the composer himself.

chapter II

TO THE FIRST PERFORMANCE (1859-1865)

The Dangers of "Tristan"

The tenor who sang the first Tristan complained of a draft that
swept across the stage during his monologue in the third act. He
developed a fever, and died a few weeks after the first performances.[1] His wife, the first Isolde, suffered for a time from
delusions. The conductor had been cuckolded by the composer:
an illegitimate daughter was born to Cosima von Bülow two months
before the first performances of *Tristan*. The baby was named
Isolde. The financier of the productions, who watched the work
from his royal box, was to find it no less unlucky for him than it
was for the singers and conductor. For Wagner's expensive demands, and his interference even in nonmusical matters of the
Bavarian government, had increased the determination of Ludwig
II's officials to drive Wagner out of Munich. Remembering the
unfortunate infatuation of the first Ludwig, the Münchners referred to the heir of Beethoven as "Lola Montez the Second."

Tristan was not performed until June, 1865, six years after it
was completed, because it was considered too difficult. Those who
finally performed it overcame the difficulty of the work only to
become aware of its dangers. Wagner foresaw both. After he had
finished *Tristan*, he confided to Mathilde Wesendonk that it was
becoming increasingly inscrutable to him how he had managed to
create such a work:

Upon reading it through again, I couldn't believe my eyes or my ears. How terribly I shall have to pay for this work some day, if I intend to see it performed! *I distinctly foresee the most unheard-of sufferings;* for in it—I can't hide the fact—I've over-stepped whatever lies within the powers of execution. Supremely talented performers are the only ones equal to the task; but they are not easily to be found in the world. Yet I cannot resist the temptation, if only to hear the orchestra![2]

Earlier, while Wagner was composing the third act of the work that had begun as something "practical," Mathilde had received the following unusually brief note:

Child! This Tristan is turning into something *dreadful [furchtbares]*! That last act!!! — — — — — — —
I'm afraid the opera will be forbidden—unless the whole thing is turned into a parody by bad production—: only mediocre perform-ances can save me! Completely *good* ones are bound to drive people crazy,—I can't imagine what else could happen. To such a state have things come!!! Alas! —
I was just going full steam ahead!
Adieu!
R. W.[3]

The *Tristram Shandy* punctuation was often part of Wagner's use-ful technique of articulating the distractions of genius before ask-ing for an emergency loan. But here the enthusiasm and impatience are genuine, and one can readily believe that Wagner encountered his new music with surprise, and a kind of fear. The composer was disinterestedly overwhelmed by the intensity of his own opera.

Renunciation

Wagner's favorite mood in the middle fifties seems to have been the elegiac, and his first written reference to *Tristan* occurs in the course of a lament for unrequited love. At the end of his *quietus* letter to Liszt, Wagner announced his new plans:

Since never in my life have I tasted the real happiness of love, I intend to raise a monument to that most beautiful of dreams, in which, from beginning to end, that love shall be for once thoroughly satiated.

I have in mind a plan for a *Tristan and Isolde*, the simplest but most full-blooded musical conception; in the "black flag" that waves at the end I shall then enshroud myself—to die.[4]

The black flag, which figures in the death of the medieval Tristan, dropped out in the course of Wagner's early sketches, but the sequence of ideas in this passage is carried over into the music-drama. A reference to death follows immediately upon a reference to fully satisfied love: desire fulfilled suggests suicide. Isolde dies with the word for desire, *Lust*, on her lips. Wagner starts out with the central conception of the myth: the *Liebestod*—a label, incidentally, which he used to describe the *Prelude* to *Tristan* and not Isolde's final solo, which he called the *Verklärung*. The fact that in the letter to Liszt Wagner is referring not to the medieval lovers but, hyperbolically, to himself foretells that his desire for a consuming passion will be objectified not only in music but in a personal love affair carried on, as far as its bourgeois setting will allow, according to the pattern of the myth. It will be fated, dominated by the idea of renunciation, and adulterous in spirit but not in fact. Some of the entries in Wagner's Venice diary even indicate that the parallel might not have stopped short of the love-death—indeed Wagner begins the diary with a vision of being kissed by Mathilde on his deathbed.[5] But Wagner was a busier man than Tristan or later Tristan-obsessed lovers, like the hero of D'Annunzio's *Triumph of Death*. He wrote four more music-dramas after *Tristan* and built a festival theater; and Mathilde Wesendonk survived the affair well enough to send Brahms the text of a cantata on the subject of cremation.[6]

Wagner was only fifteen when he wrote the first of his works in which the hero dies in a *Verklärung*, this time in the lap of a lady he has just stabbed. The lady's Brangaene-like maid dies at her feet, and the equivalent of King Mark eulogizes the dead.[7] Renunciation in one form or another runs through all Wagner's works from *The Flying Dutchman* to *Parsifal*. The Dutchman gains redemption, according to Wagner's explanation of the plot, "through *a woman* who shall sacrifice herself for the love of him. Thus it is the yearning for death that spurs him on to seek this woman."[8]

This Senta-mentality is carried over into *Tannhäuser* and *Lohengrin:* if there is one poetic theme expressed in these works, Wagner observed, "it is the high tragedy of . . . imperative and redeeming abnegation of the will."[9] He discovered at this time that he had been speaking Schopenhauer all his life. Phrases and ideas from an unfinished renunciatory work, *Wieland der Schmied,* reappear in *Tristan,* and long before *Parsifal* Wagner had contemplated writing a renunciation-drama about Jesus of Nazareth.*

The moods as well as the ideas that led to the composition of *Tristan* long antedated the arrival of Mathilde Wesendonk to fulfill what her biographers call her "special mission." Well before he went to live at the Wesendonk "Asyl" Wagner was regularly succumbing to "melancholy broodings . . . upon the innate tragedy of the cosmos."[10] And that sense of "mystical abstraction from the real world" which Tristan and Isolde express can be seen, according to Ernest Newman, as "merely the sublimation of a frame of mind that was quite common with Wagner."[11] Especially during domestic quarrels Wagner was able to abstract himself psychologically from his intolerable surroundings; and at moments of extreme tension—such as when he gave a funeral oration at Weber's grave, and when the bells rang to announce the start of the Dresden revolt of 1849—he could see and hear himself as someone else. The idea of using E-flat major arpeggios to represent the Rhine in the Prelude to *Das Rheingold* was, he tells us, conceived in just such a cataleptic condition—which Newman oddly considers "the prime condition of all artistic creation of the highest kind."[12]

Biographers of Mathilde Wesendonk like to suggest that she was the main source of inspiration of *Tristan*. That *Tristan* inspired the Wesendonk affair is closer to the truth, in the sense that Wagner allowed notions related to the opera to affect his behavior. Cyril Connolly could have had Wagner in mind when he generalized that "the welling up of the desire for artistic creation precedes a

---

* Wagner read *Wieland,* incidentally, to Jessie Laussot, one of the intelligent, sympathetic, and beautiful married women who anticipated Mathilde Wesendonk's role of inspirer and listener.

love affair. Women are not an inspiration of the artist but a consequence of that inspiration."[13]

Mathilde

The many biographies that deal with the Wesendonk affair are often hard to tell apart from the even more numerous romances about it. This is partly because the history of Wagner's relationships with women seems to fall neatly into three acts, of which the second, the affair with Mathilde, is provided with the prettiest heroine and the best love letters, and is the only one unspoiled, like *Tristan*, by consummation or marriage. Minna Wagner endured the difficulties of Wagner's early career, never comprehending that genius excused constant lack of funds. Cosima Wagner shared the struggles of his later career and protected the fortress of Wagnerism that she helped to build. Mathilde Wesendonk quietly stands between the two wives, a "pure" love uninvolved in domestic tedium or theater building.

Typical of the tendency thus to pattern Wagner's life is Julius Kapp's book—by no means the worst—about the three women, in which each is found to have the qualities the other two lacked.[14] Each had her "special mission" to fulfill, and each happily turned up at the moment in Wagner's career which was best suited for her particular task. The three-act symmetry is neat, as though Wagner had composed it himself: "One he married, one was his *unsterbliche Geliebte*, and one married him."[15] So evenly divided are the ladies' merits that Kapp cannot decide who should get the prize:

They all, each in her own way, rendered imperishable services to man and artist and have a claim to the gratitude and respect of posterity. Then why not at this point [the end of the book] drop all petty rivalry and jealousies and admit that without these women Wagner's work would hardly have assumed for us the greatness and breadth of appeal it has today? All honor, then, to the triple constellation:

MATHILDE

MINNA   COSIMA[16]

But dispite this final flourish of impartiality, Kapp had already, in the course of his narrative, awarded the prize—to the lady whose name is at the apex of his little triangle. It is Mathilde whose "life counted for most in relation to the creative artist":

As [Wagner's] muse, she possessed the secret power of setting all the strings of his magic harp in vibration and bringing out the highest revelations of his genius. This is perhaps to be ascribed less to the direct influence of her personality on the Master than to the workings of destiny, which turned their love-bond into tragedy, forced them to sorrowful renunciation and thereby induced in Wagner a state of mind which offered the most favorable opportunities possible for the development of his genius.[17]

Like most Wagnerian biographers, Kapp follows Wagner himself in sentimentally projecting Tristanesque values into the life of the composer: renunciation, for example, is somehow a stimulant to genius. The conclusion is usually that *Tristan* was the product of sublimated love. Indeed Kapp guilelessly asserts that it is to the "non-fulfillment" of Wagner's "profound passion" for Mathilde that we owe "the fevered raptures of *Tristan*, his most imperishable masterpiece."[18]

The Wagnerite who introduced the Venice diary to English readers, William Ashton Ellis, went further in the deification of Mathilde. At the turn of the century it was difficult to idealize the heroine of the *Tristan* years at the expense of Cosima, who out-lived her husband by half a century and, like Wagner after his second marriage, seldom mentioned her romantic predecessor. Indeed, in his later years Wagner preferred to forget Mathilde's part in the writing of *Tristan* and to emphasize the role of Cosima in getting the work produced.[19] But for Wagnerites like Ellis there was ready to hand the very real contrast between Mathilde and the unfortunate Minna, who had few defenders. The best that Ellis could say for Minna was that (as Wagner himself had put it) "she would have been happier with a lesser man."[20] She emerges from Ellis' portrait as a vulgar woman whose petty and poorly expressed jealously can be explained partly on the grounds that she was addicted to opium. Compare her with Mathilde, that "placid, sweet Madonna, the perfect emblem of a pearl, . . . her eyes still dreaming of Nirvana." Ellis is anxious to point out that *this* woman "could not have once been swayed by carnal passion." In this respect she is like Isolde—and Wagner is like the most chivalrous of Tristans:

In these letters all is pure and spiritual, a Dante and a Beatrice; so *must* it have been in their intercourse. For my own impression of their recipient—whom I first met in that sad year at Bayreuth when the master was no more—it was that of the silver moon reflecting a sun that has set long since. Not a word ever fell from her lips on such a love as is revealed here; but every accent of her voice, the gathering moisture in her eye, spelt worship, and from her it was, I earliest learnt a truth which added years have simply verified: that in Richard Wagner we have more than a great,—a profoundly good man.[21]

In this way the "bourgeois drama" enacted by the Wagners and the Wesendonks is converted into an idyll about a romantic genius and his Platonic love.[22] The amount of falsifying this requires is evident when one considers the banal and sordid details that must be glossed over in order to make the affair resemble the myth: Wagner's sponging on Otto Wesendonk, the compromising letters and unheroic indiscretions. And throughout the story sounds the *basso ostinato* of Wagner's egotism. During the Wesendonk years Wagner did not give up his lifelong habit of reading his prose to others, whether they wanted to listen or not. That Mathilde was an attentive listener only increased his desire to stir her responsive soul with the breath of genius. Mathilde notes in her "Recollections" that shortly after they met "the Master began to initiate me more closely into his intentions." The course was planned: "First he read his 'Three Opera Texts,' which were delightful, then the introduction to them, and gradually all his prose works, one after the other."[23] As in the second act of *Tristan*, love-making took the form of reciting lengthy discourses. Anti-Wagnerians have not hesitated to point out that the music-dramas are inflicted upon an audience in the way Wagner inflicted his prose-readings upon his friends, without regard for their time or the limits of their patience. Mathilde was a good Wagnerian, and listened attentively.

By the time *Tristan* was begun, Wagner was in love with the devoted listener. As he indicates in the famous letter to Liszt, the attempt to find "the real happiness of love" was a leitmotif of his life, which became increasingly recurrent in the 1850s. It is sounded repeatedly in his letters, even apart from those to Liszt and Mathilde. To his niece Johanna he succinctly described his state of mind: "My one need is love! Fame, honor—nothing of that kind can refresh me: only one thing can delight me and reconcile me to life—a sign that I am loved, even if it comes only from a child!"[24] At about the same time, in the course of an argument with friends about a theory that wine is poisonous, Wagner maintained that wine was "an evil and barbarous substitute for the ecstatic state of mind which love alone should produce." Only someone who had experienced "the intoxication of love" could "raise his spirits in the noblest sense of the word."[25] In *Tristan* Wagner would attempt to induce the intoxication musically.

Tristanizing

Throughout the early years of his friendship with Frau Wesendonk, Wagner was at work on the middle operas of the *Ring*. While he was scoring the second act of *Siegfried*, the Brazilian consul in Leipzig visited him with a commission from the emperor of Brazil. Pedro II greatly admired his operas and wanted him to conduct them in Rio—the emperor apparently regarding it as an easy matter for Wagner to translate the librettos into Italian, the language for opera in Brazil. Wagner's thoughts turned to *Tristan*, this time as a "passionate musical poem which would turn out quite excellently in Italian."[26] (One wonders what Nietzsche would have thought of *Tristan* in a Mediterranean language.) Nothing ever came of the offer, although Wagner did send the emperor piano scores of his early operas in the hope of some kind of imperial payment.*

---

* Dom Pedro was present at Bayreuth in 1876, and listed his occupation in the hotel register as "Emperor."

Royal patronage had to wait until 1864, when it would come from a source equally unexpected but closer to home.

Thus it happens that Rio de Janeiro heads the long list of cities which were considered possible homes for the first production of *Tristan*. The second was Gottfried's Strasbourg, which was to house not the passionate Italian but the practical German work that was supposedly within the scope of any ordinary theater. For the leading roles Wagner wanted the great tenor Albert Niemann and the soprano Luise Meyer; the orchestra could be borrowed from nearby Karlsruhe. In June, 1857, he wrote Liszt that he could complete the work for production in the summer of 1858.[27] But Wagner's new work would by no means be ready for production—difficult or practical—by the following summer.

Wagner moved into his "Asyl" on the Wesendonk estate in February, 1857, and in August the Wesendonks took up their residence next door, in the main house on Green Hill. Among the many visitors to Wagner's newly settled rent-free cottage were Hans and Cosima von Bülow. The conductor had married the younger daughter of Liszt and the Countess d'Agoult in mid-August, and the young couple were allowing their honeymoon to be dominated by the strong personality that was later to destroy their marriage. Bülow was already an apostle of Wagner, as he had once been of Liszt and was later to be of Brahms. At the age of twelve he had been thrilled (and temporarily deafened) by a performance of *Rienzi*.[28] Throughout the 1840s the young musician tried to convert first his aristocratic family and then everyone else to the New German Music. By the end of the decade he was one of the chief Wagnerian propagandists, willing to risk his health and his career in the polemic against the Master's enemies. Even on his honeymoon Bülow could think of nothing better calculated to bring him "a sense of blessing and refreshment" than to be with "this glorious, unique man, whom one must venerate like a god."[29]

If the composer of *Tannhäuser* inspired adoration, the composer of *Tristan* would demand sacrifices. After struggling with the reduction of *Tristan* for piano, and later, amidst very difficult conditions, preparing the first performances, Bülow knew the work better than anyone except Wagner, and he was among the first to be dazzled by it. In the course of a brief introduction to Bülow's letters, Count du Moulin Eckart, an orthodox Wagnerite and the biographer of Cosima, twice refers to *Tristan* as the tragedy of Bülow's life.[30]

With the Bülows in Zurich, the three women in Wagner's life met each other for the first time. "Could anything be more dramatic," asks Ellis, "than this daily gathering under the *Tristan* poet's roof of the only three women who ever had or were to have a share in his human destiny?"[31] At the end of each week during their visit, Wagner read to Cosima and her husband the completed poem of an act of *Tristan*. The entire poem was finished in mid-September, the detailed prose sketch having been begun a month before.[32] Wagner immediately imposed a complete reading of the verses upon the first available audience, which happened to include Georg Herwegh, who in 1852 had been treated to a similar reading of the *Ring;* the architect Gottfried Semper, who was later to design the projected festival-theater for Munich and help design the Bayreuth theater; Professor Ludwig Ettmüller, a specialist in the northern sagas (Wagner called him Eddamüller); and the great Swiss poet and novelist Gottfried Keller.[33] The Wesendonks, of course, also attended. Apart from Mathilde, the distinguished audience was apparently wearied and puzzled by the bare poem, unaccompanied by the music which could either in some way elucidate the verses or drown them out. Wagner admitted that much of the dialogue in the second act was incomprehensible without the music.

The composition sketch (an outline of the music) of the first act was finished by the beginning of December. The Prelude had already been written: Wagner took it immediately to Mathilde, laying at her feet "Tristan and Isolde, what they bewailed and renounced, their tears and their kisses, in music's chaste gold," according to the dedication written in the breathless rhymes of the opera's text:

. . . was sie sich klagten
und versagten,
Tristan und Isolde
in keuscher Töne Golde
ihr Weinen und ihr Küssen
leg' ich zu Deinen Füssen.[34]

Three of the five "Wesendonk" songs, set to texts by Mathilde, had been composed earlier; they were at the same time musical love-making and studies for the chromaticism of *Tristan*. "Träume," based on the wonderful A-flat music of the love-duet, was performed by a small orchestra under Mathilde's window on her birthday (December 23). The orchestral sketch (a full layout, with indications of the orchestration) of the first act was finished in mid-January, 1858, and the full score of that act was ready in April. With two thirds of the music still unwritten, Breitkopf and Härtel undertook to publish the score, the poem, and the piano reduction, and even paid Wagner in advance. Wagner expected to have the second act ready by the end of June, and the third by the end of September. Actually the publishers didn't get the completed score until August of the following year.

In January, 1858, Wagner had briefly visited Paris, to settle copyrights and incidentally to escape from some embarrassment with Otto Wesendonk, who was, according to Wagner's account, "anxious lest, as he imagined, everything in his house would soon go my way rather than his." Otto also occasionally made the mistake of interrupting the Master: he exhibited "that peculiar oppressiveness [*Wucht*] with which a man who thinks himself slighted throws himself into every conversation in his presence, something like a snuffer on a candle."[35] There are many such passages in *Mein Leben* which reveal Wagner's retrospective ingratitude toward the man who helped him in every way but unfortunately happened to be married to the composer's immortal beloved. Wagner stayed in Paris only about four weeks, spending much of the time with Emile Ollivier, who had recently married Cosima's sister Blandine. He also visited Berlioz, and at a reading of *Les Troyens*

Wagner was "filled with a dismay" that made him wish that he and Berlioz "might never meet again."[36] The aesthetic antipathy was no doubt reinforced by the consideration that *Les Troyens* could be produced only at one of the theaters where Wagner wanted to float his own works. The visit of a composer to Paris for any purpose also of course included attempts to get works produced—in Wagner's case, "for the benefit of the Parisian public in general and myself in particular."[37]

On his return to Zurich in early February Wagner immediately began the full scoring of the first act, which he sent off to Breitkopf on April 4. Three days later he sent Mathilde, as a memento, the original pencil sketch of the Prelude, accompanied, according to *Mein Leben,* by a *Briefchen* which communicated his mood at the time.[38] Most of the "little note," which ran to eight pages, was a description of Wagner's annoyance that on the previous evening Mathilde's time had been monopolized by a visiting Italian scholar; it also included a long discussion, which Wagner himself calls "nonsense," of Goethe's Gretchen. Minna Wagner intercepted the letter, "readily gave a vulgar interpretation to it," burst into her husband's room, and made a jealous scene. Wagner countered her bourgeois fury with tragic calm, asking only that she refrain from repeating the scene with the Wesendonks.[39] But Minna went to Mathilde with the letter, and later to Otto, debasing into a marital brawl what had up to then been an awkward but accepted situation.

Minna held on to Wagner's letter all her life and bequeathed it to her daughter. The outraged wife described it to her cronies as though it were the passionate postscript to "a wild night of love," but actually it is not an ordinary love letter at all.[40] In it Wagner is mysticizing, "Tristanizing"—the term is Newman's—as he had been doing for a year past and was to do for another year to come. But Minna was an unimaginative woman close to fifty who had never understood love as a mystical conception, and missed the point of lovers finding their consolation in "resignation." When Wagner tried to explain these subtle matters to her, she found his analysis merely another example of his "vortreffliche

Suade"—his "remarkable gift of the gab"[41]—an observation that readers of Wagner's prose ought to find exhilarating. In more letters to Mathilde, and later in the Venice diary, Wagner went on Tristanizing. For the composition of *Tristan* required the expression to a confidant of excess emotion, and of a sense of wonder at the work's power.

In her sentimental memoirs Malwida von Meysenbug makes the following judgment of Minna Wagner:

[Wagner's] wife was little suited to him; . . . she was not capable of raising him above the many petty and sordid cares and conditions of life, nor of lessening them with greatness of soul and feminine charm. This man, so utterly dominated by his daemon, should always have [had] a high-minded, understanding woman by his side—a wife who would have known how to mediate between his genius and the world by understanding that these are always hostile to one another.[42]

And Malwida notes that Blandine Ollivier, Cosima's sister, agreed with her. According to the lady Wagnerites, Minna, upon discovering what seemed to her to be the proof of the Wesendonk affair, ought presumably to have behaved as Emma Herwegh had, when she assisted her husband in continuing his affair with the wife of Alexander Herzen.[43] Wagner, at any rate, thought so. Never, he informed his sister in August, 1858, did Minna have "a better opportunity of showing herself worthy of the dignity of being my wife than when I needed all that is highest and dearest to support me."[44]

But Minna was not a Wagnerite. And it ought to be remembered that at the time of the Wesendonk affair no one, except the composer, Bülow, Liszt, and Mathilde, knew even part of the new music that had been written. Consequently few people—and least of all Minna—could be expected to excuse Wagner's improper behavior with the indulgent observation that the genius was Tristanizing. Even the part of the *Ring* that had already been written had never been performed. Hence, to excuse Wagner's behavior because of the greatness of his later work would have been to depend for evidence on the Prelude to *Lohengrin* and iso-

lated passages in that opera, *Tannhäuser* not having yet been revised. There is no harder practical question, as Shaw observes, than
how much selfishness one ought to stand from a gifted person for
the sake of his gifts or on the chance of his being right in the long
run.[45] Only Wagner himself knew the power of his unperformed
works, and could predict the importance of those still unwritten.
Perhaps the most remarkable thing about him is that he so con-
fidently borrowed on the credit of future accomplishment.

Minna left Zurich for a "cure," and Wagner, gradually recover-
ing from the harsh intrusion of Day, was at last enveloped enough
in Night to find the music of the second act flowing easily from
his pen. The composition sketch was written between May 4 and
July 1. But on Minna's return the domestic scenes dawned again,
the final showdown between Wagner and his wife, and between
Minna and Mathilde, postponed only because of the succession of
visitors to the Asyl: the Bülows again, the Countess d'Agoult, the
pianists Tausig and Klindworth. By August Wagner was determined to leave, in order to find the quiet necessary for com-
pleting *Tristan*. Hence it was in Venice that Tristan and Isolde
were to move toward their consummation in Death. In a run-down
Giustiniani palace on the Grand Canal Wagner finished the orchestration of the second act, and consoled himself for the absence of
his Zurich audience by keeping the diary in the form of letters to
Mathilde.

Still the Music of the Future

The poem of *Tristan* was issued in an edition of 2,000 copies in
late December, 1858 (the title page is dated 1859), and so a number of people knew the text months before the score was completed.
Wagner sent a copy to Schopenhauer, but there is no record that
the philosopher bothered to read it—not even a laconic comment
about the versification of his doctrine in the second act. The publishers were already engraving the full score of Act I, as well as
part of the piano score arranged by Bülow, who was engaged in
his first struggle with the music. He even set himself the problem

of making the piano reduction more difficult than it would have been according to Wagner's suggestions.[46] Although it is an exaggeration to consider the Bülow score unplayable, there is no doubt that even a good sight reader must study many of the passages for a while before he can play them with facility. The more pianistic Klindworth version has made the work available to generations of students with only the ordinary ten fingers.[47] But the Bülow score* served to introduce *Tristan* to the young Nietzsche and his friends, who were good musicians but not expert pianists; and the copies still available in secondhand music stores show signs of frequent use by singers.[48]

Part of Bülow's reward was a copy of the full score. Wagner called *Tristan* his "child of sorrow";[49] but in later years Bülow

---

* Unpianistic as Bülow's score may be, it is fair to note that Liszt's virtuoso rendition of the *Liebestod* (he gave it the name) is worse. Liszt's repeated chords at the famous climax, for example, are more difficult to execute, and yet less sonorous, than Bülow's tremolos; and other passages in the Liszt arrangement sound curiously old-fashioned—even without the glittering pyrotechnics that are still acceptable in works that are frankly show-pieces, like the *Rigoletto* paraphrase. Even Liszt could not make *Tristan* into facile piano music. Bülow did not even try, for he was interested far more in including all the inner voices than in piano sonority. Wagner (who must have known how to make his scores "sound" on the piano) had to suggest to him the doubling of octaves in the bass—at the cost of eliminating some of the inner voices. There is evidence that Bülow did not fully understand the score: he was discomforted by certain dissonances, and occasionally "corrected" what he thought were misprints. In a postscript to a letter to Wagner he supposes that he "need not puzzle out any accompaniment (in small notes)" to the shepherd's English-horn solo at the start of act three. Wagner replied with the amusing suggestion that the melody be harmonized in sixths and thirds, Oberon style! Bülow has also been criticized for overlooking the leitmotif of the "Death Potion" in the bass of the Prelude. But the search for leitmotifs as a scholarly pursuit had at that time barely begun, and even though his phrasing of the three notes is inaccurate, Bülow does at least note that they constitute a "characteristic bass," and he phrases the motif correctly when it appears in the first act. There is no record that Wagner was bothered by the slip in the Prelude. Bülow, rightly insisted that musicians who could not afford the expensive full score deserved to have a piano score *with text*. "Let Härtel," he wrote to Wagner, "have the arrangements 'without words' turned out by his men in the usual way. You know I refused it as the last profanation." The "sublime night-music (in A-flat major) cannot be popularized into a 'Star of Eve.'" In what he considered a striking analogy, he observed that *Tristan* stood in the same relation to *Lohengrin* as the last quartets of Beethoven to his first. The present-day cultists of Beethoven's Spiritual Development may very well consider such a comparison profane; but there have been cultists of *Tristan* who would have considered it insufficient praise of Wagner's masterpiece. For Wagner, who was humble at the altar of the C-sharp minor quartet, it was praise enough.

took upon himself the responsibilities of that paternity, as he did in the case of Cosima's illegitimate daughters. Wagner also gave full scores to Berlioz and Gounod. Berlioz was sent one of three advance copies, the day after Wagner received them, suitably inscribed to the "grand et cher auteur de Romeo et Juliette." One would like to construe this as at least a veiled acknowledgement of the debt owed by *Tristan,* for both detail and conception, to the Dramatic Symphony which Wagner had heard at its debut twenty years earlier.[50] In the light of this debt, Berlioz's three-week delay in letting Wagner know that he had received the score scarcely seems the great offense that some Wagnerite biographers (following a letter written by Bülow) have made of it. The gift of the score to Gounod was a rare if unimposing instance of Wagnerian gratitude to someone who had championed his cause—given despite the fact that "no feeling of friendship had ever been able to induce me to hear . . . *Faust.*"[51]

The gifts of the score serve to remind us that almost immediately after he finished *Tristan* Wagner was involved in the maneuverings of his most celebrated sojourn in Paris, and the famous performance of *Tannhäuser,* which was speedily refurbished with new music in his latest style. The Venusberg scene of the "Paris" *Tannhäuser,* with its rich scoring and prolonged dominant ninths, reveals that Wagner could go on writing *Tristan*-music after the death of Tristan and Isolde. Indeed the healthy change to a very different kind of libretto was required to bring about the remarkable transformation of musical atmosphere announced by the opening C-major chord of *Die Meistersinger.* Meanwhile the *Tannhäuser* fiasco and frequent *Lohengrins* by German companies hardly compensated for the fact that *Tristan* lay unperformed.

From Paris Wagner wrote to Mathilde* and to Liszt that his only goal in life was the production of *Tristan*—somewhere.[52] In order to open the German theaters to him, he even contemplated going to Dresden to stand trial—unnecessarily, for the Dresden

---

* Mathilde is now no more than a "good friend," and in the letters of this time Wagner sends his love to his friend Otto.

amnesty was issued a few months later, partly as a result of Napoleon III's patronage of the Paris *Tannhäuser*. In the course of the next years, before the miraculous intercession of Ludwig II, the list of prospective places for the performance of *Tristan*, which began with Strasbourg and Karlsruhe (not to mention Rio), grew to include Dresden, Hanover, Stuttgart, Prague, and Vienna. For a while there was even the quixotic hope of a Paris production, despite Wagner's understandable distaste for a *Tristan* in French. Only Karlsruhe and Vienna, however, got past the planning stage.

The young grand duke of Baden and his newly-wed wife, the daughter of the crown princess of Prussia, were both music lovers with an enthusiasm for Wagner. But their singers and orchestra took fright at the difficulties of *Tristan*, and Wagner's old friend Devrient, the manager of the Karlsruhe theater, soon learned that it was by no means an "easy" work. He also feared losing control of his theater to Wagner. The work was shelved, and a Berlin paper was the first to comment that at last the title of "music of the future" was justified, for it was unperformable in the present. Ironically the future Munich Tristan and Isolde, Ludwig Schnorr von Carolsfeld and Malvina Garrigues, later Frau Schnorr, were at this time members of the Karlsruhe company.[53]

Vienna displayed more endurance, but in the course of the protracted preparations Wagner managed to alienate almost everyone concerned with the production. He had gone there shortly after the failure of the Paris *Tannhäuser*, to refresh himself with a well-done *Lohengrin* (it was the first time he heard this opera, written thirteen years before) and scout for singers for a possible renewed attempt to do *Tristan* at Karlsruhe. The good singers and the friendliness of the opera intendant suggested that *Tristan* might be done directly in Vienna. Rehearsals began, but by mid-August of 1861 the tenor, Aloys Ander, who had sung a beautiful Lohengrin, was terrified of the role of Tristan, which the Vienna press had already pronounced impossible.* It should interest modern purists that Wagner conceded transpositions and extensive cuts—

---

* Ander died insane at the end of 1864.

142 bars in the third-act monologue.[54] Neither Tichatschek, who had sung the first Tannhäuser, nor Schnorr was available at the time, and an Alsatian tenor named Schrumpf, who called himself Morini, proved too stupid for the role.[55]

For a while the soprano, Luise Meyer-Dustmann, was more co-operative, and she and the Brangaene satisfied Wagner at an open rehearsal of selected passages, in October. But a month later Wagner appeared in Vienna with Frau Dustmann's sister, the actress Friede-ricke Meyer. Since the soprano and her sister were on bad terms, Wagner's association with the actress quickly cooled Isolde's enthusiasm for *Tristan* and its composer.[56]

The prospects of getting *Tristan* produced were further weakened by the hostility of the press, which Wagner increased by insulting the man who was then and would remain for three more decades the most influential critic in Vienna.[57] Hanslick's reputation as a sound critic and good stylist has until recently been blackened by Wagnerites who were apparently more shocked by his misjudgments than by Wagner's rudeness. After snubbing Hanslick twice, Wagner gave a reading of the text of *Meistersinger* in his presence, before an audience who undoubtedly knew, even without the hints in the text, that Beckmesser was originally named "Hanslich." Thenceforth the critic had any number of opportunites to earn the immortality bestowed upon him as opponent of Wagner and of composers in the Wagnerian camp. The hostility of Hanslick and others, Tristan's timorousness and hoarseness, and Isolde's diminishing zeal made it clear to the Opera personnel that a production was impossible.* Hope for it was abandoned, until a year later the Bavarian *deus ex machina* called Wagner to Munich.[58]

Lola Montez the Second

The strange story of Ludwig II and Wagner has been retold in books of fact and fiction that outnumber those about the Wesendonk affair. In them Ludwig is known as the Tragic Idealist, the

---

* It is usually reported that the Vienna rehearsals numbered seventy-seven—a number too large to represent stage or action rehearsals, and too small to represent coaching sessions for the singers.

Mad Monarch and the Hamlet-King.[59] But without the elucidation of the many theories about Ludwig's "madness" and Wagner's motives, the correspondence (in five volumes) between the king and the composer reveals at least two important facts about the men.[60] Ludwig, though not at the time insane, was abnormally sentimental. And Wagner eagerly made use of this defect in Ludwig's character by pretending that it was a virtue.

Not long after they met, Ludwig was writing to Wagner in terms that, allowing for the warmer tone of friendly letters a century ago, render his letters to the middle-aged composer often indistinguishable from those to his adolescent favorites:

I can only adore you, only praise the power that led you to me. More clearly and ever more clearly do I feel that I cannot reward you as you deserve: all I can ever do for you, can be no better than stammered thanks. An earthly being cannot requite a divine spirit. But it can love, it can venerate: you are my first, my only love, and ever will be.[61]

In almost every letter of a correspondence that lasted twenty years can be found equally disturbing examples of what has been called Ludwig's "idealism," which remained remarkably unaffected by political interference, personal betrayal, and madness. It is a proof of Wagner's single-minded eagerness to get his works performed that he accepted this adulation without embarrassment.

Ludwig's lifelong melancholy took the form of a longing for abdication and for death.[62] Hence *Tristan* was perfectly suited for the inaugural of his operatic reign. Right after the first performance he wrote to Wagner the following note, which epitomizes *Liebestod*-infatuation:

Einziger!—Heiliger!—

Wie wonnevoll! — *Vollkommen.* So angegriffen von Entzücken! . . . . .Ertrinken. . . . .versinken — unbewusst — höchste Lust. ——

Göttliches Werk! ——

Ewig

treu — bis über
den Tod hinaus! —[63]

Yet there is ample contemporary evidence (including the testimony of his childhood tutor, his piano teacher, and Wagner himself) that Ludwig was unmusical, and that what captivated him was not the music so much as the romantic texts of the operas. His characteristic quotations are from *Tannhäuser* and *Lohengrin*, and they show his special fondness for statements about sin and salvation made by "spiritual" characters such as Wolfram. Nor does he distinguish between the early operas and the later: the music seemed to him all of a piece.[64] That he sometimes said *Tristan* was his favorite—which Newman suggests as an indication that Ludwig was not unmusical[65]—could be explained on the grounds that he associated the production of that work with the years of his most intense Wagner-worship.

Certainly Ludwig's sense of the works of Wagner seems to have derived more from the content of *Lohengrin* than from the music of *Tristan*. His favorite symbols were those of the earlier saga, from the time of his childhood at Hohenschwangau, where tableaux of the legend decorated the walls, to the time of his eccentric withdrawal from affairs of state, when he fed the swans at his private pier on Starnberg Lake. Before he was thirteen, a governess had thrilled him with accounts of *Lohengrin* at Munich, and three years later he persuaded his father to command a performance of that work—the title role sung by Ludwig Schnorr von Carolsfeld. By the time he had read the 1863 Preface to the *Ring*, Ludwig was determined to answer Wagner's call for model performances.

When shortly after he ascended the throne Ludwig told his cabinet secretary to find Wagner for him, the composer was financially at perhaps the lowest point of his career. No novelist could invent a better detail than that Wagner (eventually traced to Stuttgart) at first refused to see the "Secretary to the King of Bavaria" because he suspected a ruse on the part of one of his many creditors. Soon, however, Wagner was solvent. But his reputation for evading debts preceded him to Munich, and of course his political past was known. When he began to boast of his influence over the young king, suspicions were understandably aroused. And as he called to him a court of old musical associates he began to alienate the musicians of Munich too.[66]

Wagner gathered around him not only the artists, like Bülow and the Schnorrs, who would be directly involved in the first *Tristan*, but also many of the young writers and musicians who formed the entourage that gratified his demand for undivided attention. Among them was the composer Peter Cornelius, who infuriated the Master by refusing to come to Munich until he had finished writing his opera *Der Cid*. Cornelius's healthy instinct— which he unfortunately did not follow completely—was to stay clear of the influence of Wagner and his works. "Wagner is a Venus, I a Tannhäuser" he wrote to a friend, in the course of a correspondence filled with expressions of his fear of Wagner. Again, in a simile drawn from the work he felt he most had to avoid, "Wagner merely wants me to be his Kurvenal. He does not understand that although I have many qualifications for that role—including doglike fidelity—I also unfortunately have a bit of independence in my character, and too much talent to be merely the zero behind his one."[67]

To complete his entourage, Wagner needed what he often called "sympathetic female companionship." At first it was Mathilde Maier, an intelligent young woman whom he had met in 1862, who was asked to come to Munich to provide it. Her refusal coincided with the arrival, in advance of her husband, of Cosima von Bülow with her two children. Wagner and Cosima had not met since late November, 1863, on a day which Cosima later described as "the day when we found each other and were united in *Liebes-Todesnot*."[68] She did not go to live permanently with Wagner until 1866 (after the death of Minna) and they did not marry until 1870. Nevertheless her arrival in Munich marks her acceptance of the "call to destiny" to become the lover of Wagner, his companion and secretary, cocreator of his empire, and guardian of the imperial stronghold after his death.[69] It is a neat biographical coincidence that just as the composition of *Tristan* was inseparably bound up with the Wesendonk affair, the more practical matter of mounting it should concur with the beginning of Wagner's most successful liaison. Of the three marriages associated with *Tristan*—those of the Wagners, the Bülows, and the Wesendonks—only the last survived. Mathilde's final letter to Wagner—in response to Cosima's request for some manuscripts in her possession—is dated January 13, 1865.[70]

Once he was settled in Munich, Wagner's troubles increased in proportion as his friends settled around him and his comforts multiplied. Bülow, the musicologist Ludwig Nohl, and others of Wagner's circle were guilty of public indiscretions, and Wagner himself went on referring to the king as "mein Junge." The composer's doubts that *Tristan* and the *Ring* would be within the capacity of Munich singers led to plans for a new music school, set out in a detailed memoir to the king, which proposed that the Bavarian state finance a Wagnerian festival theater. The ostentatious luxury of Wagner's home also worried the treasury and scandalized the citizens. Forgotten creditors from earlier eras came to Munich. Wagner thoughtfully had his portrait painted for Ludwig, who awkwardly regarded it as a gift. Sober and self-interested bureaucrats clustered into anti-Wagnerian factions. Attacks on Wagner appeared in the papers and parodies of his activities in *Punsch*.[71] And most of the outrage and resentment focused on the preparations to perform an opera about two lovers who deny the world for love.

"Tristan" in Munich

In January, 1865, Wagner outlined for Ludwig a revised schedule of productions for the next nine years, beginning as follows:

May and June 1865. *Tristan* in the Residenz Theater, before an invited public: three to six performances, with Schnorr and his wife (Dresden), Mitterwurzer (Dresden) as Kurvenal, Beck (Vienna) as Marke, and Sophie Stehle (Munich) as Brangaene.[72]

Only the Dresden singers were in the actual performances. It is not known why Sophie Stehle declined the part of Brangaene: it was sung instead by Anna Dienet, a new member of the Munich company, whom Bülow considered very capable. Since Beck could not obtain leave from Vienna, the part of Mark eventually fell into the hands of Zottmayer, from Hanover. "Weak in the head but strong in the lungs" was Bülow's opinion of him, and his singing struck others as "uncouth"—qualities that indicate he was less than adequate for the role. Mitterwurzer had been the original Wolfram in the Dresden *Tannhäuser* of 1845: he had a fine baritone, but tended to overact.[73]

A series of mistimings had prevented Wagner from knowing the Schnorrs much earlier. In 1856 Tichatschek had told Wagner about his young colleague, then twenty, who had already made his debut at Karlsruhe. Schnorr not only had an extraordinary voice, but as the son of a famous painter (Julius Schnorr von Carolsfeld) was more cultured than the average tenor of the time. He married Malvina Garrigues in 1860—she was ten years older than he, and as early as 1848 Wagner had heard her sing another sort of love-death, as Norma. They were still in the Karlsruhe company at the time of the first projected *Tristan*, but they left for Dresden in 1860, before Wagner's second attempt to produce *Tristan* at Karlsruhe.[74] Wagner could have borrowed Schnorr from Dresden, but he had heard sufficiently dreadful reports of Schnorr's corpulence to dampen his desire to meet the intelligent tenor who was also a good actor—good enough, it may be remarked, to overcome the discrepancy between his enormous size* and King Ludwig's idealized envisionment of Wagner's heroes.[75]

Wagner did try to get Schnorr to save the Vienna production, but at that time the singer's obligations held him at Dresden. A guest appearance as Lohengrin at Karlsruhe in May, 1862, at last gave Wagner an opportunity to hear the tenor whom he henceforth judged the only possible Tristan. That summer the Schnorrs visited Wagner at Beibrich, where Bülow and Cosima were also visiting. The singers sang long stretches of *Tristan* with Bülow at

---

* There are photographs of Schnorr as Tristan, in which he looks rather as Brahms did thirty years later.

the piano, anticipating the performance for which all three were summoned to Munich in 1865. Schnorr, already an ardent Wagnerian, fell under the influence of Wagner's dominating personality.[76] Thus by 1865 Wagner had strong control over tenor, conductor, and financier—a complete reversal of the situation in Vienna.

Wagner therefore had every reason to regard the coming performances as the first of his "art festivals," and he issued an open invitation to the "friends of his art from far and near" who wanted to share in the highest and deepest artistic event in a manner quite different from the usual relationship between theater and public.[77] But mounting the model production continued to present unusual difficulties, among them the choice of the theater. Although Ludwig wanted *Tristan* in the Court Theater, which held 2,000, Wagner preferred the "cosy Residenz Theater," where the acoustics were lucid and the nuances of miming could be distinguished. Orchestral rehearsals proved that the work was out of scale in the small theater, and Wagner had to move it to the larger house, at what would seem to have been the negligible sacrifice of the miming effects. "For the first performances," Wagner wrote, "I had wished for a smaller and more select audience. I have to give this up in order to achieve musical clarity. Oh for my invisible, sunken, transfigured orchestra in the theater of the future!"[78]

Instead of his theater of the future Wagner got more creditors from the past, and he had to appeal to the treasury in order to save his furniture. Bülow, who was on the verge of a nervous breakdown, increased the difficulties with an almost catastrophic indiscretion.* He had been told that his request for an enlargement of the orchestral area would require the sacrifice of thirty stalls. "What does it matter," he shouted, "whether we have thirty

---

* Bülow had much earlier drawn Wagner's disapproval with an indiscretion about *Tristan*. "I deprecate as impractical," Wagner told him in 1859, "your expression of doubt [in an article on *Tristan*] as to the likelihood of the opera's popularity. Such words are not spoken simply *among ourselves* but spread to those who do not understand us, or who are more or less permanently hostile, and this fact should always be considered in writing for publication. Härtels are already becoming difficult on account of the expressed doubts of—my friend. What have you, I, and our few real friends to do with this tiresome question of popularity?"

Schweinehunde more or less in the place?" Despite his public apology, most Munich journals made use of this expression of "Prussian insolence" in their campaign to drive Bülow (and Wagner with him) out of town. Every day for a week, in larger letters each day, the *Neue Bayerischen Kurier* displayed the slogan "HANS VON BÜLOW IS STILL HERE!"[79]

The first performance was scheduled for May 15. Wagner's "friends from far and near" converged on Munich, as though rehearsing for their later pilgrimages to Bayreuth: Gasperini, representing the Paris Wagnerites; Heinrich Porges, who later wrote a guide to *Tristan* for King Ludwig; August Röckel, Wagner's old revolutionary colleague; the indiscreet musicologist Richard Pohl; the composers Adolf Jensen, Joachim Raff, Karl Eckert, Johann Kalliwoda, and Felix Draeseke. Eduard Larsen, who was later to conduct the first performance of *Tristan* outside Munich, and Leopold Damrosch, who brought the opera to New York, were also among the six hundred invited guests who attended a dress rehearsal on the eleventh, lasting from ten in the morning until after three in the afternoon.[80] Wagner spoke: "To the poison-filled heart that perchance may come to our work let us tender the love potion"—a sentiment which Ludwig reinforced by granting a pardon to those who had been imprisoned for participation in the revolution of 1849![81]

The open dress rehearsal was the only performance many of the guests heard, because the debut on the fifteenth had to be postponed. On that morning Wagner had scarcely finished borrowing money from the treasury when he received the news that Malvina Schnorr had become hoarse. It was inevitable that the postponement should occasion the widespread observation that the music had ruined Isolde's voice, and the by now overworked quip about the Music of the Future. Among the other speculations about what really caused the postponement was the rumor that the orchestra had gone on strike, led by the anti-Wagnerian hornist Franz Strauss (the father of Richard). Frau Schnorr did not recover for some weeks, during which time Munich could attend, instead of

Tristan, a parody called *Tristanderl und Süssholde.*[82] On June 10 the unperformable opera was at last performed. Although most of the more illustrious guests had to leave before then, there is, in retrospect, some compensation in the knowledge that the delayed performance was attended by the most profound and original post-Wagnerian symphonist, Anton Bruckner. Already past forty, Bruckner got to meet the Master he adored (to whom he later dedicated his Third Symphony); and on the occasion of this Munich visit he showed the manuscript of his First to Bülow.[83]

In comparison with their preparation and their aftermath the three performances—on the tenth, thirteenth, and nineteenth— were uneventful. Apparently both of the Schnorrs and the orchestra were excellent, the other singers (perhaps with the exception of Zottmayer) more than adequate. A "Schweinehund" demonstration against Bülow never materialized, and there were even some favorable notices in the press. Wagner, Bülow, and both Ludwigs were in a state of high elation. Cosima gave the king a cushion, which she embroidered with symbols of the music-dramas: the Dutchman's ship, Tannhäuser's staff, Ludwig's favorite Lohengrin swan, and the cup which contained the love potion.[84] But in a month Schnorr was dead, and within six months Wagner had been driven out of Munich. After the death of Schnorr, Wagner could associate *Tristan* with a new sort of renunciation:

How can I think [he wrote in his diary] of the only pleasure I have ever had from any of my works, how can I think of *Tristan,* without renouncing all joy henceforth for ever? I shudder when I think of *Tristan!* And that was the only time, the only time, when I was happy![85]

"Tristan" here can refer to the opera, the hero, and the tenor who created the role.

The Death of Tristan

The death of Ludwig Schnorr and the subsequent delusions of his widow bring to mind Wagner's early apprehension that only the healthiest natures could deeply involve themselves in *Tristan* with

safety. Wagner's recollections of Schnorr minimize the role played
by the exertions of singing and acting in the tenor's death—stress-
ing the fact that the carelessness of the stagehands, not the demands
of the composer, was responsible for the fatal draft that swept
across the stage. And Wagner supports his point by referring to
Schnorr's deathbed anxiety that his illness not be attributed to
overexertion.[86] These recollections, however, were written three
years after Schnorr's death;* and the disjointed entries in Wagner's
diary at the time of the death indicate that he shared the general
impression that Schnorr had sacrificed himself to *Tristan*: "My
Tristan! My Beloved!" Wagner wrote, "I drove you to the
abyss. . . . I lay hold of him to check him, to draw him back, and
I push him over. . . . And myself? My head does not swim. I look
down: it even delights me. But—the friend? Him I lose! Mein
Tristan! Mein Trauter!"[87] A year later Wagner succinctly characterized Schnorr's devotion: "For me he lived, for me he died."[88]
There is no doubt that Schnorr had died in a delirium of Wagner-
worship. "O Siegfried, Siegfried, farewell!" he cried, referring to
the role he was preparing. "Console Richard!" And again: "My
Richard loved me! I die happy: *He* loved me." In his penultimate
paroxysm he sang passages from the role of Siegfried, and cried
out a wish to see Wagner once more.[89] Wagner had a genuine
feeling of friendship for Schnorr, and in addition he regretted the
loss of his greatest tenor. Hero worship, however, nourished his
egotism, and there is in his reaction to Schnorr's death a hint of
gratification that there can be death-devoted Wagnerians.

One effect of Schnorr's death was to drive his widow to spiritualism. Malvina began to believe that she was in communication
with her dead husband, and she eventually turned up at Triebschen
with a young lady who served as her medium. Apparently Schnorr
had announced to his wife from beyond the grave that henceforth
she was to play a guiding part in Wagner's life. This "mission"
would justify her husband's self-sacrifice for the Wagnerian cause.
Tristan as much as spiritualism determined the nature of Malvina's

---

* After the death of Schnorr, Wagner retired to a quiet hut on the Hochkopf,
and read the *Ramayana*.

delusions.[90] She and Wagner were to effect a Platonic union of souls: he would find redemption through the love of the "pure divine womanliness" he had so often celebrated in his works. She idealized herself just as Wagner had idealized Mathilde Wesendonk a decade earlier: Tristanizing had returned to plague its inventor.

It is therefore ironic that Wagner should have behaved as Minna had done in the earlier affair: he interpreted Malvina's behavior in the crassest way—as a mad passion with the object matrimony, converted into crazed jealousy upon the discovery that Cosima was Wagner's mistress. To be sure, Malvina had already begun to feel that Cosima was an "evil spirit" who prevented Wagner from properly responding, and this feeling grew into one of plain hatred of Cosima. But Wagner and Cosima had a more urgent reason for picturing Malvina as Phaedra rather than as Senta or Isolde: the woman had to be discredited as mad with jealousy before she exposed their adultery to the king. There followed a long series of deceitful attempts to suppress Malvina and get her evicted from Munich.[91] She, in turn, tried to tell Ludwig about the illicit liaison. The king was hard to convince. It took four years for him to acknowledge the plain fact that Wagner and Cosima had not been living according to the rules of the chaste friendship he idealized.

The chief victim of all this was Hans von Bülow. He remained at Munich as *Kapellmeister* long enough to conduct the second set of *Tristan*s in 1869. Once again a child was born to Cosima and Wagner on the eve of *Tristan* performances: their only son, Siegfried, on June 6, 1869.* On the fifteenth Cosima wrote to her husband asking for a divorce. Bülow replied on the seventeenth— three days before the scheduled first performance. His chivalric reply is generous to Cosima, whom he cannot blame for preferring to devote "the treasures of her mind and affection" to a superior being.[92] Towards neither his wife nor Wagner does he display any resentment. Instead it is turned toward himself, and toward the work with which he associated the whole nightmare:

---

* The "Meistersinger" daughter, Eva, was born in February, 1867. Bülow conducted the debut of that opera in Munich in 1868.

My intensive work on *Tristan*, that gigantic but devastating production, has literally finished me. . . . My stay in Munich will end where it began. This constitutes a kind of rounding off (a fateful rather than a vicious circle), and will make it easier for me later to look back on the series of events and on my sufferings (the punishment of my faults towards you), which fall between the four years' interval between the two representations of this same work, as a nightmare.

Yes, without any reproach to its mighty creator, *Tristan* has given me the *coup de grâce*. . . . Poor Eberle, Richter's pet *répétiteur*, was driven mad during the rehearsals by the opera itself (we tell the public it was an excess of beer); as for me, who confess always to have lacked the necessary courage in my very numerous arrangements for taking my life, I assure you I could not have resisted the temptation if anyone had offered me a few drops of prussic acid.[93]

Du Moulin Eckart tells us that "Frau Cosima and the Master smiled together at this curious indictment of a great and mighty work, in the service of which nobody had laboured so nobly or so congenially as Hans himself."[94] Perhaps Wagner, remembering the remarks he had once made about musical intoxication, was amused by the public explanation of the *répétiteur*'s "madness." There is certainly nothing amusing about the anxieties, overwork, personal bitterness, and loss of self-esteem that lie beneath Bülow's outburst against the opera—or about the danger that suicide might have been added to death, delusion, and divorce in the chain of disasters that trailed after *Tristan* in Munich.

Bülow was, after all, reiterating the apprehensions that Wagner himself had always had about the dangers of *Tristan*—apprehensions that the performances of 1865 had confirmed. The Schnorrs, it must be admitted, had been especially vulnerable—Ludwig physically and Malvina mentally—and Bülow was notoriously hypersensitive. In the following years, however, the Master would have a chance to try his "great and mighty work" on a stronger nature. For Friedrich Nietzsche had already begun to visit Triebschen.

chapter III

NIETZSCHE PRO TRISTAN (1868-1888)

The Pattern of Criticism

It is well known that Nietzsche went to Bayreuth in 1876, heard parts of the *Ring*, observed the audience, and left in acute physical distress. It is not so well known that before then Nietzsche had ceased to be an uncritical Wagnerite. Bayreuth was less a sudden revelation than it was a vivid confirmation of cultural evils Nietzsche had already observed—evils which *Parsifal*, still later, confirmed again most notoriously. Nietzsche had been ready for revulsion and disappointment, and the Festival simply dramatized his apprehensions.[1]

Nietzsche's sister has offered the opinion that his disappointment would not have been so great if, instead of the *Ring*, the work performed had been *Tristan*.[2] Of course *Tristan* would have been an unlikely choice for the opening of Bayreuth in 1876. It is not so obviously Germanic as the *Ring*, and it lacks the elaborate scenic magnificence that could demonstrate, as the opening of Bayreuth required, all the mechanics of the Wagnerian system in full operation. And it would not have been suitable to inaugurate the grand project which owed its realization to the patience and energy of Cosima Wagner with the work that was supposed to have been inspired by Mathilde Wesendonk.

Nor is it prudent to consider the conjecture of Frau Förster-

Nietzsche seriously, when one can't even trust her facts. Her campaign to pervert the meaning of her brother's philosophy, and to establish for him a reputation that would attract as disciples precisely those people of whom he would have most disapproved, included an attempt to minimize the importance and severity of Nietzsche's break with Wagner. This she did in her edition of the Nietzsche-Wagner correspondence, in which fragments of the letters (some of them reconstructed from Nietzsche's rough drafts) are connected by a great deal of editorial material, designed, as Frau Förster boldly informs the reader, "to set in vibration only the tenderest chords of the closest friendship, which even though they be written in a melancholy minor, at least reveal no harsh dissonances on either side." The dissonances, which were sounded after the correspondence ceased, must, as the editor helpfully notes, be looked for "in other places."[3]

The other places are, of course, the later works of Nietzsche— particularly the paragraphs of insight and invective that were collected under the title *Nietzsche contra Wagner*, and the wittiest and most incisive critique of Wagnerism that has yet been written, *The Wagner Case*. Both books were published in 1888, five years after Wagner's death. It has often been pointed out—Nietzsche said so himself—that criticism so violent and so penetrating could only have been written by someone who had once been a devotee, that the denunciation in *The Wagner Case* is the counterpart of the extravagant praise in *The Birth of Tragedy*. Some critics have decided to disregard Nietzsche's anti-Wagnerism because it derived from disappointment.[4] But Nietzsche's polemic was a surer acknowledgment of Wagner's powers than the praise of Wagnerites. "Savage as he is"—the observation is W. H. Auden's— "Nietzsche never allows the reader to forget for one instant that Wagner is an extraordinary genius and that, for all which may be wrong with it, his music is of the highest importance."[5]

As Auden suggests, it was for the *music* of Wagner that Nietzsche retained his respect. But it is possible to be more specific. For it appears that with a particular kind of Wagnerian music—the chromatic music of *Tristan*—Nietzsche remained in a state of infatuation. This would support Frau Förster-Nietzsche's hypothesis about Bayreuth, 1876; indeed, Walter Kaufmann, whose understanding of Nietzsche corresponds in no other way with that of the sister-editor, notes the philosopher's particular love for the music of *Tristan*. And the dependable Nietzsche scholar Kurt Hildebrandt has observed that *Tristan* remained an effective experience for Nietzsche long after he had ceased to be a Wagnerian in any party sense of the word.[6] It appears that *Tristan* was exempt from Nietzsche's disenchantment with Wagnerism—or, more accurately, that the power of the music remained a more formidable danger than the bombast, the mechanical philosophy, and the sentimental Christianity which one can so easily follow Nietzsche in condemning.

The unique importance of the *Tristan* music is recorded in *Ecce Homo*, the autobiographical work written in the same year as *The Wagner Case* and *Nietzsche contra Wagner*—the last productive year of Nietzsche's life:

All things considered, I could never have stood my youth without Wagner's music. . . . When one wants to rid oneself of an intolerable pressure, one needs hashish. Well, I needed Wagner. . . . From the very moment when there was a piano score for *Tristan*—my compliments, Herr von Bülow—I was a Wagnerian. I considered Wagner's previous works beneath me—they were too common, too "German." But to this day I am still looking for a work of equally dangerous fascination, of an equally shivery and sweet infinity, as *Tristan*—and I look in all the arts, in vain. . . . This work is by all means the *non plus ultra* of Wagner; the *Meistersinger* and the *Ring* were merely relaxation to him. . . . I regard it as a particular good fortune to have lived at the right time and to have lived precisely among Germans, in order to be *ripe* for this work. . . . The world is poor for those who have never been sick enough for this "voluptuousness of hell": it is permissible, it is almost imperative, to have recourse to a formulation of the mystics.[7]

In this passage Nietzsche sets the pattern of criticism for others who also came to Triebschen under the spell of *Tristan* and discovered that the spell survived their departure. Here is what may be

described as a moral revulsion to what one is attracted to aesthetically: "dangerous" is a moral judgment of the aesthetic "fascination." If Nietzsche had not been extremely sensitive to the kind
of harmonic lushness characteristic of the *Tristan* music, then he
would have been able fully to reject the attractions of *Tristan* along
with those of the other operas he not only rejected but outgrew. A
distaste for the ingenious pastiche of motifs that constitutes most of
the musical texture of the *Ring* can naturally follow upon a rejection of the work's eclectic message. *Tannhäuser* is early and uneven;
and *Lohengrin*, stylistically consistent as it is, displays a sameness of
texture that serves to remind musicians of the great advance in
technique evident in *Rheingold*. The parts of *Parsifal* that are not
Tristanesque are for worshipers who have never doubted the
Master's perfect rightness. And if everyone liked *Meistersinger*—
it was the favorite Wagner opera of Brahms and of Hanslick—
there is at least nothing dangerous about its sunny C major.
Nietzsche even thought of it as gay. But the fascination of *Tristan*
is dangerous because it is indelible: one cannot eradicate one's
responsiveness, but only disapprove of it. And Nietzsche seems to
have responded to its sensuousness as strongly at the end of his
career as when he and his fellow students first decoded Bülow's
piano score.

Coming to Triebschen

It was the fall of 1862 when Nietzsche and his friends Wilhelm
Pindar and Gustav Krug read through *Tristan* at the piano, and
although Bülow's score was no longer hot off the press (it had
been published in 1860) the three young men of eighteen were
probably among the first to study the work. They were already
enthusiastic followers of the new music, subscribers to Franz
Brendel's pro-Wagner *Zeitschrift für Musik*, and authors of papers
on the relationship between music and poetry and on the art-work
of the future. Frau Förster-Nietzsche recollects that her mother
(like the parents of Pindar and Krug) considered the piano-play-
ing "a frightful noise"—probably because the pianists "did not

understand how to make the melody stand out from the rich harmonic background."[8] One may wonder which melody she is referring to, since the "unending melody" of *Tristan*, which is inseparable from its harmonic context, scarcely contains the sort of tune likely to catch the ear of a household listener. And presumably the harmonic texture was what most interested the students of the new work. "Even I," Frau Förster-Nietzsche confesses, "could not get up any enthusiasm about it at first"; but happily she was converted when her brother and his friends succeeded in getting across the effect of the hunting horns at the beginning of the second act.[9] She reports that her brother insisted that "everyone *must* be enraptured" by the music; and even though it is doubtful that she could accurately remember Nietzsche's words —not to mention her mother's long retort, which is reported verbatim—it may be assumed that, like many discoverers of *Tristan's* harmonies since, he tried to make converts.

Apparently Nietzsche did not hear an orchestra play any excerpt from *Tristan* until six years later, during the last year of his classical studies at Leipzig and three years after he had encountered the works of Schopenhauer. In October, 1868, the Euterpe Society of Leipzig performed the Prelude, along with the Overture to *Die Meistersinger*. Nietzsche wrote to his friend Rohde that he could not bring himself to keep critically cool toward the music, which "set every fiber and every nerve tingling"—the words, as Hildebrandt observes, not of a doctrinaire Wagnerite but of someone who is carried away by music.[10] He was so ardent a music-lover that he wanted to combine his enthusiasm with his professional activities: according to a letter written that summer, he was already in search of "some philological matter that could be treated musically." On finding it he would "stammer like a baby and pile up images, like a barbarian lost in dreams in the presence of an antique Venus-head."[11]

If this was the dawn of the ideas that would lead to the Basel lectures of January, 1870, on the Greek Music Drama, and thence to *The Birth of Tragedy*, then Nietzsche's meeting with Wagner, less than two weeks after the Leipzig concert, came when the time was ripe; especially so because the following year, after he received his professorship at Basel, he was near enough to Wagner's home at Triebschen to be a frequent and favorite visitor. He quickly became devoted to Cosima. For Wagner he adjusted his ideas on music and Greek tragedy so that they would seem perfectly in tune with the Master's belief that his music-dramas were embodiments of Greek aesthetic ideals. Add to this a shared enthusiasm for Schopenhauer, and it seems inevitable that the Master should have found a philosophical disciple, and the philosopher a musical hero. Of all the works of Wagner, *Tristan* best represented the wedding of Schopenhauer and Dionysus: the striving Schopenhauerian will of the lovers embodied in music of Dionysian frenzy.

A letter to Wagner of November, 1870, epitomizes Nietzsche's hero worship. It is a brief commentary on Wagner's *Beethoven* essay, which Nietzsche received shortly after he had returned, in ruined health, from his service as an orderly in the Prussian army. Nietzsche is happy to find that Wagner's ideas are perfectly harmonious with those of Schopenhauer: together, theirs is "the *only* philosophy of music." But even *cognoscenti* of Schopenhauer will have difficulty in recognizing Wagner's profound discipleship. In fact a genuine appreciation of Wagner, Nietzsche insists, is reserved for a select few, not philosophical so much as musical— namely, "those to whom the message of *Tristan* has been revealed."[12]

A year later Nietzsche is still thinking of himself as among initiates: "To only a few hundred people of the next generation will the music of Wagner mean what it does now to me." This is in a letter to Rohde describing a concert in Mannheim—the first of the fund-raising concerts for Bayreuth—which included on the program the Prelude and *Liebestod*. "It is precisely this," he writes, "and nothing else, that I mean by the word 'music' in describing the Dionysian."[13] By this time *The Birth of Tragedy*, with its freshly rewritten Preface to Wagner,[14] and its appended chapters about *Tristan and Isolde* and the music of the future, was already in print, ready for publication in January, 1872.

The Rebirth of Tragedy

The later chapters of *The Birth of Tragedy* are the first important literary expression of Tristanism. But even the earlier part of the essay, which deals with the origins of Greek drama, would have been different, and presumably more circumspect in its assertions, if Nietzsche had not known Wagner's masterpiece.[15] For *Tristan* was probably the chief source of Nietzsche's recognition of music as the Dionysian art. Nietzsche does not mean the graceful, melodious, "Mediterranean" music, which he would later endorse as the antithesis to Wagner; in *The Birth of Tragedy* that is merely Apollo's music—"plastic rhythm" and "Doric architecture of sound"—with which the Greeks had long been familiar before the music of Dionysus "spread abroad terror and a deep shudder." Dionysian music is characterized by a "heart-shaking power of tone," and by a "constant stream of melody" (as opposed to an ordered tune). Above all it makes use of "incomparable resources of harmony"—particularly harmonic *dissonance*, which is a source of primal Dionysian delight. In its full force it is music of frenzy [*Rausch*] and excess.[16] In short, it is the Tristanesque.

Just as Schopenhauer had criticized as unmusical the imitative passages in the *Creation* and the *Seasons* of Haydn, Nietzsche belittled the sort of music that is only a "paltry replica" of phenomena, which "simply tries to beguile us with external analogies between some natural event and certain rhythmical and acoustical combinations."[17] In 1871 Nietzsche did not foresee that Wagner's popularity among the educated Philistines would derive in great part from his ability at just this sort of tone-painting, and that he himself would come to consider it a sign of Wagner's decadence. In *Tristan*, at any rate, there is very much less literal imitation (Isolde's waving, Tristan's heartbeat, the sea motif, conceivably) than there is, say, in the *Ring*; and therefore more of the Dionysian music which "offers us a universal mirror of the world will"—and is the source of tragedy.[18]

The recognition of the Dionysian origin of tragedy, and of the

special character of music as the Dionysian art, enabled Nietzsche
to inspect the problem of tragedy from a point of view that was
not derived from conventional aesthetics—which misguidedly expected music and tragedy to answer to criteria of beauty proper
only to the plastic arts.[19] Music stimulates the imagination to em-
body the immaterial world—"which speaks to us . . . and yet
remains invisible"—in images that in turn gain heightened significance because of their association with the appropriate music.
Music can, that is to say, give birth to myth—notably to the tragic
myth, in which the symbolic images are endowed with supreme
significance by the music which suggested the images in the first
place. In tragedy the characters of the myth and their action are
invented by the Apollonian imagination—which may be thought
of as the Nietzschean version of the form-giving power that the generation of Winckelmann and Goethe had extolled as the genius
of Greek art. But music and the chants of the chorus—the elements
of Dionysian frenzy—supply the life, the "everlasting lust for becoming," as though "illuminating the stage figures from within."
And at the tragic catastrophe the Dionysian fury shatters the organized Apollonian stage-world and triumphs in destructive joy.[20]

In passages of similarly poetic metaphysics, Nietzsche gave his
revolutionary account of the birth of Greek tragedy from the
spirit of music, and of its subsequent murder by the rationalizing
spirit of Socrates and Euripides. In the last chapters of the essay
Nietzsche turned his attention from Athens to Central Europe.
The Wagnerian section (chapters 16-25) might better have been
called the Rebirth of Tragedy from the Spirit of Music.[21] For they
describe the renaissance of a new tragic art, the music-drama,
recently arisen out of the ashes of the typical art-form of modern
Socratic culture—the opera.

The difficulty of Nietzsche's criticism of opera is that he never
says which operas he has in mind. Wagner is the only composer
mentioned by name; and any twentieth-century reader must
wonder where, at this stage in the development of his musical ideas,
Nietzsche would have placed the greatest composer of dramatic

music, Mozart. Part of Nietzsche's attack is against the recitative, and against the theory—which he seems to have associated with the alternation of recitative and aria—that the text, rather than the music, was the soul of opera.[22] Now the eighteenth-century opera of, say, Gluck was theoretically supposed to have already reasserted the aesthetic ideals of Greek tragedy. Among these ideals were those of perfect proportion and moderation which an Augustan age selected as most in harmony with its own rationalism. They persisted as a set of clichés, despite the efforts of Heine and others who anticipated Nietzsche in recognizing the Bacchic Greece. A chief purpose of Nietzsche's essay was to extol the Dionysian values of Greek art as against what may be called the "Grecian-urn" aesthetics of eighteenth-century and romantic Hellenism. One of the dicta of Gluck's famous Preface to *Alceste*—it was, as we know, reiterated by Wagner in his early theory—was that in opera the music should be put in the service of the text and the action. "I have striven," Gluck wrote, "to restrict music to its true office of serving poetry by means of expression and by following the situations of the story, without interrupting the action or stifling it with a useless superfluity of ornaments."[23] For Nietzsche, one of the signs of the victory of the anti-Dionysian spirit in Greek tragedy had been just this sort of subordination of the music to the other elements—"the victory of the particular over the general." Euripides, for example, had concentrated on single character traits, and the spectator had ceased to be aware of myth at all and attended instead to the amazing lifelikeness of the characters.* All that then remained for the musical elements of tragedy was either decoration or tone painting—at its Euripidean best it depicted fiery emotions in place of representing Dionysian transports —and when the Dionysian genius of music had departed from tragedy, tragedy was dead.[24] Similarly, an operatic art whose ideal is a semimusical declamation—in which the music is "wholly ex-

* Yet it may be remarked that in the *Hippolytus* Euripides gave us the closest classical parallel to *Tristan*. Phaedra is obsessed with an impossible object, and in her suicide-condemnation of Hippolytus achieves a kind of consummation in death.

ternal and incapable of reverence"—merely produces a superficial and mosaiclike conglutination of elements. The Dionysian profundities are replaced either by a rationalistic rhetoric or by an indulgence of vocal virtuosity.[25] Nietzsche thus rejects not only the subordination of music to text which was required by Gluck's theory (though it was not always his practice), but also the unsubordinated but "ornamental" music to which Gluck himself, for different reasons, objected.

Fortunately a new Dionysian spirit had arisen that promised to release music from its enslavement to a Socratic art. A power had sprung out of the recesses of the German soul—it could first be detected in the chorales of the Reformation—and revealed itself in the orchestral music of Bach, Beethoven, and Wagner. Socratism, bent as it is on the extermination of myth, dreads the potency of this nonoperatic "monster that has risen out of the infinite depths." Wagnerian music-drama—which Wagner and Nietzsche both considered to be in the tradition not of opera but of the symphony—heralds the new age of tragedy that will replace the Alexandrian opera with German myth from German music.[26] The nineteenth century is thus moving through the phases of Greek cultural history in reverse order—a reversal prefigured by Socrates himself, when in his old age he recognized that he must practice music.[27] At the end of his career Nietzsche will extol the French, "southern" gaiety of Bizet as the antithesis to the Teutonic ponderousness of Wagner. In *The Birth of Tragedy* it is presumably French and Italian opera that represents the decadence of an art into which German music, culminating in Wagner, will inject new life.

Dionysian

When Nietzsche is ready to illustrate his point with Wagnerian quotation he addresses himself only to those of his readers who are genuine musicians—listeners, that is to say, who, like Nietzsche himself (and unlike the later Wagnerian audiences), are in the habit of responding almost exclusively to what he calls "unconscious musical relations," without the need of words, actors, or scenery to reinforce their response.[28] The third act of *Tristan*, apart from word and image, is like the movement of a powerful symphony. Is it possible, Nietzsche asks, for any of his selected hyperaesthetic listeners to hear this music without being shattered? In asking this question, Nietzsche piles image upon image in the manner of a turn-of-the-century Tristanite; D'Annunzio in particular comes to mind:

How is it possible for a man who has listened to the very heartbeat of the world-will and felt the unruly lust for life rush into all the veins of the world, now as a thundering torrent and now as a delicately foaming brook—how is it possible for him to remain unshattered? How can he bear, enclosed in the paltry glass bell of his individuality, to hear the echoes of innumerable cries of weal and woe sounding out of the "vast spaces of cosmic night," and not wish, amidst these pipings of metaphysical pastoral, to flee incontinent to his primordial home?[29]

Sixteen years after he wrote this, in the preface to a new edition, Nietzsche rightly noted that his language had been "terribly diffuse and full of unpalatable ferment." He observed that his first book exhibited "every conceivable fault of adolescence"—the sort of judgment a number of mature critics have made about their early jottings on the wonders of *Tristan*.[30]

The answer to Nietzsche's question is that the listener is not shattered by his disconcertingly intense reaction to the music precisely because he must become aware of words and images. As the listener is about to expire in a paroxysm of feeling, Apollo comes to the rescue:

It is at this point that the tragic myth and the tragic hero interpose between our highest musical excitement and the music, giving us a parable of those cosmic facts of which the music alone can speak directly. . . . The Apollonian power, bent on reconstituting the nearly shattered individual, asserts itself, proffering the balm of a delightful illusion.[31]

Nietzsche gives some examples of what happens when the ideal listener becomes a spectator. At the beginning of the third act he hears music that is like "a hollow sigh echoing from the womb of things." But when he becomes aware of the scene, with Tristan lying mortally wounded, the music connotes the presumably more bearable image of the abandoned and empty sea. Again, later, the jubilation of the shepherd's horn would cut the listener to the quick if he did not see Kurvenal rejoicing at the arrival of Isolde's ship. We are moved by joy and pity, but "no matter how deeply pity moves us, that pity saves us from the radical 'pity of things,' even as the parable of myth saves us from the direct intuition of the cosmic idea, as idea and word save us from the undammed pouring forth of the unconscious will."[32]

Kurvenal has sighted Isolde's ship, and Apollonian illusion has triumphed over Dionysian frenzy. But the supreme scene of the *Liebestod* is yet to be described. It seems that Apollo's victory was not complete: "In the final effect of tragedy the Dionysian element triumphs again: its closing sounds are such as were never heard in the Apollonian realm." Ultimately "the world of appearance is pushed to its limits, where it denies itself and seeks to escape back into the world of primordial reality."[33] In so far as they mean anything at all, the final words of Isolde's swan song, which Nietzsche at this point quotes, seem to be describing this very process, as well as the strange transfiguration of Isolde herself:

> In dem wogenden Schwall,
> in dem tönenden Schall,
> in des Welt-Athems
> wehendem All,
> ertrinken, versinken,
> unbewusst,—höchste Lust![34]

Clearly Dionysus triumphs in the end, as the oboe sounds the motif of desire for the last time. Yet in some way the Apollonian illusion is still present, having undergone a transformation that Nietzsche can describe only in metaphor. "The difficult relations between the two elements in tragedy may be symbolized by a fraternal union between the two deities: Dionysus speaks the language of Apollo, but Apollo, finally, the language of Dionysus;

thereby the highest goal of tragedy and of art in general is reached."[35]

It is perhaps an unwitting criticism of Wagner's dramatic technique that there is more action in the metaphorical drama enacted by Apollo and Dionysus than there is on the stage of Tristan and Isolde. The difficulty of Nietzsche's metaphor is compounded by the fact that in his later works it is Dionysus alone who symbolizes what is represented here as the union of the two gods. In *Zarathustra*, for example, the original opposition of the gods seems to be repudiated, and the Will to Power—the one force in the universe which is both striving and form-giving—is called Dionysian.[36] As Erich Heller has observed, the attempt to unravel the complex of historical reminiscences and insights associated with these Greek gods is doomed to failure: "A scholar's guarded steps cannot possibly keep pace with the rush and dance of the passions of the mind swirling around these names and arrested only for brief moments in innumerable figurations."[37] It is equally impossible to fix and label the leitmotifs in the third act of *Tristan*. But Nietzsche's puzzling description of the struggle and union of symbolic gods does at least make it clear that the drama of *Tristan* lies in the music. And the figurations of Nietzsche's early essay accurately characterize his response to that music's frenzy and sensuousness. In his later work Nietzsche denied the healthiness of that response. But the intensity of *Tristan* did not diminish between the time he judged it good and asked the world to listen, and the time he judged it bad and warned the world of its dangers.

Nothing but the Orchestra

Despite the great critical attention that has been given to *The Birth of Tragedy* and the circumstances of its composition, one surprising fact is never mentioned. Nietzsche could not have attended any stage performance of *Tristan* until after the book was in print.* He

---

* Only six performances of *Tristan* were given before 1872, all in Munich. Four were in 1865: the debut on June 10, and three repeats on June 13 and 19 and July 1. Presumably all this time Nietzsche was in Bonn. There are letters of his dated (or judged to have been written on) June 11, 16 (or 23), and 27, and

therefore had an extrinsic reason for restricting his discussion of *Tristan* to those readers who did not need scenery and actors to help them to understand the work.[38] They would have had to be musicians who could, as he did, get a symphonic thrill from playing the piano score—which was the only source of his knowledge of the music, apart from orchestral performances of the Prelude and *Liebestod*, and perhaps Wagner's private piano performances at Triebschen.

When Bülow invited him to attend the new performances of *Tristan* in the summer of 1872, Nietzsche could look forward to testing his recently published assertions about the work.[39] ("Take off your glasses!" Wagner wrote him, with what may be taken to be a humorous allusion to *The Birth of Tragedy* as well as to the quality and appearance of the singers: "You must pay attention to nothing but the orchestra.")[40] Nietzsche enthusiastically invited his friend Carl von Gersdorff to meet him in Munich: "Quickly, quickly. . . . We must hear the work twice!"[41] The performance did not belie the extravagant claims of his essay. " 'Tristan' was indescribable," he wrote Rohde, later adding (it was a judgment he never repeated) that of all the works he knew it was "the noblest and the most chaste (*die höchste Reinheit*)"! "One fairly floats in bliss and exaltation!"[42]

Contra Wagner

It was not long, however, before Nietzsche began jotting down the criticism of Wagner that grew into his great anti-Wagnerian essays. These essays contain surprisingly little specific textual criticism.[43] When particular references were occasionally needed to substantiate the charges, *Parsifal* was most conveniently at hand, as

---

July 6, all from Bonn; and there is no record of his having left Bonn at the time. In the letters of June 11 and mid-June he does describe in detail a music-festival he had attended in Cologne during the first week in June, at which were performed works by his then favorite composer, Schumann. Two more performances of *Tristan* were given in 1869, on June 20 and 23. Nietzsche wrote letters from Basel in mid-June, on the 16th and at the end of the month; and apparently he did not at the time leave his professorial duties, but was living "a life of seclusion."

the sacrosanct fetish of the Bayreuth cultists. Hence *Parsifal* is usually thought of as Nietzsche's chief aversion. But Wagner's last work was not completed until 1882, and, as we know, Nietzsche had begun to doubt the health of Wagnerism well before he wrote the laudatory (but colorless) essay on *Richard Wagner in Bayreuth* in 1876.[44] In the essays contra Wagner, the case against any one of the music-dramas is subsumed under the case against Wagnerism as a whole, just as the diseases of Wagnerism itself were seen as the symptoms of a general cultural decadence. At least three of Nietzsche's charges may nevertheless be isolated as particularly applicable to *Tristan*—and they have been the source of the most intelligent criticism of *Tristan* in the twentieth century. The first has to do with the defects of Wagner's rhythm and melody: Nietzsche generalizes these defects as "German" and compares them with the rhythmic and melodic inventiveness of French music. The second is the accusation that Wagner was primarily an "actor," who depended upon rhetoric for his mass appeal. The third consists of various objections to Wagner's sensuality. If the first attacks *Tristan* where it fails, in rhythm and melody, the third attacks it where it succeeds too well, in the lushness of its harmony.

In *Nietzsche contra Wagner* the effect of Wagner's famous "infinite melody" is described in a simile: "One walks into the sea, gradually loses one's secure footing, and finally surrenders oneself to the elements without reservation: one must *swim*."[45] Nietzsche had once praised such surrender to the elements as properly Dionysian, and in *The Birth of Tragedy* he had displayed a Swinburnian fondness for images of musical drowning.* Now Wagnerian swimming had become a symptom of decadence, a musical disease of which the healthy counterpart was dancing. One dances to rhythms. But infinite melody, according to Nietzsche,

---

* Someone in Hollywood, for a film called *Humoresque*, thought of accompanying the scene of a suicide-drowning with the *Liebestod*—the vocal line played on a solo violin! In a proper performance, incidentally, it quite suits the meaning and style of *Tristan* to *allow* Isolde's voice to be "drowned out" by the orchestra during her final solo. Conductors who hold the orchestra down at the climaxes overlook the fact that Wagner could have written the voice line "above" it if he had wanted to.

seeks deliberately to break all evenness of time and force and even scorns it occasionally; it marks the complete degeneration of rhythmic feeling, chaos in place of order.

Infinite melody is not only unrhythmic—it is also not melody. Nietzsche might have observed that the two criticisms are really one, for rhythm defines the form and movement of successful melody. This is evident in the Bellini-like regular periods of Chopin and in the irregular long lines of Berlioz—to mention two of the great melodists, significantly Mediterranean in style, in comparison with whom Wagner's inadequacies as a melodist have recently been pointed out.[46] Nietzsche, of course, thought of Chopin as Slavic rather than French. "I still have enough of the Pole in me," he wrote in *Ecce Homo*, "to let all other music go, if only Chopin is left to me." But this is in a passage where all other musicians— Slavs, Croats, Italians, Dutchmen, Jews—are contrasted favorably with the Germans.[47]

That Wagner sought deliberately to avoid melody is a generous suggestion. Actually "infinite melody," like other features of Wagner's system, was a technique he devised to cover up for a lack of gift. Schumann noted Wagner's deficiency in melodic invention[48] even before *The Flying Dutchman, Tannhäuser*, and *Lohengrin* indicated that Wagner would never tire of repeating the same four-crotchet tune first heard in the Overture to *Die Feen*. It is reported that Wagner himself was amused (and presumably disconcerted) by the prevalence of the rhythmic cliché

in most of the important "arias" in his earlier operas.[49] Only 96 bars in all of *Lohengrin* are in triple time (ten minutes in three and a half hours).[50] From *Rheingold* onward, the inadequacy is disguised by setting leitmotifs—not melodies but phrases—end to end to form a continuous pseudo-melodic texture. Above the texture, at the surface of the harmony, the vocal line, following the rise and fall of verbal declamation, is attached to convenient series of notes, sometimes complete leitmotifs, more often fragments of them—never melodies, as one can test by playing the vocal line without its harmonic support. The vocal line of the third act of *Tristan*, for example, played apart from the orchestral harmonies, can sound as unmelodic as any of the purposely unmemorable vocal lines of Schoenberg. In the later music-dramas this substitution of sung declamation for melody was so well done—and so effectively provided with a rationale by Wagnerian propaganda*—that it established a new method of vocal composition, carried on faithfully even by composers (like Hugo Wolf) who could also employ a true melodic talent.[51]

In *Tristan* the melodic clichés of the earlier operas can still be detected behind various disguises. To take one of the most cleverly disguised examples, the tune that each of the lovers sings near the end of Act II (beginning "Dem Land, das Tristan meint," after "O König") may be very much better than, say, the love-duet of Lohengrin and Elsa, but it would be no less monotonous rhythmically if it had not been forced into triple time and patched up with an interpolated reminiscence of the *Liebesnacht*.[47] Isolde's Narrative and the orchestral prelude to the second act fall into four-square sequences which would be as tedious as examples of the same rhythmic defect in Scriabin or César Franck if the harmonic coloration did not command the listener's attention. Even the *Liebestod* can be easily fitted into the rectangles of a quadrille, as Emmanuel Chabrier proved in a loving parody called *Souvenirs of*

---

* Henry T. Finck, author of a turn-of-the-century *Wagner and his Works*, was among the Wagnerites who were outraged by the criticism that *Tristan* is lacking in melody. For him *Tristan* is a "forest of melodies which the myopic cannot see on account of the trees." He goes on to show that the melody is "emancipated," "continuous," and so forth—certainly never a trite geometric tune. In extravagant language Finck points out the harmonic beauties of *Tristan* and insists on calling them "melodic." Bernard Shaw takes a similar position: symmetrical tune-turning is easy—the hard way is to weave leitmotifs symphonically. Yet he elsewhere observes that Sarastro's (symmetrical) tunes provide the only music fit to be sung by God.

Munich. What few genuine melodic stretches there are in Wagner arise, it would seem, almost inadvertently out of the tone color of an instrument, like the English horn solo that creates the desolate atmosphere of the third act. Nowhere is Wagner's inability to write a natural tune more evident than at places where the plot requires one apart from any special kind of harmonic coloration—unless Cecil Gray is wrong as well as heretical when he observes that the Prize Song in *Meistersinger* is one of the most forced and cragged tunes ever constructed.[52]

Any one of Nietzsche's criticisms can thus set off a chain re-action of examples that embellish his point. He, on the other hand, directly exposes the cultural diseases which Wagner's faults symptomize. The trouble with "infinite melody" is that it gives us infinity *instead of* melody: there is no thought in Wagner, only the chaos that precedes thought. Wagner deprives one of the intellectual pleasure of music—a pleasure, Nietzsche might have added, for which there is no substitute in the recognition and tracing of leitmotifs. As the cure for the cancer of "infinity without melody" Nietzsche recommends "light feet, wit, fire, grace; . . . logic, the dance of the stars, exuberant intellectuality, the vibrating light of the South, calm sea—perfection"; in short, all the characteristics of *la gaya scienza*.[53] If even the wit and gaiety of *Meistersinger* is ponderous and labored, certainly the darkness and gloom of the endless night in *Tristan* is the antithesis of Southern daylight and dancing. What more effective foil than *Tristan* to set off the glittering qualities of French art—whether the composer chosen be Nietzsche's Bizet, André Gide's Chopin, or the Berlioz who has been rediscovered in recent decades?

Historians of European music often like to distinguish two traditions—a "playing North" and a "singing South."[54] Despite the inevitable intermingling, the first is orchestral and harmonic, the second vocal and melodic. When repudiating the first, Nietzsche took up the second with the enthusiasm of rediscovery. In addition to *Carmen,* he returned to Schopenhauer's Rossini; and he chose as the only city that was truly musical, Venice[55]—not, presumably, the Venice of the second act of *Tristan*. But perhaps Wagner's faults—"Northern" and "German" as they may be—are in a still more general way representative of the faults of European music taken as a whole. In comparison with Near-Eastern complexity, our rhythms are, after all, confined within simple duple or triple patterns; and compared, let us say, with the subtle quarter tones of the music of India, our melodies require little attention to pitch. Indeed, equal temperament requires a certain dulling of the sense of pitch—a loss that is compensated for, of course, by the possibilities of modulation in our uniquely *harmonic* music.

More Air!

Wagner had one talent that might have been associated with Southern wit—a talent for miming. He was brought up in a theatrical family, and early in life married an actress. To the end of his life his favorite hobby was the devising of stage effects; and he never gave up his desire to dominate the stage, even when it was only his own parlor, draped in the heavy velvet hangings that were his favorite *décor*. Nietzsche recognized this actor's instinct as the chief explanation of the character of Wagner's art. In the music itself there was *Schauspielerei: "espressivo* at any price, and music in the service, the slavery, of poses."[56] Worse still, effect-mongering was part of the Wagnerian system; hence the musician who would follow in Wagner's school would also become an actor, and develop his talent for *telling lies*.[57] Thus Nietzsche is critical in advance of the seductive but superficial effectiveness that mars the music of even the greatest of post-Wagnerians, Mahler and Richard Strauss.*

When the striving for effect at any cost is combined with the greatest harmonic powers, there is clearly a danger: witness the

* Wagner himself, it is important to remember, similarly criticized Meyerbeer for having relied too much on "effects." Meyerbeer, Wagner, Mahler, Strauss: there is a tradition of large-scale "expressiveness at any cost"; yet the vulgar and the theatrical are often, as Sir Kenneth Clark observes about Rodin, an extension of the true. Nietzsche recognized this when he wittily called Wagner "the ventriloquist—of God"!

female Wagnerite who "with will suspended lets *Tristan and Isolde* 'come over' her."[58] At the time of *The Birth of Tragedy* only a few initiates could appreciate the frenzy of that music. Now large audiences wallow in Wagnerian lies, and the educated Philistines are especially satisfied when their easy pleasures are elevated into what they think of as spiritual experiences. Hence the success among the Wagnerian ladies (Nietzsche knew Malwida von Meysenbug) of *Parsifal*—where the harmonies of *Tristan* are rendered acceptable by the religious message. "He who overthrows us is strong," they think; "he who elevates us is godly; he who makes us wonder vaguely is profound."[59] What overthrows best is *passion;* and Nietzsche sees Wagner as a mass seducer, who seduces by "convincing the nerves." This he can do because of his disinclination to have done with an intense feeling: "his terrifying habit of dwelling on a situation in which every instant almost chokes one."[60] Indeed the music can even at times cause Nietzsche physical distress: "irregular breathing, disturbance of circulation, extreme irritability with sudden coma."[61]

"Air, more air!" Nietzsche cries, repeating Isolde's seaboard outburst.[62] Clearly he has *Tristan* in mind. It is there that Wagner proves himself the "connoisseur . . . of all that thrills, of extravagant excesses, of all the feminism out of the vocabulary of happiness."[63] There a single situation is dwelt on longest. There we hear loudest the theatrical scream of passion, unmelodic and suggestive of infinity. We are prompted to call for air, for there is too much water.

Self-Mastery and Self-Denial

When he found the mass responsiveness to Wagner's harmonies decadent, Nietzsche's criticism of his age was self-criticism. He was, in fact, proud to claim that he had discovered in himself all the pathological symptoms of his era, because he believed that he had won his battle to overcome them. "I think I know better than anyone else," he says in the *Tristan* passage of *Ecce Homo,* "how Wagner achieves the . . . fifty worlds of strange enchantments which none besides him had the wings to reach: and such as I am

—strong enough to turn to my advantage even the most question-able and the most dangerous and thus become stronger—I call Wagner the great benefactor of my life."[64] To disavow Wagner was painful and isolated Nietzsche in loneliness; it was to take sides against himself, to prefer being right to enjoying what he no longer approved.[65] In the Preface to *The Wagner Case* he calls it self-mastery. But he also calls it self-denial.[66] He had to deny himself not only Wagner's friendship, and the sympathy of Cosima,* but the enthusiasm of his youthful Wagner-worship—a repudiation that struck his friend Rohde as scarcely credible. He also had to relinquish the pleasures of Wagnerian harmony. Here his self-mastery was not completely successful."I can perfectly well under-stand," he said, "a musician of today who says 'I hate Wagner but I can endure no other music.' "[67] Nietzsche himself was like this musician. For his praise of wit and melody in music is never as convincing as his acknowledgment of the rival power of musical sensuality. *Tristan* could still affect him. But now its fascination seemed dangerous, and the pleasure it gave a sign of weakness.

In a passage that might have been written by a less fair and cir-cumspect Wagnerian, Ernest Newman—for whom *The Wagner Case* was "venomous nonsense" written in a crazed frame of mind[68] —concludes that it was Nietzsche's departure from the Wagnerian camp, and not his former devotion, that indicated weakness. The emotional impact of Wagner's middle works had once "set a fire raging" in the youthful Nietzsche: "But his musical arteries were unable to stand for so long so high a blood pressure; and when the reaction came the world was treated to the edifying spectacle of the pint-pot capacity railing peevishly at the impermissible magni-tude of quarts."[69] Apart from the (Nietzschean) ill temper of these remarks, Newman misses the point.[70] Nietzsche did not stop re-sponding to *Tristan*, but began to judge the quality of his response.

* One of the last letters Nietzsche wrote (in January, 1889) was to Cosima. It reads simply "Ariadne, I love you"; and is signed "Dionysus." A few days earlier he had reminded his friend, the composer Peter Gast, not to miss the "tremendous page on *Tristan*" in *Ecce Homo*.

Then he recognized that to lose oneself in sweet infinities is immoral. The dissonances of *Tristan*, like the Eros they accompany, paralyze the intellect; hence they are life-denying, and fully to give in to them is to be seduced into a suicidal drowning, like Isolde's, in mounting waves of chromatic harmony.

chapter IV

WAGNER AND TRISTAN IN PARIS (1850-1900)

Lekeu and Mallarmé

Nietzsche sometimes looked to France for the gaiety and wit that would save European culture from the Music Without Any Future.[1] Yet Wagner had already begun to dominate much of French music. *Carmen* itself was accused of Wagnerism in 1875, by which time conservative critics had learned this new way of labeling the slight innovations that shocked them. A decade later the Parsifalian gloom of César Franck's chromaticism had settled over an influential group of young composers; and if Nietzsche had known the school of Franck he would probably have concluded that sanctimonious Philistinism had driven wit and gaiety even from Paris. Perhaps Wagner's endless *melos* was preferable to the wingless and reiterative twofold tunes of Franck.

In 1889 Guillaume Lekeu, a pupil of Franck not yet twenty, fainted during the Prelude to *Tristan* and had to be carried out of the Bayreuth Festspielhaus.[2] Earlier Lekeu had made his pilgrimage to Triebschen—"where Wagner wrote *Tristan*"—and before he died at the age of twenty-four he had improvised countless encomia of Wagner in letters to friends. Each note of Mark's lament, he wrote, "can break one's heart."[3] Perhaps Lekeu and his master Franck were, as Belgians, more susceptible than the French to Teutonic influence. Yet Henri Duparc and Ernest Chausson, both

Parisians, were equally subject to an oppressive Wagnerism, the latter surpassing Lekeu as a writer of Wagner-obsessed letters. And Emmanuel Chabrier, the most Gallic of composers, struggled for years with the completion of a Wagnerian opera that was as heavy as his few works still in the current repertory are light. Neither Chabrier, Chausson, nor even Vincent d'Indy had the conviction of Debussy, who could tear up pages of the manuscript of *Pelléas and Mélisande* and strike off on a new line when "the ghost of old Klingsor . . . appeared at the turning of one of the bars."[4] It is reported that, at the performance of *Tristan* which overpowered Lekeu, Chabrier burst into tears.[5]

Yet the composers who made pilgrimages to Bayreuth, and who could not write a love-duet without echoing *Tristan*, were not the most notorious Wagnerites. Symbolist poets and naturalist novelists alike advertised themselves as the heirs of Wagner; and their programs, if not their works, were better known than those of the quieter musicians. After 1885 few writers could issue an aesthetic manifesto without mentioning the synthesis of the arts, while critics discovered in parallel scenes and repeated phrases examples of leitmotif, not always so obvious as the Lohengrin swan which floats across verse after verse of Symbolist poetry. The atmosphere of Montsalvat was often as oppressive in Villiers and Verlaine as it was in César Franck.

Painters like Odilon Redon and Fantin-Latour deserved to be known as Wagnerian, for, like Beardsley in England, they produced and advertised lithographs of scenes from the music-dramas. But other painters as monochromatic as Whistler and as unsymbolic as Degas were similarly labeled, and the young Cézanne, with his friend Zola, was a member of the Wagner Society in Marseilles—and did a painting called *Overture to Tannhäuser*.[6] Even the spirit of *revanche* learned, for a time, to exempt Wagner from anti-German sentiment: *Eine Kapitulation*, Wagner's tasteless farce about the Siege of Paris, may have been hard to excuse, but *Judaism in Music* was after all a less flippant and more characteristic work. Or perhaps Wagner could be classed with Goethe, Kant, Hegel, and Schopenhauer, as representing "l'esprit allemand, si sage, si libre" which would prevent Germany from being absorbed by Prussian militarism.[7]

But despite the vogue of Wagner in literary and artistic circles and his notoriety among the public, the music-dramas were rarely performed. The people who purchased the lithographs of Redon and Fantin-Latour recognized, no doubt, that it is easier to contemplate a black-and-white impression of, say "L'Evocation d'Erda" than it is to listen to that low-voiced lady predict the doom of the Gods.[8] Between the unfortunate performances of *Tannhäuser* in 1861 and its revival in 1895 only two Wagner operas, *Lohengrin* and *Die Walküre*, were produced in Paris.* "Should we not long since have become acquainted with the entire Tetralogy?" asked Debussy as late as 1901. "For one thing, we should then be rid of it, and the Bayreuth pilgrims would cease to annoy us."[9] They did well, he adds, to produce *Die Meistersinger* at the Opera (in 1897. in French); but "it would have been even better to give *Tristan and Isolde* (in which Chopin's charming soul appears, reflected here and there in the music directing its passion.)"† By the time Parisians did hear *Tristan* in German, it had become part of the repertory of seventy cities on three continents (not counting performances in Italian, French, English, Russian, Hungarian, Czech, and Danish). Berlin saw its hundredth *Tristan* only eight years after Paris saw its first, and seven years before Paris heard it in German. There were, to be sure, private recitals of the music-dramas—sometimes preceded by lectures—with piano accompaniment: Debussy played *Tristan* and *Parsifal* in society to finance the composition of *Pelléas*.[10] And there may have been some reluctance on the part of cultists to see the sacred music-dramas

---

* Not counting *Rienzi* and concert performances. The comparative dates of the first performances in the major European and American cities are listed in Appendix A.

† There remains, Debussy goes on to say, "only *Parsifal* to fear; and for family and mercenary reasons, Mme. Cosima Wagner reserves, in this case, the right of production to herself." The idea that there was Chopin in *Tristan* would have disconcerted the younger Mme. de Cambremer in *Swann's Way*, who, as a lady Wagnerite, used to make her Chopin-loving mother-in-law feel ignorant and old-fashioned.

performed along with Massenet at the "frivolous" Opéra.[11] Whatever the reason, to hear proper performances composers had to
make their annual pilgrimages to Bayreuth or Munich, while most
of the poets and painters who styled themselves Wagnerites were
content to remain in Paris listening to *morceaux*—the *Tannhäuser*
overture, the *Chevauchée des Walkyries*, and the overture to
Le Vaisseau-Fantôme (which the more accurate Wagnerites preferred to call *Le Hollandais Volant*).

These accepted repertory selections could scarcely elicit the
kind of emotional response displayed by Lekeu and Chabrier at
Bayreuth. Here is a description of how the most celebrated literary
Wagnerite attended the Sunday Wagner Concerts:

Sitting there among the other listeners, bent over in an attitude of
meditation and concentration, the music made him seem far away;
and slowly he took out a pencil from his pocket and solemnly began to
write, on a worthless scrap of paper which he hid from sight with
elegant modesty. The orchestra dictated and Mallarmé wrote.[12]

Mallarmé's devotion to Wagnerian theory was not above suspicion;
but one may entirely question his devotion to the music. Certainly
his economical and enigmatic poems were not "dictated" by the
Wagnerian orchestra, which here seems to be providing nothing
more than background music.

Lekeu in a faint and Mallarmé aloof and irrelevantly inspired:
the oversensitive composer and the inattentive poet typify the
opposite extremes of French Wagnerism. The literary kind of
Wagnerism predominated, which accounts for the odd fact that
while Wagner's name was invoked everywhere his best music
was seldom performed. For the literary Wagnerites were for the
most part not passionate music-lovers. The *Revue wagnérienne* and
the later organs of the Symbolists did not specialize in musical
exegesis, and it was admitted in their pages that close knowledge
of Wagner's scores was not required for admission to the Wagnerian
ranks.[13] The plots and characters mattered more than the music:
"We studied his characters," wrote Léon Daudet, "as if Wotan
held the secret of the world and Hans Sachs were the spokesman
for free, natural, and spontaneous art."[14]

What mattered most was the System. Only by misreading Wagner's theories—and remaining conveniently ignorant of how the music of the later operas belies them—could the French poets of the 1880s seriously adopt Wagner as a champion and precursor. To be sure, the union of the arts expounded in *Opera and Drama* was superficially similar to the *correspondances* of Baudelaire. And the primacy of music expounded in Wagner's later works seemed to support the notion that poetry should aspire to the condition of music. Wagner, as we know, tried to minimize the differences between his earlier and his later theories. The Symbolists tended to confuse them, pulling out of the grab bag of notions those that persuasively but inaccurately resembled their own. In his theories, Wagner had appropriated the whole realm of art for Wagner's sake. In theirs, the Symbolists appropriated Wagner for Art's sake.

The composers would not have said with Daudet that they admired above all the librettos. Nor did they show a special interest in Wagner's theories. It was the music that moved them to tears, and made them question their own capacity for original musical thought. The chromaticism of Klingsor-Wagner was the enchantment. The literary Wagnerites, on the other hand, often failed to discriminate among the various operas. Sonnet sequences in the *Revue wagnérienne* assign equal space, and presumably equal quality, to *Rienzi* and *Tristan,* and in some of the sonnets there is scarcely a clue to indicate which opera has evoked the rhymed reverie.[15]

Thus Tristanism may be distinguished from literary Wagnerism in the narrative that follows. The former, culminating in the operas of Chabrier and Chausson, was the result of responsiveness to Wagnerian harmony. The latter, culminating in the *Revue wagnérienne* and the Symbolist movement, invoked the Wagnerian Idea as the battle cry of aesthetic innovation. French Tristanism was a private problem, French Wagnerism a public pose.

Preludes and Evenings

Wagner went to Paris for the first time in September, 1839. The long trip from Riga had included the rough voyage from the coast of Norway to London, which inspired *The Flying Dutchman*. Wagner was twenty-six, married and destitute; but the only commission he received, apart from hack work, was 500 francs for the *Dutchman* libretto, to be set by a French composer named Dietsch.*

Twenty-one years and five visits later, Napoleon III commanded a performance of *Tannhäuser* at the Opéra. Baudelaire thought it was ironic that only after it had come under despotism would France produce the work of a revolutionary.[16] But Wagner's revolutionary days, like those of Louis Napoleon himself, had ended in the early fifties; and there is something fitting in the association of the two democratic dictators—even though in 1871 Wagner would exult at the fall of the weaker empire. Wagner wouldn't meet his Sedan, someone remarked after the Franco-Prussian War, for there was no prospect of finding a "musical-dramatic Bismarck or Moltke."[17]

During the two decades between the *Dutchman* libretto and the *Tannhäuser* production Wagner's French reputation had grown very slowly. When the first version of *Tannhäuser* had been premiered in Dresden, in 1845, the cursory notice given it in the Paris press included the information that it was in five acts, and that the first name of "M. Wagener," the composer, was Robert.[18] In the next dozen years, with the exception of a few favorable notices by Berlioz, only two articles significantly promoted the Wagnerian cause. Both were by Parnassian poets, inspired by foreign performances. In 1850 Gérard de Nerval reported on the Weimar debut of *Lohengrin* in the Paris *Presse*, and in 1857 Théophile Gautier discussed *Tannhäuser* at Wiesbaden in the *Moniteur*.[19] Gérard's concern with the relationship between the words and the music anticipates that of the Symbolists; he seems, however, far more responsive to the music than Gautier, who did not have the success that Baudelaire had a few years later in switching from art criticism to music criticism.[20] Another review of the Wiesbaden *Tannhäuser*, containing some accurate musical analysis, appeared

---

* The same Pierre-Louis-Philippe Dietsch turned out to be the conductor of the 1861 *Tannhäuser* performances. Despite his twenty-five masses, it is these two points of contact with Wagner's career that assure him his place in music dictionaries, where he is usually noted as having conducted *Tannhäuser* incompetently.

in the *Courier de Paris*. It was written by the critic-composer Ernest Reyer, who twenty-five years later composed *Sigurd*. *Sigurd* is often (carelessly) cited as the first French Wagnerian opera; Gautier's more effective contribution to the Wagnerian cause was, as we shall see, his remarkable daughter Judith.

During the fifties Wagner probably got most of his publicity from the hostile press. A series of articles in the *Gazette Musicale* by the veteran musicologist and critic François-Joseph Fétis began the war against Wagner—waged in the name of God, humility, and melody—which led to the Battle of *Tannhäuser* in 1861.[21] In what Baudelaire called an "indigeste et abominable pamphlet," Fétis says all the right things, if perhaps for the wrong reasons: Wagner lacks rhythm and melody; his System is designed to cover up a lack of inspiration; his egotism shows what happens to the godless disciples of Feuerbach. *Opera and Drama* was already in print, but apparently the only facts generally known about that enormous work were that it expounded a System and that it included an extended and unprovoked attack on Meyerbeer. The older composer therefore had good reason—along with the money and the experience in public relations—to encourage the press in its resistance to Wagner.[22]

Around the hostile press and the growing group of literary Wagnerites formed rival parties, ready, when the projected *Tannhäuser* was announced, for another *Hernani*.* Once settled in Paris for his longest stay (on money received from Otto Wesendonk for the rights to the *Ring*), Wagner entertained his literary supporters at Evenings: in a letter of March, 1860, to Mathilde, he lists as being among his devotees Alpénor de Gasperini, Frederic Villot, and Champfleury.[23] Villot, to whom Wagner dedicated "The Music of the Future," was conservator of the Louvre. Gasperini, a physician turned man of letters, had already written an enthusiastic pro-Wagner article in the *Courier du Dimanche*, and went on to become one of the most effective propagandists—particularly in a

---

* Simultaneously in Berlin were planted the seeds of a greater rivalry: the Brahms-Joachim "manifesto" of 1860 against Liszt and Wagner.

book on Wagner published in 1866.[24] His reservations about *Tristan* —"Tristan est une erreur, mais une erreur qui sera féconde"—his endorsement of Wagner's theoretical works, and his disapproval, on musical as well as practical grounds, of the revision of *Tannhäuser*, indicate that he was a literary Wagnerite of the kind for whom *Lohengrin* represented perfection.[25] Like Gasperini, the realist novelist Champfleury (Jules Fleury-Husson) was praising Wagner in print before he had heard more than a few concert numbers.[24] The novelist's instant adoption of the composer's half-known theories serves to remind us that it is historically and aesthetically inaccurate to think of Wagner as being among the romantics. For the realists and Parnassians found in Wagner a spirit akin to their own revolt against the older generation of romanticism. In a collection called *Grandes figures d'hier et d'aujourd'hui*[26] Champfleury reprinted his essay on Wagner along with a study of Courbet.* The juxtaposition suggests the affinity between those masters, who belonged to the same generation. During the years of the Orleans monarchy, Berlioz had equaled the achievement of Delacroix; and in the last years of the century Debussy would match the achievement of the postimpressionists. But there was no French composer of the intervening generation to equal Courbet, and after him Manet. Wagner was imported to fill the gap.

It was Champfleury who introduced Baudelaire to the Wagnerian circle. Wagner also lists among his supporters Gustave Doré (who could have done fine illustrations of Nibelheim); the composer Stephen Heller; Gounod, whom Wagner found "good but not deeply gifted"; and "a really profound musician . . . Sensale" (Saint-Saëns).[27] Almost all the supporters had attended the concert of January 25 at the Théâtre-Italien, at which the Prelude to *Tristan* was introduced to the world. Berlioz, Meyerbeer, the Belgian composer Gevaert, and the seventy-eight-year-old Auber were also present at this important debut.†

* Champfleury may be seen, along with Proudhon and Baudelaire, among the friends of the painter in Courbet's *L'Atelier* of 1853.

† There were two more concerts on February 1 and 8. The programs included the overtures to the *Dutchman* and *Tannhäuser*, and the Prelude and Wedding Music from *Lohengrin*.

The *Tristan* Prelude made a far greater impression on Wagner than on his distinguished audience. The unfavorable reviewers chanted in chorus that Wagner "a tué la mélodie"—one accused him of the murder of music itself—and Scudo in the *Revue des Deux Mondes*, for whom the *Tristan* Prelude was "un entassement de sons discordantes," was enraged by everything except the marches from *Tannhäuser* and *Lohengrin*. The audience at one of the concerts is said to have burst into applause after the first sixteen bars of the *Tannhäuser* March, presumably in appreciation of an unexpected melodic period. Gasperini analyzed each number for the *Courier du Dimanche*, but few of the favorable reviewers singled out for special comment the one piece on the program that had been written after 1850.* Those who attempted to defend Wagner against the murder charge certainly had to point elsewhere to indicate an "abundance of melody." The reviewer for the *Moniteur* was probably generalizing correctly when he noted that the Prelude to *Tristan* "n'a produit aucun effet."[28]

Berlioz excepted the *Tristan* Prelude from his general praise in the *Journal des Débats*. "I have read and re-read this strange piece of music," he wrote; "I have listened to it with the profoundest attention and a lively desire to discover the sense of it: well, I have to admit that I still haven't the slightest notion of what the composer was driving at."[29] It was certainly not the form of the piece that baffled Berlioz, for he noted that it was constructed on a long crescendo-diminuendo arch, like the *Lohengrin* Prelude, which he rightly considered a masterpiece.† He found the *Tristan* Prelude themeless, except for "a sort of chromatic moan, full of dissonant chords, of which the long appoggiaturas that replace the real note only increase the cruelty."[30] It was, in short, the almost complete replacement of melodic means by harmonic that dis-

* One exception was Paul Challemel-Lacour, who referred to the *Tristan* "overture" as "beautiful and superb music." He was apparently not similarly impressed by the libretto, when given the task of translating Wagner's poetry into French prose: "I translate very much as I would rule paper, turning the ecstasies of *Tristan* into French as best I can and thinking all the while of Garibaldi."

† The two Preludes were not exactly identical in form at these concerts, because Wagner tacked on to the *Tristan* Prelude a concert ending consisting of the end of Isolde's "Verklärung."

turbed him*—and Wagner might at least have been grateful for the only accurate observation of the profound difference between his new music and what were by now his war horses. Despite his confession that he found the piece incomprehensible, Berlioz had described it exactly and concisely. It was to this review that Wagner replied in an open letter which led to the famous split between the composers.[31]

Berlioz had been far more concise than Wagner himself, whose elucidation of the Prelude for the 1860 audience reads like an attempt to reproduce the effect of the music in words—in case the orchestra (which he had to lead through the score "note by note, as if exploring for gems in a mine")[32] should break down. The program notes, happily, can be skimmed.[33] The prospect of performing *Tristan* seems to have revived Wagner's delight in talk about final redemption and the bliss of dying. In the midst of a practical letter to Mathilde we find him "wistfully looking towards the land of Nirvana"—which "soon changes into *Tristan*."[34]

Wagner's only foretaste of the *Tristan*-Nirvana of 1865 was an informal performance of the second act in the summer of 1860, at the home of Pauline Garcia-Viardot, the famous singer whose remarkable career spanned three eras.† Mme. Viardot sang Isolde and Brangaene, Wagner taking Tristan and Mark. Klindworth came from London (at Wagner's expense) to accompany. The performance did not impress the audience of two: Mme. Marie Kalergis, the guest of honor, who had helped liquidate the debts of the winter concerts, and Berlioz, who had been invited by Mme. Viardot "with the avowed object of restoring harmony" between the composers (melody would have been more to the point). Mme. Kalergis, the niece of Nesselrode (once she had been a pupil of Chopin, and she was the friend of Liszt and Delacroix, and an admirer of Berlioz), wrote that *Tristan* was "quite plainly im-

---

* The Prelude later reminded Hanslick of "the old Italian painting of a martyr whose intestines are slowly unwound from his body on a reel."
† She had begun her career in the circle of George Sand, corresponded with Turgenev, created roles for Meyerbeer, Gounod, and Massenet, and had a daughter who was engaged to Gabriel Fauré.

possible; it is an abstraction, intriguing to study, and with beauties in it in which one can perceive a sound idea; but as a dramatic work it will be rejected by the public everywhere." *Chez* Viardot she didn't say a word about it. Berlioz restricted his remarks to a laconic compliment about the warmth of Wagner's delivery.[35] On another occasion Wagner heard the *Liebestod* sung by the Neapolitan Princess Campo-Reale, skillfully accompanied by Saint-Saëns.[36] But however distinguished the performers and audiences, such Evenings scarcely satisfied Wagner's desire to put the *Tristan* music before the public. It was some consolation that his adeptness at musical eroticism would be publicly displayed in the new Venusberg scene which he was inserting into the old and tired *Tannhäuser*.

"*Divertissement par M. Pétipa*"

Wagner improved the Venusberg scene with doses of the new chromaticism. The motifs he retained from the original scoring are developed symphonically; the languorous song of the sirens now shimmers in the alternating voluptuous colors of the *Liebesnacht;* and a new ascending phrase in half steps sounds like an extension of the *Tristan* "Desire" motif. Although Wagner patched and improved elsewhere in the score, the scene seems like an independent work; and to find a brilliant dramatic contrast, as some critics do, between the erotic chromaticism of Venus (foreshadowing Kundry) and the measured diatonic tunes of the Dresden-1845 hero (foreshadowing Parsifal) is to imagine a defect a virtue.[37] The ironic fact about the 1861 *Tannhäuser* is that the Venusberg music caused a stir not because of its intensity and novelty, or its stylistic discrepancy, but because of its placement at the beginning of the opera.*

The story of the Jockey Club's successful effort to ruin *Tannhäuser* is well known. The members' fury that the "divertissement par M. Pétipa"†—we know it as Wagner's Bacchanal—was

---

* The novelty of the Venusberg scene was probably less than it ought to have been, for the ladies of the court of Venus wore pink ballet dresses.

† Pétipa was, of course, the ballet master.

scheduled for a time before they customarily arrived at the theater was fanned by anti-Austrian sentiment: here was a clear and at the same time safely indirect way of demonstrating the unpopularity, both personal and political, of the Princess Metternich, who was Wagner's patroness at the court of Napoleon III.[38] Wagner's difficulties were doubled by the hostile press and the resentment occasioned by his refusal to hire the opera claque. He was further encumbered by an incompetent conductor, an uncooperative *Heldentenor* and a stout Venus. The catcalls and dog whistles of the Jockey Club grew louder at successive performances: by the third —and last—hawkers of toys were selling "Wagner whistles" on the boulevards.[39]

It is not surprising that in the midst of the whistling the mixture of styles went virtually unnoticed: the discords in the audience drew attention away from those in the orchestra. Berlioz, who in a private letter wrote that he considered himself "cruelly avenged," discreetly turned over his public column in the *Débats* to someone else.[40] The lighter journals specialized in caricatures of Wagner and parodies of "Les Tribulations du Tannhäuser"; but even the respectable *Gazette musicale* alluded to an obvious and off-color pun on the word "Venusberg." Prosper Mérimée, in the audience, found the whole thing a "colossal bore"—although he went on to report the gossip, including Auber's remark that the opera sounded like Berlioz without melody. There was only one defense of Wagner in the daily press. Many of the weeklies, however, took Wagner's side against the rioters, and some went so far as to print the reviews of outright Wagnerites.[41] Malwida von Meysenbug was in Paris, and reported on the performances for the London *Daily News*. "It was a known fact," she later observed with indignation, "that the ladies of the ballet had their wages increased by these gentlemen" (of the Jockey Club) "and that the latter were accustomed to go to the opera after dining, not to hear the beautiful harmonies, but to see the most unnatural and most terrible production of modern arts, the ballet. After the performance, they became better acquainted with the dancing nymphs behind the scenes." What, asks Malwida, did these aristocratic rakes care about "a chaste work of art, which celebrated the victory of sacred love over the frenzy of emotions?"[42]

But the Wagnerian cause profited from the fiasco. For the initial enthusiasm of the literary Wagnerites was now reinforced by righteous indignation: they could defend the art of the future against the bad manners as well as the bad musical taste of Paris society. In the catcalls of the audience many writers and poets recognized a familiar sound; and when Baudelaire wrote of the immensity of the injustice perpetrated by the Jockey Club, his indignation was no doubt increased by memories of similar injustices to himself.

Correspondences

Baudelaire discovered the music of Wagner when he desperately needed a new enthusiasm. His sense of failure and his ennui required the healthy antidote of an artistic discovery which would revive the sensations he had felt when he first read Poe. That had been in 1846; and after attending the Wagner concerts of 1860 he wrote to his friend Poulet Malassis that it was fifteen years since he had felt so carried out of himself.[43] As before, he forced his friends to share his enthusiasm—not to attend the Wagner concerts was as great an offense as it once had been not to have read Poe. But their weariness must have been tempered by surprise at the fact that this time the hero was a composer.

For up to then the chief source of aesthetic *volupté* for Baudelaire had been the visual arts. As a critic he was usually occupied with painting rather than poetry, and his essays on the *salons* are examples of the rarest kind of writing—art criticism of the first rank. In contrast, his knowledge of music was negligible. He was pleased when he learned that Beethoven and Weber were the idols of Wagner's youth: they are the only composers whose names appear in his poems. Weber occurs most memorably in the beautiful stanza about another member of Baudelaire's pantheon:

Delacroix, lac de sang, hanté des mauvais anges,
Ombragé par un bois de sapins toujours vert,
Ou, sous un ciel chagrin, les fanfares étranges
Passent comme un soupir étouffé de Weber.[44]

"Wagner" is just as good a rhyme; and if "Les Phares" had been written after 1860 the strange fanfares might well have sounded like a *Wagnerian* stifled sigh. For, despite the fact that they belong to different ages, it is Wagner whom Baudelaire, in his later criticism, considers the counterpart of Delacroix. Before the concerts of 1860, Baudelaire had not chosen any composer to rank with Delacroix and Poe, even though Berlioz was available as the obvious choice. After hearing *Tannhäuser* Baudelaire had a triumvirate— and if the composer of total-art-works does not seem the best partner for the two romantics of an earlier generation, it must at least be noted that a generation later Nietzsche, in agreement with Baudelaire, called Delacroix "Wagner's closest relative."[45] But Baudelaire must also have noticed Wagner's kinship with later and less "romantic" painting, for, echoing the Wagnerian epithet, he later hailed Edouard Manet as the Painter of the Future.[46]

Behind the analogies which Baudelaire drew between composers and painters lay the famous doctrine of *correspondances*. Baudelaire thought that there are more or less exact reciprocal relationships among the objects of the various senses—an idea which he developed from romantic sources in Poe, De Quincey, Hoffmann, and Swedenborg, not to mention neo-Platonism and perhaps a tendency toward synaesthesia.[47] The doctrine is at the core of the essay on *Tannhäuser*. There Wagner is praised as a *painter* of space and depth, and as an adept at the art of *translating* subtle emotions into music.[48] A great part of the essay is given over to an informal proof of the doctrine. Baudelaire demonstrates that his own "translation" into visual imagery of the Prelude to *Lohengrin* is similar to programs of the piece written independently by Wagner and Liszt. Hence the music must have suggested the same images fairly accurately to all three. He nowhere replies to the obvious objection that, apart from the matter of accurate correspondences, the piece of music is very much *better* than any of its equivalents in prose-poetry.[49] His concern is to reaffirm the observation that we necessarily express ourselves by means of the reciprocal analogies among the senses: it would really be surprising, he insists, if sound could *not* suggest color, and if colors could *not* give one the idea of a melody—and if both sound and color were unsuited to the translation of ideas.[50] And he includes in the Wagner essay two quatrains of his sonnet "Correspondances," which was to become part of the aesthetic canon of the Symbolist movement.

Baudelaire, who knew the theories of *Opera and Drama,* clearly intended in some way to connect the doctrine of correspondences with what was known about the doctrine of the *Gesamtkunstwerk.* But it is difficult to see how he could have found more than a superficial resemblance between Wagner's project of combining all the arts in a substantial supermasterpiece, and his own idea that the various sense images are hieroglyphics of an invisible reality. However this may be, the next generation of poets could find in his essay confirmation of their inclusion of Wagner's theories among their own.[51] The Symbolists could also easily mistake Baudelaire for a doctrinaire Wagnerite like themselves. For there are symptoms of literary Wagnerism in the *Tannhäuser* essay: the avoidance of musical jargon; the remarks about the leitmotifs as a "système mnémonique"; and the analysis of the myths of *Lohengrin* and *The Flying Dutchman* without reference to the music, for these were works which Baudelaire knew only through the librettos and the fragments performed at the 1860 concerts.

Yet Baudelaire differs fundamentally from the later literary Wagnerites. His art criticism always began with the direct experience of the painting, an experience then modified and cultivated by theoretical analysis. With Wagner's music the procedure was the same, and Baudelaire would no more have allowed that the proper criticism could begin with a study of Wagnerian theory than he would have allowed that the operas themselves could have been written to demonstrate the theories. There were among his readers those who had heard that Wagner composed according to a theoretical recipe, and therefore could not compose spontaneously. Baudelaire makes it a special point to remind them that the theories were the product of Wagner's critical reflection upon completed works. It would be amazing, Baudelaire tells them, if a critic became a poet, but it is impossible for a poet not to engage in theorizing.[52] In Baudelaire's own aesthetic experience, *volupté* preceded *connaissance*.[53] When he undertook to read Wagner's theoretical works it was in order to enlighten his sense of delight, before the stage performance had furnished him with complete elucidation.[54] His Wagnerism began, as he told Wagner in a famous letter of February, 1860, with "the greatest musical joy I have ever experienced"; and at the orchestral concerts he had allowed himself to be "penetrated and overcome by a joy almost sensual, like the feeling of rising into the air, or of floating on the sea."[55] ("La musique," he wrote elsewhere, "souvent me prend comme une mer.")[56] The similes anticipate those of Nietzsche, and were later overused by Baudelaire's diffuse English reflection, Swinburne.[57] "In matters of art," Baudelaire says about Wagner's music, "I admit that I do not dislike excess; moderation has never seemed to me to be the sign of a vigorous artistic nature."[58] It is the Venusberg and not the garden in Cornwall which prompted the following passage of prose-poetry:

Langueurs, délices mêlées de fièvre et coupées d'angoisses, retours incessants vers une volupté qui promet d'éteindre, mais n'éteint jamais la soif; palpitations furieuses du coeur et des sens, ordres impérieux de la chair, tout le dictionnaire des onomatopées de l'amour se fait entendre ici.[59]

But the criticism has entered the *Tristan*-drenched atmosphere of *The Birth of Tragedy*. Thus Baudelaire foreshadows the Tristanism of the French composers rather than the Wagnerism of the *Revue wagnérienne* and the Symbolists, even though the latter happened to find in the essay on *Tannhäuser* their two favorite texts about the interrelationship of the arts, conveniently set side by side.

Wagnerites

After the 1861 *Tannhäuser* no full-length Wagner was heard in a major Paris hall for more than twenty-five years.* During that time three channels were open for the dissemination of Wagnerism: popular concerts, accounts of foreign performances, and books by and about Wagner. In May, 1862, Jules Pasdeloup included the *Tannhäuser* March in one of the Sunday programs of his recently formed Concerts Populaires. In the course of twenty years other pieces from the operas were cautiously added to the repertory, but it was not until the eighties that an extended Wagnerian repertory could be heard, owing to the efforts of Edouard Colonne and especially Charles Lamoureux.[60] The latter, who in 1881 founded the Societé des Nouveaux Concerts (the celebrated "Concerts Lamoureux"), provided almost all the music of Wagner with which the Symbolists were familiar; and his concert performances of two acts of *Tristan* and all of *Lohengrin* gave firsthand experience of the music to Chabrier and d'Indy, who were assistant conductors.[61]

Only the elite of early Wagnerians made excursions to foreign performances before Bayreuth was enshrined in 1876. Munich was the Mecca in the sixties: *Tristan* in 1865 and 1869, *Die Meistersinger* in 1868, *Das Rheingold* and *Die Walküre* in 1869 and 1870. At the debut of *Tristan* no more than five Frenchmen were counted in the audience: Gasperini, the critic Léon Leroy, Edouard Schuré, and two chance tourists. Gasperini was disconcerted by the new harmonic style. Leroy, though he regretted the influence of Schopenhauer on the poem, was carried away by the music: never before, he said, had the symphonic art been extended to include such richness of color.[62] Leroy's enthusiasm was exceeded by the extravagance of Schuré, a twenty-four-year-old Alsatian who had already drafted a history of German folk song. Sixty-three years after the performance Schuré remembered his reaction to it:

* There is one minor exception: a run-through of *Rienzi* in 1869.

An immense desire, a compelling nostalgia has dominated my entire life: to realize completely the Divine in art. After having attended a performance of Wagner's *Tristan*, I felt that I had seen this ideal realized in the theater through the threefold magic of poetry, music, and drama, in the hands of a titanic creator. It left a deep and terrifying impression. For years I renounced writing poetry myself. I told myself that after work like Wagner's, after such completeness of expression, there was nothing further to do.[63]

Just as Nietzsche appended his youthful praise of Wagner to *The Birth of Tragedy*, Schuré, only a few years later, devoted to Wagner the second volume of his major work on *Le Drame musicale*.[64] And Schuré's central idea is that great (Wagnerian) art is spontaneous and natural—Dionysian.* But unlike Nietzsche, Schuré never unconverted: not even the ingratitude displayed in *Eine Kapitulation*, where Wagner included him among the cast of characters, could drive Schuré from the camp of the Master.[65] He frequently visited Triebschen, and his *Drame musicale* became the authority on Wagner during the most prolific years of French Wagnerism. Dujardin, the editor of the *Revue wagnérienne*, said he learned all his Wagnerism from it.[66] Thus Schuré's initial experience of *Tristan* led to the composition of a textbook that would, in the case of many devotees, provide a substitute for listening to the music.[67]

Neither Schuré's books nor Lamoureux's concerts did more for the cause than the ramified career of Catulle Mendès. In 1861, at the age of nineteen, Mendès asked Wagner to contribute to his newly formed *Revue Fantastique*. The magazine lasted less than a year, but the young Portuguese Jew found other ways of advertising Wagner—who nevertheless continued to maintain that the Jews were responsible for his failures in Paris.[68] In 1867 Mendès married Gautier's daughter Judith, and afterward the couple frequently visited Wagner at Triebschen, usually in the company of their friend Villiers de l'Isle-Adam.[69] Wagner's fulminations against the French at the time of the Franco-Prussian War did,

---

* Schuré spoke with Nietzsche at Bayreuth in 1876, and provided one of the best accounts of Nietzsche's mood at the time of his unconversion.

however, alienate Mendès, who was especially disgusted by the gratuitous insult to Victor Hugo in *Eine Kapitulation*. Thereafter Mendès made the necessary separation between Wagner the man and Wagner the artist:

Je ne lui tendrai pas la main qui l'applaudit.

True to the sentiment of his alexandrine, he attended the Bayreuth festival of 1876 but did not enter the gates of Wahnfried.[70] In a roman à clef called *Le Roi Vierge* (1881) Mendès took mild revenge on the Wagner circle. King Frederick II of Thuringia is obviously Ludwig II (the novel was banned in Bavaria); the Abbé Glinck is Liszt; and Wagner, who is vividly depicted in one of his tantrums, goes under the appropriate name of Hans Hammer. *Tristan* figures in the story as an opera called *Floris et Blancheflor*.[71]

Yet Mendès' books and articles on Wagnerian theory were required reading of the Symbolist avant-garde. In a dialogue between "le jeune prix de Rome" (Debussy?) and "le vieux Wagnériste" (Mendès himself) which he wrote for the *Revue wagnérienne*, Mendès discussed his curious blend of theoretical Wagnerism and French cultural nationalism.[72] A great name, he writes, awaits the French genius who has absorbed Gallic folk music and at the same time assimilated "all those points of Wagnerian theory which are compatible with the French genius." Alone or with the help of a poet, this genius would rid French opera of outmoded and ridiculous operatic conventions. Mendès' description of the opera of the future is a compendium of what he and his colleagues must have thought were the components of the Wagnerian System. The long-awaited genius will achieve a unity between poetry and music for the sake of the drama:

The poet in him will boldly reject literary ornament, the musician all those vocal and symphonic beauties which can hinder the flow of dramatic action. He will reject recitatives, airs, strettos, even ensembles, unless these are demanded by the dramatic action, to which everything must be sacrificed. He will break the back of the old four-square melody and his melody—without becoming Germanized—will stretch out unbroken, following the poetic rhythm. In a word, his music will become language, but a language which is music.

Moreover, he will transform his orchestra into a "great cauldron, in which the themes which represent his characters or their emotions will be mingled and developed and all the elements of the drama will be molten and welded together." The stage action will be steeped in the "tragic atmosphere" created by this orchestra: "manifold, yet springing logically from a single idea," the action will move "amidst violent passions, unexpected happenings, smiles ands tears, relentlessly towards some great final emotion."[73] What Mendès wants is a French Wagner:

Whoever creates such a work will be a great man and he will earn our love. For, even though he borrows his forms from Germany, he will modify them and, in his inspiration, he will remain a Frenchman. Then when the Germans extol the great name of Richard Wagner, we shall proudly acclaim this name—as yet unknown—but which we shall soon hear greeted with cries of applause and welcome.[74]

Mendès had at least recognized the simple truth that none of the Symbolist poets was prepared to admit: that a complete conversion to practicing Wagnerism was only possible for an artist prepared to write not simply poems but music-dramas.[75] But it is difficult to envision what, apart from the use of Gallic rather than Teutonic legend—and "Tristan," even so, is Gallic by adoption—would make such music-dramas French. If the composer-poet had to follow strictly the Wagnerian recipe Mendès prescribes, then "remaining a Frenchman in inspiration" would be an empty phrase. One could not follow the prescription without imitating the music.

Mendès might have recognized the inconsistencies of his requirements in the failures of two operas for which he himself wrote the librettos: Chabrier's *Gwendoline* and Debussy's *Rodrigues et Chimène*. In *Gwendoline* Chabrier is neither Gallic nor spontaneous. Debussy, on the other hand, abandoned *Rodrigues* after having written two acts, apparently because the ghost of Klingsor could not be exorcised from its pages. Not long afterward *Pelléas* fulfilled some of the milder requirements of Mendès's prescription. But Mendès—perhaps because he resented the abandonment of *Rodrigues*—professed to find in *Pelléas* an insufficient wedding of music and drama, and would have preferred to hear instead "Debussy's score performed by one of the symphony orchestras, and to see the charming lyrical tale of . . . Maeterlinck, lyrical in itself without singers or musical instruments, on the stage of one of the Parisian theaters."[76] The libretto of *Pelléas*, which was taken over with very few changes from Maeterlinck's play, is admittedly lyrical and perhaps charming without Debussy's music; it can of course be played as straight drama—whereas no one ever attempted to perform as a stage play one of Wagner's librettos. But according to Mendès' other criterion, Debussy's represents the happier wedding of music and drama, for *Pelléas* is far less easily adaptable for independent orchestral treatment than *Tristan* or *Parsifal*.

In 1869 Mendès had introduced his young wife Judith to Wagner and Cosima at Triebschen. She was already a Wagnerite, her father, Théophile Gautier, having taken her to the 1861 *Tannhäuser* when she was eleven.* Judith has described the feelings she had when she first visited Wagner's home:

What this wonderful genius meant to us it would have been difficult to make clear even to those who were not of us, at that time when only a little group of disciples stood by the Master upholding him against the jeers of the masses who failed to comprehend him. . . . We had the fanaticism of priests and martyrs—even to the slaying of our adversaries! It would, in fact, have been impossible to convince us that we should not be entirely justified in annihilating all those scoffers—blind to the new radiance which was so clear to us.[77]

Villiers, who was with her, threw himself upon the seat beside her and pressed her hand between her own: "It is to you, my dear Judith, that we owe this incredible good fortune."[78]

Wagner was immediately and permanently enchanted with the most talented of lady Wagnerites, who could write critical studies

---

* This was not the only exotic influence she was exposed to: at seventeen she published a collection of poems translated from the Chinese, which she had learned from a mandarin who lived with her family.

of his "oeuvre poétique." Although their correspondence is devoted mainly to Wagner's orders of luxuries from Paris, it is full
of sentiment. Wagner alludes to an "emotional episode" that
occurred between them during the opening of Bayreuth: and at
the time of *Parsifal* Judith briefly played a role similar to that of
Mathilde Wesendonk twenty-five years before.[79] Ernest Newman
would have it that Wagner was Tristanizing again: "What he was
really in love with was in the earlier case his *Tristan,* in the latter
his *Parsifal:* it was merely that from the immensity of his artistic
passion something flowed over to the mere woman and glorified
her in his eyes."[80] Wagner's affair with Judith Gautier is another
indication, at any rate, that *Parsifal* is related to *Tristan.* Cosima
was far more understanding than Minna had been; and Judith
was much better than Mathilde at advancing Wagner's cause.
In addition to writing articles and books, she gave lectures on the
music-dramas illustrated by singers accompanied on four pianos.[81]

Judith tried to account for the resistance of the French to Wagner: their quick intelligence, "so light, so mobile, so disposed to
mockery," deprives them of that quality so indispensable to the
comprehension of master works—simplicity. They cannot refrain
from finding something to ridicule in sublimity, and in noble and
terrible passions. Not only is Wagner unrecognized, but the French
have also forgotten Shakespeare and Victor Hugo. The trouble
with her countrymen, Judith concludes, is that they consider art
an amusement.[82]

Despite the efforts of propagandists like Judith, Mendès and
Schuré, one could not properly speak of Wagnerism as a vogue
in France until the 1880s. The machine of Wagnerism, which
moved slowly in the sixties, came to a long halt at the time of the
Franco-Prussian War and did not easily regain momentum. In
1869 *Rienzi* at the Théâtre Lyrique drew favorable notices; but
that the decade which had begun with a renovated *Tannhäuser*
should have been ushered out with the earliest and worst of Wagner's performable works indicates the very slow progress, if not
the retrogression of French Wagnerism. As one reviewer put it,

the reception of the early work could prove nothing: it was better to fail with *Lohengrin* than to succeed with *Rienzi*.[83] A performance of the *Rienzi* Overture earlier that year had, incidentally, prompted what is perhaps the most famous caricature of Wagner —the drawing by André Gill (in *L'Eclipse* of April 18) of a megacephalic Musician of the Future hammering a note into an enormous ear.

Even some of the favorable reviewers of *Rienzi* made the distinction, already familiar among those who knew him, between Wagner the musician and Wagner the man.[84] One source of the personal hostility was *Judaism in Music*, which had been reissued in French in March, 1869. It was perverse timing on Wagner's part to remind the world of this essay just before a performance of the opera which most obviously demonstrated his indebtedness to Meyerbeer and Halévy. Similarly mistimed was the publication in 1868, in both German and French, of *German Art and German Politics*, a series of articles that had appeared the year before in the *Süddeutsche Presse*.[85] The book opens with a quotation from Konstantin Frantz's *Inquiry into the European Balance of Power* (1859), announcing that the mission of Germany was to destroy the materialistic civilization of the French and replace it with the nobler culture of God's own people. Wagner expands this thought with vague, dangerous, and wearisomely familiar bombast about the German Folk, the German Youth, and the German Spirit— all leading, of course, to the project of renovating European Culture by means of model performances of great works (his own). Thus, well before *Eine Kapitulation* and the *Kaisermarsch*, Wagner offended the honor of the French, and advertised where his sympathies would lie in the event of a Franco-German War.* "According to Wagner," wrote Bizet, after reading *German Art and German Politics*, "it is the destiny of Prussia to destroy France politically, and that of Bavaria, under its King, to destroy her intellectually. . . . This pasteboard republican would amuse me

---

* The final articles of the original series were repressed as a danger to Franco-Bavarian relations.

vastly if he did not make me sick. I would like to rub his nose in his article."[86] (Yet not much later Bizet must admit that he cannot forget the immense pleasure he owes to Wagner: "The charm of his music is unutterable, inexpressible. It is voluptuousness, tenderness, love!")[87]

As in the case of *Judaism in Music*, the vitriol of Wagner's personal resentment was mixed with the venom of his political and cultural nationalism, just as his egotism identified his own triumph with the triumph of Germany—a *hybris* that Bayreuth later seemed to justify. French nationalism responded by making anti-Wagnerism an ingredient of patriotism; and critics of Wagner's views or of his music could fortify their animosity with patriotic sentiment. Born in Saxony and successful in Bavaria, Wagner was now associated with victorious Prussia—three chapters of Victor Tissot's *Les Prussiens en Allemagne* (1876) were devoted to Bayreuth; and, as one observer put it, the anti-Wagnerian press would have its readers believe that the Saxon composer was responsible for the annexation of Alsace-Lorraine. If the works of Wagner were not sufficiently familiar to provide examples of the vulgarity of German culture, descriptions of them, or of the interior decoration of Wagner's home, or of his tampering with the score of Gluck's *Iphigénie en Aulide*, were evidence enough of the superior refinement of the French.[88]

In the year following the war, when *The Birth of Tragedy* was written and the German cities were holding fund-raising concerts for the founding of Bayreuth, no Wagner was heard at the popular concerts in Paris. Late in 1873 Pasdeloup cautiously included the *Tannhäuser* Overture in one of his programs. Thereafter his purely musical proselytizing often occasioned patriotic demonstrations. In October, 1876, when he included fragments of the *Ring* on his program, brochures of *Une Capitulation* were sold in the boulevards. A claque booed the Overture to *Der Freischütz*, thinking it was the Funeral March from *Die Götterdämmerung*. The mistake could not have been entirely due to the blurred acoustics of the Cirque d'Hiver. Pasdeloup protested against the demonstration in the press, and it was suggested as a remedy that he perform the works of Wagner without identifying them as such in the program notes.[89]

It is difficult to determine what turned the tide in the eighties. No doubt the enthusiasm of independent Wagnerites helped to do so; and the success of Bayreuth, with its international audience, was well publicized. The sure-fire appeal of some of the *morceaux* inevitably led to an interest in others. It is significant that the first popular success of Colonne's newly founded Concerts Nationaux was with the *Chevauchée der Walkyries*, in 1881 (although on the same program the *Liebestod*, with Isolde's part played on a cornet, was poorly received). In the same year Lamoureux founded the Société des Nouveaux Concerts, and so there were three weekly concert societies playing Wagner—a sign of the new vogue. Lamoureux's orchestra performed with a rare perfection, which must have served to clarify for the public works like the *Tristan* Prelude. In 1884 he presented all of Act I in concert form, with explicative programs, and in the following year most of Act II. In October, 1882, in honor of the debut earlier in the year of *Parsifal* at Bayreuth, the Prelude to that work, in spite of its un-captivating slow tempo, was played by Pasdeloup at the Cirque d'Hiver, by Colonne at the Châtelet, and by Lamoureux at the Château-d'Eau—all on the same day.[91]

Between 1879 and 1886 more than twenty serious Wagnerian books were published in French: translations of Wagner's auto-biographical writings, studies of the works, summaries of the theories, accounts of visits to Bayreuth, and novels with Wagnerian themes. By 1886 the young critic Georges Servières could write a survey of the criticism of Wagner in France, elaborately divid-ing his history into six periods, and sufficiently sure of the right-ness of his position to remark that the ineptitudes of anti-Wag-nerians were worthy of a new supplement to *Bouvard et Pécuchet*.[91] Sets of the Wagnerian lithographs were on the market; and the Wagnerian Woman had established herself as a Parisian as well as a Central European figure. According to *La Vie*

Parisienne there were three types: *l'excentrique, la haute banque,* and *la femme chic.*[92] By the late eighties, wrote Romain Rolland, Wagnerism had begun to influence the thought of the most distinguished people in Paris: "writers not only discussed musical subjects, but judged painting, literature, and philosophy from a Wagnerian point of view. . . . The whole universe was seen and judged in the thought of Bayreuth."[93]

The thought, but not the music of Bayreuth. "With these new admirers," noted Maxim Léroy, "music completely disappeared under social comment and philosophical discussion."[94] The Opéra's avoidance of Wagner was extended to include the debuts of Wagnerian operas by Frenchmen. Although Reyer's *Sigurd* (which was Wagnerian in subject, if not in style) appeared in 1883, and Chabrier's *Gwendoline* in 1886—anticipating by a decade Humperdinck's *Hänsel und Gretel* (1893), Strauss's *Guntram* (1894), and Hugo Wolf's *Corregidor* (1895)—both French operas were first performed in Brussels. D'Indy's *Fervaal* also had a Belgian debut, and Chausson's *Le Roi Arthus* was introduced where *Tristan* itself was once supposed to be done, in Karlsruhe. In Paris poets and theorists celebrated Wagner Without Music; and they announced their new aesthetic creed in the pages of the oddest of doctrinal magazines—the *Revue wagnérienne.*

A Wagnerian Review

The *Revue wagnérienne* was founded in February, 1885, by Edouard Dujardin. It was published monthly for three years, and afterward many of its causes were taken over by the more famous Symbolist *Revue indépendante.* Dujardin's long and unusual career covered three literatures and many of the arts. He had been a student at the Paris Conservatory with Debussy and Dukas, but after he heard the *Ring* in London (1882) he abandoned musical composition, presumably because he felt he could not surpass Wagner. He turned instead to novels; to lyrical tragedies which anticipate the esoteric "wagnéries" of Joséphin Péladan; and even to biblical exegeses, one of which was dedicated jointly to Houston

Stewart Chamberlain and Lenin.[95] George Moore used him as a consultant for his Wagnerian novels: Dujardin read the successive drafts of *Evelyn Innes*, looking for musical howlers. His best-known contribution to English literature, however, was his use of interior monologue in the novel *Les Lauriers Sont Coupés* (1888), which is supposed to have influenced James Joyce. The device links *Ulysses* and Wagner, for Dujardin's interior monologue was an attempt to translate Wagner's "unending melody"— leitmotifs included—into prose.

Dujardin's attendance at Mallarmé's "Mardis" brought him into touch with many of the poets and writers who would contribute to the new review: Verlaine, Villiers, Catulle Mendès, J. K. Huysmans, and the American Stuart Merrill. Chamberlain and Hans von Wolzogen represented the Bayreuth Wagnerians in the *Revue*. The busiest contributor was the young Téodor de Wyzewa, later the biographer of Mozart.[96] Dujardin's account of the inception of the *Revue* illustrates how a mystique may arise out of semi-ignorance. The *Ring* in London had been "four evenings of ecstasy": "j'étais pris," Dujardin tells us, using a familiar simile, "comme dans le flux d'un océan; et je suis resté pris toute ma vie."[97] Two years later he was in Munich, striking up a friendship with Chamberlain and other high priests of the cult. Dujardin did not speak German well, and considered himself ignorant of Wagner's thought. He and Chamberlain studied the texts together: " 'Vous savez? tel passage? eh bien, je crois que j'ai compris'. . . . What rapture it was to enter into this new world of which day by day we began to perceive the profound meaning!"[98] Dujardin's initiation into the depths of Wagnerian thought—and of the German language as Wagner used it—brought him to a conclusion quite different from that of the composers who were at about the same time being initiated at Lamoureux's concert-performances of *Tristan:*

With the music, after all, it is enough to let one's heart respond to the incantation; but the poems, that great efflorescence of legends, the myths . . . which we felt were so charged with ideas! The philosophical thought which we recognized behind the poem and the music! And the new conception of art, or rather the renovation of art, which would replace an ordinary evening's diversion with a great spiritual festival, like those in Hellenic antiquity and in the Middle Ages of our cathedrals![99]

Later on Dujardin criticizes those "music lovers" who, once captivated by Wagner's music, go no further.[100] But he means further into the "philosophy" and not into the study of the music, to which, after all, it is sufficient to let one's heart respond.

There was clearly an irrationalist element in the program of the *Revue wagnérienne* to penetrate and propagate the "profound significance" of Wagner's works. On the one hand the music was thought of as a purely emotional experience, which could not be elucidated; and there was even the suggestion that analysis might spoil it. On the other hand, the seemingly rationalistic attempt to penetrate a philosophy was really not far from being an excuse for immersing oneself in vague and verbose glosses, much as one might immerse oneself in the music. "I am sure," wrote Dujardin, "that Wagner would have been the first to encourage disciples who . . . not only investigated his works but also investigated their own minds, rather than following his."[101] As a result of this attitude the theories were propounded inaccurately, and "so imperfectly understood"—as a recent scholar of the period has put it—"that the symbolists of 1885-95 were able—indeed forced—to make up a great part of them."[102] Much of the so-called Wagnerian philosophy of the *Revue* was Symbolist theory decked out with Wagnerian terms. Wyzewa, the chief theorist, contradicts Wagner's writings at every turn of his thought; his long articles on Wagnerian literature and painting were actually expositions of the neo-Platonic aesthetic of Mallarmé and Wyzewa himself.[103] The rest of the Wagnerizing in the review is less easily identifiable: one gets the sense that the writers have entered some foggy region of thought, and that the Frenchmen who sat around the oracular Chamberlain in the cafés of Munich had retained a good deal of their original awe.

The single article of musical analysis that appeared in the first year of the *Revue* might have been more accurately described as an appreciation of the technical perfection of the System. Pierre Bonnier's "experimental critique" of "Le Motif-organe de *Maîtres Chanteurs*"[104] included a fold-out "Tableau de l'orientation des 83 principaux aspects du motif-organe"—charted in tree-form to indicate the "organic generation" of all the motifs (some of which appear only once in the opera) from the *Ur-Motiv.* "If a work is living," Bonnier concludes, "it is because it is organized."[105] In a later issue the same operation was performed on *Parsifal.* The "tableaux" anticipated by a decade those intriguing charts in the Bayreuth handbooks of Albert Lavignac, on which black dots in decorative patterns indicate the scenes where each of the leitmotifs recurs.[106] Hero worship often leads to such busywork: pseudo analysis, no less than vague panegyric, is the product of the cult of art as a mystery. The eulogies of Wagner in the *Revue wagnérienne* may impressionistically reproduce in odd French prose certain moods and symbols of Wagner's world, but they teach us very little about his technique or his meaning. The presumably analytical articles pick out and reorder certain details of that world, as an astrologer might plot the movement of stars in the heavens he barely understands.

Symbolism

All the contributors would probably have agreed that the most important article to appear in the three years of the *Revue* was a brief essay called "Richard Wagner, rêverie d'un poète français."[107] The poet was Mallarmé. The reverie is usually thought of as the high-Wagnerian counterpart of Baudelaire's *Tannhäuser* essay: the greatest poets of two successive generations each wrote only one essay on a composer, in both cases Wagner; and Mallarmé had the precedent of Baudelaire's essay in mind when he undertook to write his own.[108] But the two essays are very different. Baudelaire's originated in an intense musical experience. Mallarmé's, in contrast, was solicited by members of his circle who wanted a contribution to the Wagnerian cause from their leader. Baudelaire described and analyzed a work he knew. Mallarmé does not refer to a single passage of Wagner or even mention the name of a music-drama.

He had never seen any of the works of Wagner, didn't know the scores and, according to many reports, was not particularly sensitive to music.[109] "I have spent all of yesterday and today on the study," he wrote to Dujardin:

It is half article, half prose-poem, but I haven't been able to finish it. It has been more difficult than anything I have ever done, I think. . . . I have never seen any Wagner, and yet I want to write something original, something accurate, something important on him. You must give me time.[110]

The essay was delivered two weeks later. Since there were no performances to rush off to see, the time was probably spent polishing the diction of what turned out to be one of Mallarmé's most impeccable prose-poems.

The praise of Wagner in Mallarmé's difficult essay is as unspecific as it is complex and elegant; Mallarmé was perhaps the coolest of French Wagnerites, and he had not contributed to the sonnet sequences on the music-dramas.[111] The criticism of Wagner, a bit clearer, reveals the great difference between the Symbolist aesthetic and Wagner's. According to Mallarmé, Wagner had indeed revived the lifeless and empty theater with the life-giving breath of music. He sees Wagner's achievement much as Nietzsche had seen it when celebrating the rebirth by symphony of the formerly "Socratic" theater. But Wagner's synthesis argued that there was a musical poverty in poetry which Mallarmé could not acknowledge.[112] And the poet had a distaste for the acted-out myth:

Does a gesture of our soul, do symbols in preparation or in blossom need any place for their development, other than the fictitious stage of vision which flashes in the glance of the audience? Myth is the Saint of Saints, but It must live in our imaginations.[113]

Mallarmé had variously described his elusive Ideal as a Theater without scenery and actors; a Book containing within it hero, place, and stage; silent Music.[114] The ultimate Nothingness exalted by the "musicien du silence" is the opposite of Wagner's fortissimo Nirvana.

However it is represented, the Symbolist aesthetic seems anti-thetical in spirit to Wagner's. Edmund Wilson speaks of the aim of the Symbolists "to intimate things rather than state them plainly," and Arthur Symons describes their attempt to "evade the old bond-age of rhetoric, the old bondage of exteriority."[115] Where the Sym-bolists intimate, Wagner is over-explicit; and art had reached the highest regions of rhetoric in the works of "God's ventriloquist." Wagner may fairly be described as having "aimed above all things at being precise, at saying rather than suggesting, at saying what [he] had to say so completely that nothing remained over." Yet these are the words Symons uses to describe that aspect of realism and the Parnassus against which Symbolism was a reaction![116] And when Mallarmé himself criticized the Parnassians he might have been writing about Wagner:

The Parnassians . . . take the thing just as it is and put it before us—and consequently they are deficient in mystery: they deprive the mind of the delicious joy of believing that it is creating. To name an object is to do away with the three-quarters of the enjoyment . . . which is derived from the satisfaction of guessing little by little: to suggest it, to evoke it—that is what charms the imagination.[117]

In the music-dramas which most closely adhere to the *Gesamtkunst-werk* ideal, Wagner not only "names the object" but translates the name into a musical label that reminds us of it each time it comes up. The symbols in Symbolism are usually a disguise for the ideas they represent, and the fleeting and vague connection between symbol and idea must be made by the imaginative reader. In con-trast, the presumption of the Bayreuth leitmotif-handbooks is that the corresponding connection in Wagner, if it is not immediately clear, can be made by looking it up.

In *Axel's Castle* Edmund Wilson has familiarized modern readers with a picture of Mallarmé at his Tuesday receptions:

Mallarmé, with his shining pensive gaze from under his long lashes and always smoking a cigarette "to put some smoke," as he used to say, "between the world and himself," would talk about the theory of poetry in a "mild, musical and unforgettable voice." There was an atmosphere "calm and almost religious." Mallarmé had "the pride of his inner life," said one of his friends; his nature was "patient, disdainful and imperiously gentle." He always reflected before he spoke and always put what he said in the form of a question.[118]

Contrast this with the typical picture of Wagner relentlessly reading one of his manuscripts to a captive audience, or singing all the roles in a makeshift debut of his latest scene: blatant, impatient, rash, assertive, and dogmatic. The contrast between the men is carried out in their works. The laconic and polished poems of Mallarmé are intentionally obscure: echoes and allusions vibrate in a mysterious half-light. If the poems were supposed to approach the condition of music, it must have been the quietest kind of impressionistic chamber music, with isolated harmonies and many silences. Symbolism began the line of modern poetry that seems to be valued in inverse proportion to the number of people who understand it.* The Music of the Future, on the other hand, was intended to impress all of posterity. If Wagner did not get the entire Folk which his program demanded as audience, he did at least, as Nietzsche discovered, get the pretenders to culture. And the Friends of Bayreuth may have had money, enthusiasm, and patience, but they were certainly not an elite of sensibility. Symbolism is abstract and aristocratic; Wagner is concrete and middle-class.

Nevertheless, the major writers whom Wilson studied as the literary heirs of the Symbolists—Eliot, Joyce, Yeats, Valéry, Proust—gleaned symbols from the Wagnerian myths, and extensively used a technique of thematic recurrence of which Wagner's leitmotifs had become the classical example. *Tristan* itself provides motifs for works as inaccessible to the Wagnerian audience as *The Waste Land* and *Finnegans Wake*.[119] But Eliot's allusions to Isolde seem no more Wagnerian in spirit than the ubiquitous references to Lohengrin in the poems of his master Laforgue; and when Joyce and Proust

---

* Wyzewa assigned the following un-Wagnerian epigraph to an article on Wagnerian literature: "La valeur esthétique d'une oeuvre d'art est toujours en raison inverse du nombre des esprits qui peuvent la comprendre."

are compared, let us say, to Thomas Mann, it should be evident that, although all three use the leitmotif technique, only the German novelist inherited the Wagnerian style (brought up to date by an ironic tone). The heirs of Symbolism rarely bothered to study Wagner's theories, for Mallarmé's synthesis superseded Wagner's. Here Wagner's position was comparable to Poe's. Both had been adopted by the French poets because of their aesthetic theories, and once these theories had been transformed and assimilated there was little need to return to the originals. T. S. Eliot has observed that "if the influence of Poe upon Baudelaire, Mallarmé and Valéry was based on a misunderstanding, it was a fecund and significant misunderstanding, for the aesthetic they erected upon this dubious foundation remains valid for their own work."[120] The same may be said of the influence of Wagner, with the qualification that, whereas Poe had once been studied carefully, Wagner had been superficially scanned or learned about at second hand.

Dans la Forêt

The *Revue wagnérienne* contemptuously attacked those composers who were content to learn from Wagner's music without going deeper into his thought. Dujardin specifically criticized Chabrier for having "never understood a word" of the Master beyond "questions of harmony and instrumentation."[121] The insinuation was that the composers were insular and unintellectual. French musicians of the 1880s were, on the contrary, as closely in touch with art and ideas as their romantic predecessors had been—and their successors of the 1920s would be. Saint-Saëns and d'Indy wrote substantial books of theory and criticism. Chausson's elegant salon was attended by Renoir and Rodin, Mallarmé and Gide. Chabrier owned eleven Manets, including the *Bar aux Folies-Bergères*.[122] That they for the most part *avoided* falling into Dujardin's "depths of thought" attests to their superior sophistication. But there was another kind of Wagnerian Deep, as Dujardin might have remembered from his first "drowning" in the *Ring*. A composer who had bypassed the profundities of the *Revue* might very well be permanently trapped in a descending sequence of altered chords.

In the process of assimilating Wagner's music, the song composer Henri Duparc was a catalyst. The first and favorite pupil of César Franck, Duparc introduced d'Indy to Franck's circle. Duparc met Wagner and Liszt at Weimar in 1869, the same year in which he, at twenty-one, and d'Indy, at eighteen, heard their first *Tristan*—Bülow conducting at Munich. Ten years later Duparc introduced the work to Chabrier. Chausson repeatedly sought Duparc's advice about the composition of the Wagnerian *Roi Arthus*; and among Duparc's other friends were Saint-Saëns and Fauré, although they belonged to neither the solemn school of Franck nor the group of composers, painters, and poets whom Fantin-Latour painted as "Petit Bayreuth."[123] As this brief listing suggests, everyone knew everyone else, and as a result the amount of musical cross-fertilization is incalculable.

Although Duparc outlived Wagner by fifty years—he died in 1933, at eighty-five—his entire output of music consisted of fifteen songs, a symphonic poem, and an orchestral nocturne, all composed between 1868 and 1885. The songs, set to Parnassian poems, are as un-Wagnerian in length and scale as they are in number. But not in harmony. Tristanesque enharmonics color the salon lyricism. As a snub to the critics who accused him (and everyone else) of copying Wagner, Duparc deliberately wrote the song *Extase* (1878) in the style of *Tristan*—an unashamed acknowledgment of discipleship comparable to Chabrier's witty *Souvenirs de Munich*, a set of quadrilles for piano on themes from *Tristan*, or Lekeu's violin sonata, "where the composer seems to be transcribing for a chamber music medium the ecstasies of the *Liebestod*."[124]

The cause of Duparc's forty-eight-year musical silence was a nervous malady which could conceivably have been aggravated by the emotional atmosphere of Franck's circle. His early musical death is curiously parallel to the actual deaths of Lekeu, at twenty-four, and Chausson, at forty-four, both of whom were excited and stifled by the humorless idealism and constant talk of Morality and

Love that surrounded the figure of Franck. "Je veux être *ému*," said Duparc—emphasizing the most important aesthetic criterion of the generation which temporarily turned French music away from the plastic, the pictorial, and the architectural. "*Espressivo* at any price" was how Nietzsche, at the same time, was describing one of the immoralities of Bayreuth—to which each of the French composers made his pilgrimage. "Pour moi," wrote the young Lekeu, "l'art est infiniment sentimental, d'où mon admiration pour *Tristan et Yseult*."[125]

In no way did the pupils of Franck display the "wit and light feet" that Nietzsche considered healthily Mediterranean. Emmanuel Chabrier, on the other hand, seemed to be a proper representative of the south. While still an amateur musician working in the Ministry of the Interior he composed humorous and sophisticated operettas; and Franck himself recognized in Chabrier's piano pieces an "eighteenth-century" wit and vitality.[126] Even during the composition of *Gwendoline* Chabrier went on writing vigorous orchestral pieces, rhythmic waltzes, and comic songs. Another opera, light, brilliant, and original, followed *Gwendoline*.[127] Chabrier's trip to Munich was happily counterbalanced by a journey to Spain, and the well-known *España* was performed at the time when he was assisting Lamoureux with the concert performances of *Tristan*.[128]

It is therefore a simplification of the facts to say, as Gerald Abraham does, that Chabrier "went to Bayreuth, heard *Tristan* and wept, and came home to write a tragic-heroic music-drama, with Danes who cry 'Ehèyo! Ehèyo!' and all the usual Wagnerian trimmings."[129] But the wish to dramatize Chabrier's conversion is understandable when one considers the discrepancy between *Gwendoline* and the rest of his music. Even while his Gallic works were supplying an antidote to Wagnerism, he considered the direct product of his infatuation with *Tristan* his magnum opus.[130] Duparc noted that after hearing *Tristan* "the jovial Chabrier parted for the night without saying a word"; he borrowed the piano score and returned it with passages underlined in admiration.[131] The admired passages turned up again in *Gwendoline,* along with Wagnerian construction and a Nordic myth. The libretto was written by Catulle Mendès, and Chabrier once half-jokingly told the conductor Felix Mottl that if the work had no other merits it at least had that of being "the joint effort of two fanatics of that great genius," Wagner.[132] Here is the story: Harald, a Dane, conquers Armel, a Saxon. To make peace Armel offers Harald his daughter, Gwendoline (who has fallen in love with her conqueror anyway). But Armel betrays Harald on the wedding day. Gwendoline, torn between her duty to her father and her love for her bridegroom, chooses to die with Harald. The plot thus provides occasion for a number of love-duets and a fine love-death (with the scene enveloped in flames). Much of the music is original. Chabrier's parallel ninth chords point forward from Wagner to Debussy; and in Gwendoline's spinning song Chabrier remembers the un-Wagnerized folk melodies of the Auverne. It is therefore the more regrettable that half the score is a compilation of Tristanesque effects. The love-duets imitate the turns and colors of the *Liebesnacht:* part of the first-act duet is in the *Tristan* key of A flat, and in the second act we hear the pulsating tied-rhythms of "O sink' hernieder."[133] The lovers repeat each other's words amidst *Tristan* appoggiaturas: "S'il meurt, mourir aussi." Ascending chromatic notes express Harald's Desire.[134] If it was a source of disappointment for Chabrier that he had not written *Tristan* himself, there was apparently some consolation in reproducing it.

D'Indy's *Fervaal* bears much the same relationship to *Parsifal* as *Gwendoline* does to *Tristan.* "Quant au wagnérisme," d'Indy wrote with reference to *Fervaal,* "J'ai vécu trop près de l'orbite de l'astre Wagner pour n'avoir pas été fatalement entraîné dans sa révolution."[135] Although the Wagnerian influence became increasingly less evident in his music, in the last year of his life d'Indy wrote a book on Wagner[136] which is in the true Bayreuth tradition, for it is inaccurate and anti-Semitic; and on the day of his death he was at work on a study of *Parsifal.* The choice of Wagner's religious drama as a model befitted the most influential disciple of Franck and later the puritanical administrator of the Schola Cantorum. *Fervaal* is a long and slow Celtic tale of symbolic characters who are concerned with incurable wounds, magic gardens, oaths of chastity, and the cult of purity. Even the key signatures are symbolic. Medieval music is incorporated into the work, and the orchestra patiently "comments" on every bit of the action.[137] As in *Parsifal* itself, there are also echoes of *Tristan*.[138] In his own text, d'Indy tried to imitate Wagnerian assonance in French. The repeated line

> *Hou! Hou!* au *loup!* au *loup!*

which was once notorious, is from d'Indy's later opera *L'Etranger*, in which music is again made the vehicle of philosophical ideas.[139] The Stranger is a Wotan-like figure who has renounced love, and at the end of the work he and a girl named Vita carry out a seaside *Liebestod* by disappearing into a vast wave.[140]

L'Etranger (1903) may be said to end the era during which serious French opera was dominated by Wagner. In the years that followed, the Wagnerian influence was modified by that of Debussy and the Russians. *Pelléas*, produced in 1902, must of course be excepted from most of the generalizations based on works like *Gwendoline* and *Fervaal*—as must Charpentier's veristic *Louise* (1900), although it is often called "Wagnerian," and the later operas of Massenet (who was known in some circles as "Mademoiselle Wagner").[141] Wagnerian harmony was equally evident in nonoperatic music of the eighties and nineties—even in the finest symphonies of the time: d'Indy's "French Mountain Air" (1886), Dukas's Symphony in C (1896), and the beautiful B-flat Symphony of Chausson (1891). "None of these works," d'Indy himself observed, "can reasonably be accused of being Wagnerian pastiches, yet every one of them betrays in some point or other the influence of the composer of *Tristan*."[142]

During most of this era Ernest Chausson was struggling with his *Roi Arthus*. Like Chabrier, Chausson had a late start as a professional composer, and his decision to take up music seriously coincided with his attendance at the Munich *Tristan* of 1879. His wealth left him leisure for introspection, for which the oppressive influence of Franck and Wagner on his delicate musical sense frequently provided the subject. One can therefore extract from his letters a series of exclamations and complaints that document the history of a *Tristan* obsession:

> I have heard *Tristan*, which is marvelous; I don't know any other work which possesses such intensity of feeling. As pure music it is splendid and of the highest order; as a way of understanding the musical drama it is a revolution. (1880)
> I have done all I could in order to avoid being too Wagnerian. (1884)
> The red specter of Wagner . . . does not let go of me. I reach the point of detesting him. Then I look through his pages, trying to find hidden vices in him and I find them. (1884)[143]

In 1886 Chausson began writing the libretto of *Le Roi Arthus*. From the start he was plagued by the fear that his story might resemble *Tristan* too closely. The fear was well grounded, for the central theme of the plot is the guilty love of Lancelot and Guinivere, and Lancelot's conflict between his loyalty to Arthur and his love for Arthur's wife. The derivativeness of the plot would not have mattered so much, according to Chausson, if only he could, in composing the music, have "successfully de-Wagnerized" himself. "Wagnerian in subject and Wagnerian in music: is that not altogether too much?" Two years later there is still "above all that frightful Wagner who is blocking all my paths." In 1893 he is still hoping to de-Wagnerize his work. Chausson's reaction to the news of Wagner's death, in 1883, had been prophetic of his difficulties: "And now Wagner is dead!" he exclaimed to a correspondent, "—but he has written *Tristan!*"[144]

Le Roi Arthus was produced, un-de-Wagnerized, in 1903, four years after Chausson's death. In the same year Debussy, no doubt with the stillbirth of such works in mind, observed in the *Mercure de France* that Wagner had been "a beautiful sunset mistaken for a dawn."[145] Debussy had once saluted the false dawn. His Prix de Rome had financed long hours at the Villa Medici where he lived apart "playing the score of *Tristan* in his room"—a score that found its way into the *Cinq Poèmes de Baudelaire* and *Rodrigues et Chimène*.[146] And Debussy had found the Bayreuth *Tristan* of 1889 no less affecting than his first encounter, on his return, with the score of *Boris* and with the Javanese gamelang at the Exposition Universelle.

Like Nietzsche he turned away from Wagner for reasons of musical and intellectual health. The recipes of old Klingsor had become poisonous. Debussy discovered that Wagner had started a "tradition of lies," most pernicious among them the false piety of *Parsifal*. The rhetorical, the overwhelming, the long-winded had to be attacked in the name of Gallic conciseness and clarity. Thus "M. Croche, antidilettante," makes the same charges as Nietzsche contra Philistinism—with the difference that while Nietzsche sounds impassioned Debussy sometimes seems dyspeptic.[147]

Again like Nietzsche, Debussy retained his responsiveness to the music of *Tristan* long after he had become officially anti-Wagnerian. He is said to have literally shaken with emotion upon rehearing the work, five years after he had written the amusing and caustic reference to the opening of the Prelude (to be played "avec une grande émotion") into the "Golliwog's Cakewalk" of the *Children's Corner Suite*. The familiar combination of responsiveness and dis-approval must account for the qualities of *Pelléas* that make it seem like a negative of *Tristan*. The plot of *Tristan* could have been the model for Maeterlinck's tenuous account of an inexplicably fated love. Pelléas is Golaud's much younger brother, just as Tristan had been Mark's adopted son. There is a love-duet and a kind of love-death. But in *Pelléas* rhetorical passion is replaced by hints of sensa-tion, just as Wagner's extraordinary German gives way to Maeter-linck's basic French. The "endless polyphonic melody" of *Tristan* becomes in *Pelléas* a mosaic of fragmentary, static, and reverbera-tive color-chords, with the elusive leitmotifs floating in the atmos-phere. The musical understatement of *Pelléas* is antithetical to the Tristanesque—purposely so.[148] If Debussy felt that the music of *Tristan* had been brutally imposed upon him, compelling his unwilling admiration, he seems to have set out to write a work which, in contrast, required a sympathetic, almost personal understanding between composer and audience. The music of *Tristan* is intended to overwhelm everybody; the music of *Pelléas* leaves unmoved all listeners except those whose imagination is stimulated by a temperamental affinity.*

In subordinating the music of *Pelléas* to the text Debussy happened to meet the requirements of Wagner's early theory of music-drama. At the same time the allusiveness of *Pelléas* and the restricted range of musical emotion belong to the aesthetic of the Symbolists. "Carry the theories of Mallarmé to a practical conclusion," wrote Arthur Symons, "multiply his powers in a direct ratio, and you have Wagner." Cecil Gray is right in substituting for Wagner Debussy.[149] In the art of vague but intimate suggestion Debussy was the Symbolist master.†

In Debussy's music-drama the separate lines of Wagner's influence converge. As a Symbolist masterpiece the aesthetic theory behind *Pelléas* may be traced back through the interpretations of the literary Wagnerites to the art-synthesis of *Opera and Drama*—the theory which in composing *Tristan* Wagner had ignored. In this respect *Pelléas* may be called the Anti-*Tristan*—a designation which is further warranted by the fragmentary harmony, emotional understatement, and simple language. But these qualities also in another respect bespeak the power of Wagner's chromaticism—for that power is no less evident in Debussy's rebellion than in the submission of Chabrier and Chausson. The excesses of *Tristan* dictated Debussy's restraint.

---

* It is interesting to note that Debussy later considered Bédier's *Tristan* as an opera subject. The project was carried out in part by the Swiss composer Frank Martin, in the oratorio *Le Vin Herbé*. Martin went farther than Debussy in avoiding the style of Wagner's *Tristan*: the medieval narrative form is retained, chanted by a chorus, and accompanied by a small orchestra of seven strings and a piano.
† This opinion is succinctly expressed by Cyril Connolly: "Debussy's faun killed Mallarmé's."

chapter V

LOVE AND DEATH IN VENICE (1883-1933)

Wagnerizing on the Isle of Wight

Proust's Madame Verdurin was a lady Wagnerite of the *haute banque* sort, with a touch of the *excentrique*. If the pianist of her little clan suggested playing the Ride of the Valkyries or the Prelude to *Tristan*, she would protest. It was not that the music was displeasing to her but, on the contrary, that it made too violent an impression. "Then you want me to have one of my headaches?" she used to ask.[1] Later on M. Verdurin would ask M. Vinteuil to play his Sonata in F sharp (Saint-Saëns? César Franck? Lekeu?). "No, no, no, not my sonata!" Mme. Verdurin would scream. "I don't want to be made to cry until I get a cold in the head, and neuralgia all down my face, like last time." The little scene, which was regularly enacted, would then continue with M. Verdurin's suggestion that the pianist play "just the *andante*." "Just the *andante!*" his wife would reply: "How you do go on! As if it weren't 'just the *andante*' that breaks every bone in my body. The 'Master' is really too priceless! Just as though, 'in the Ninth,' he said 'we need only have the *finale*,' or 'just the overture' of the *Meistersingers.*"[2]

England as well as France had its Wagner-loving ladies who had to limit themselves to small doses of Prelude and Overture. They also read novels—an art-form in which they could tolerate Wagnerian length—and were kept amply supplied with stories that contained easy, up-to-date, and elevated Wagnerian allusions. With a hint of the music-dramas, a novelist could invoke a mood that was, as Edmund Wilson describes Count Axel's castle, "half-Wagnerian, half-romantic-Gothic."[3] Simply naming a character Sieglinde, say, or Gudrun, might endow her with the romance of not only the medieval but the Wagnerian namesake. Or one could write about opera singers, or amateur musicians—or send the wealthier characters to a season at Bayreuth.

The hero of the second (and worst) novel by D. H. Lawrence is named Siegmund, and he works as a fiddler in the Covent Garden orchestra. *The Trespasser* (1912) is in part a rewriting of material by Lawrence's friend Helen Corke, who later published her own Wagnerian novel based on the same material.* Both books are about the love affair between a girl and her music teacher, and both end with the teacher's suicide.[4]

Because of the low pay at Covent Garden, Lawrence's Siegmund must take on extra jobs in orchestras that play "The Saucy Little Switzer" instead of Siegfried's Rhine-Journey. Eventually he leaves his embittered wife and unpleasant children to spend a holiday with his intellectualized—or at any rate Wagnerized—pupil Helena. According to Lawrence's description, Helena belongs to "that class of 'dreaming women' with whom passion exhausts itself at the mouth"[5]—a characterization that might suggest that she is a dramatic soprano. She is, however, merely a mediocre student of the violin, although she occasionally plays at being Isolde by humming snatches of that role and accepting nothing more than kisses from her lover.

Nineteen of thirty-one chapters are given over to the account of an unconsummated five-day love affair on the Isle of Wight. Siegmund and Helena spend their time reading German and talking a love-duet even longer than that of Tristan and Isolde, lingering over such subjects as Night, the Sea, transcendental love, "vivid soul experience," and joint suicide by drowning. Helena's musings reveal the musical cast of her mind:

* The original title of *The Trespasser* was *The Saga of Siegmund.*

All along [she says] Fate has been resolving, from the very beginning, resolving obvious discords, gradually, by unfamiliar progressions; and out of original combinations weaving wondrous harmonies with our lives. . . . The Master-Fate is too great an artist to suffer an anticlimax. I am sure the Master-Musician is too great an artist to allow a bathetic anticlimax.[6]

One would gather from the rest of the book that the Master-Musician is Wagner. The Isle of Wight is called "Sieglinde's island"; the sunlight on the sea is "the Rhine maidens spreading their bright hair to the sun"; the barking of sheep dogs reminds the lovers of "Fasner [sic] and Fasolt"; and the sound of a fog-horn is "not Wotan's wrath, nor Siegfried's dragon," but "the call of the horn across the sea to Tristan."[7]

Helena is learning German because she wants "to understand Wagner in his own language." She brings her studies with her on her holiday ("There is the Nietzsche I brought—") and practices her new words while making love: "Meanwhile she whispered over him sharp, breathless phrases in German and English, touching him with her mouth and her cheeks and her forehead." "Goethe and Heine and Uhland seemed to speak her language," but she has an antipathy to the French, which Siegmund shares: he considers the music of *Pelléas* cold.[8]

The characters in Wagnerian novels display a remarkable aptitude for performing excerpts from the music-dramas that are presumably recognizable without accompaniment. In *The Tres-passer* Siegmund usually whistles, carelessly, and Helena half-articulately hums:

"Ascribe it to the fairies," he replied, whistling the bird music out of Siegfried, then pieces of Tristan.

But he was straying ahead, carelessly whistling the Spring Song from Die Walküre.

All the time Siegmund was mechanically thinking the well-known movement from the Valkyrie Ride, his whole self beating to the rhythm. It seemed to him there was a certain grandeur in this flight, but it hurt him with its heavy insistence of catastrophe.

Helena forever hummed fragments of "Tristan." As she stood on the rocks she sang, in her little, half-articulate way, bits of Isolde's love, bits of Tristan's anguish, to Siegmund.[9]

The musical conversation is usually sentimental and critical:

"Artists are supremely unfortunate persons," she announced. "Think of Wagner," said Siegmund.

Helena lay beside him, half upon him, sad with bliss. "You must write a symphony of this—of us," she said.

"What music do you think holds the best interpretation of sunset?" ... "A Beethoven symphony—the one—" and he explained to her. She was not satisfied, but leaned against him, making her choice. . . . "The Grail music in 'Lohengrin,' " she decided.[10]

But sometimes their disagreement about a musical matter borders on bickering, as in this amusing bit of space-filler:

"What is the pitch?" asked Helena.
"Where it is horizontal? It slides up a chromatic scale," said Siegmund.
"Yes, but the settled pitch—is it about E?"
"E!" exclaimed Siegmund. "More like F."
"Nay, listen!" said Helena.
They stood still and waited till there came the long booing of the fog-horn.
"There!" exclaimed Siegmund, imitating the sound. "That is not E." He repeated the sound. "It is F."
"Surely it is E," persisted Helena.
"Even F sharp," he rejoined, humming the note.
She laughed, and told him to climb the chromatic scale.
"But you agree?" he said.
"I do not," she replied. . . .
"What is the note in 'Tristan'?" Helena made an effort to ask.
"That is not the same," he replied.
"No, dear, that is not the same," she said in low, comforting tones. . . .[11]

Tristan has given its name to a particular *chord*, but there is no single *note* with which it can be associated: Wagner was equally fond of using E and F, and even F sharp. In the course of their discussions, the lovers refer only to the mythical music-dramas: nowhere in the book is *Die Meistersinger* mentioned. Nor does Helena ever order Siegmund to climb the *diatonic* scale!

Lawrence had a low opinion of *The Trespasser*. Later he expertly incorporated images of Valhalla into the closing chapters of *Women in Love*—concerning the relationship of Gudrun and Loerke (Loki) and the *Heldentod* of Gerald. But the early novel, although unrepresentative of Lawrence, is neatly representative of the absurdities of an amateur Wagnerism that was prevalent in England at the turn of the century. Comparable quotations could be collected from the works of George Moore (or his literary heirs, like Charles Morgan),[12] although in Moore they are inconveniently scattered over many long novels, and the novels were proofread for musical mistakes by experts like Dujardin—a service which Lawrence ought to have called upon for *The Trespasser*. Graham Hough, in his recent study of Lawrence, suspects that *The Trespasser* was strongly influenced by Moore's *Evelyn Innes*, and rightly observes that "Moore's brand of worldly aestheticism sits very ill on Lawrence."[13]

The Wagnerian allusions that intrude upon the love-making of Siegmund and Helena are part of this ill-settled inheritance from the Aesthetic Movement. In 1869—the year Nietzsche went to Triebschen—Francis Hueffer had imported Wagnerism into the circle of the Pre-Raphaelite Brotherhood. A decade later, in one of the earliest expository articles on "Aesthetic Culture," Wagner was classed with Botticelli, Chippendale furniture, Queen Anne houses, and medieval lamps as among the delights of those who have "inward and spiritual grace." "In music," this defense of aestheticism informs its readers, "the Aesthetes affect Liszt, Rubinstein, and Wagner, who are all most consummately intense"—and there follows an account of how myth and unending melody had bridged the chasm between natural truth and the ludicrous conventions of opera.[14] With this pedigree, fashionable Wagnerism suited the talent of Lawrence no more naturally than, say, illustrations by Beardsley would suit *Sons and Lovers*.

The Wagnerism that seems so out of place on the Isle of Wight had been transplanted from an artificial paradise, where allusions to the music-dramas had added piquancy and suggested profundity. There Wagner connoted passion with a touch of decadence. In a similar way references to him intensify the tone of religious sensuality in the novels of Moore and other British reflections of Villier's *Axel* and the world of Huysmans. It was Dorian Gray who used to sit "listening in rapt pleasure to Tannhäuser, and seeing in the prelude to that great work of art a presentation of the tragedy of his own soul."[15] George Moore's Evelyn Innes had sung Isolde (and taken lovers) before she entered a convent as Sister Teresa, thus giving up one religious vocation (to sing in a cut version of Wagner was blasphemous) for another.[16] And in *The Lake*, which Moore dedicated to Dujardin, a priest falls in love with a young girl who writes to him about the profundity of the *Ring*.[17] Wagner added zest to forbidden love, just as Richard Strauss's chromatics enlivened Wilde's *Salome*.

Above all Wagner represented the Artist, and Wagnerism an acknowledgment of the supremacy of Art. "Shakespeare absorbed dramatic poetry," wrote Moore, "Balzac the novel, Wagner absorbed dramatic music—we are the moths that flutter in the light of suns that shall have no setting."[18] Moore needed no experts to correct his references to Shakespeare and Balzac; but in the case of dramatic music he had not seen the light of other suns by which Wagner's brilliance could be measured. Mozart and Beethoven are scarcely mentioned in Moore's works, and his taste for Bach was probably "no more than a tribute to his general love of the eighteenth century."[19] In a casual letter which no expert revised, he refers to the operas in terms that are revealingly inadequate: they are, he writes, his "delight and relaxation"—not simply the Forest Murmurs and the Peaceful Slumber Music, but "the operas" in general. Once again a Wagnerite proves to be ignorant of the music. "The members of our family," wrote Moore's brother, "were all unmusical . . . ; George no better than the rest. He could not hum a tune correctly, and what he wrote about music was what he heard others say. Perhaps he had some taste, but he had no ear."[20] Dujardin himself observed that Moore did not like music. "It always semed to me," he is reported as saying, "that Moore's interest in Wagner, about whom we had endless conversations, was mainly literary."[21]

Tristanizing Along the Adriatic

In contrast, the cult of Wagner as practiced by Gabriele D'Annunzio was mainly musical. D'Annunzio's works, like his life, belong to the fashionably aesthetic world Moore liked to portray. At his worst, he had no taste; but, unlike Moore, he had an ear.[22] As a consequence, his aesthetic gardens are overgrown with chromatic lushness. He did not have to flatter his readers with factitious reminders of all the music dramas; he could present them with exuberant passages of fictional Tristanizing.

In the course of an unconsidered outburst against the clumsiness of foreign fiction (Turgenev, Flaubert, Dostoievsky) as compared with the subtlety of the novel in English (Fenimore Cooper and Hardy), D. H. Lawrence makes the following remark: "Take even D'Annunzio and my Trespasser—how much cruder [and] stupider D'Annunzio is, really. No, enough of this silly worship of foreigners."[23] The Wagnerism in *The Trespasser* indicates a reason for the seemingly farfetched comparison. Siegmund and Helena echo the aestheticism for which D'Annunzio, in his autobiographical novels and his novelistic life, was the chief European advertisement. Most likely Lawrence had in mind a particular novel by D'Annunzio, the *Trionfo della Morte*,[24] which in addition to being Wagnerian—Moore admired it during the writing of *Evelyn Innes*—is curiously similar to *The Trespasser* in other ways.

Both Lawrence's novel and D'Annunzio's are devoted to the analysis of a love-affair, which in each case is described largely in the conversation of the lovers. The seashore provides the setting for both novels, and the sea one of the central symbols. And in each work the best chapters are those that do not deal directly with the love-affair (and are therefore not Wagnerian): in *The Tres-*

passer the description of Siegmund's home life; in *The Triumph of Death* the remarkable account of a pilgrimage to a religious shrine.

Both heroes commit suicide. But while Lawrence's Siegmund wearily hangs himself at home, D'Annunzio's Giorgio jumps off a precipice into the sea, carrying with him his unwilling beloved. Siegmund is a failure from the lower middle class; Giorgio an aristocratic murderer. A meager income makes it impossible for Siegmund to divorce his wife and marry Helena; all he can afford is a brief holiday on the Isle of Wight. Giorgio, living on an independent income inherited from an eccentric uncle, has the leisure to fall obsessively in love, and to travel with the victim of his obsession from villa to villa along the Adriatic. Unbothered by the dreary financial problems that drive Siegmund to suicide, D'Annunzio's hero can afford to leap to Nirvana in a love-death that is in part the invention of idleness. Giorgio is the upper-class and high-aesthetic model for Siegmund's unsuccessful imitation of the romantic hero.

The difference between the heroes is, in short, this: Siegmund is a Wagnerite, Giorgio a Tristanite. Siegmund keeps alluding to Wagner to prove his sensitivity, just as Helena does to indicate that she is an intellectual. They attempt to aggrandize their brief affair by Wagnerizing a hopeless holiday into a retreat of mythical lovers. D'Annunzio's hero is too elegant for this sort of cultural display; he does not need Wagner as material for pretensions. But he is insane, and *Tristan* contributes to his delusions.

D'Annunzio postpones his florid retelling of *Tristan* to the penultimate chapter of *The Triumph of Death*, in which the hero recalls a performance of the work at Bayreuth. At that point in the novel, the impressionistic translation of the music provides a set of images by means of which the reader may more precisely understand the nature of the hero's insanity. In the course of the novel music has been linked with madness and murder, and obsessive love with decadence and death. The *Tristan* chapter gathers together all these associations in what may be called a final orchestral statement of the novel's themes. It coincides with Giorgio's resolution to carry out his suicide-murder, which occurs in the next and last chapter. The description of Tristan and Isolde's love-death is followed by Giorgio's parody of it.

The novel had opened, as it ends, with a suicide. Scenes of violent death and mutilation punctuate the narrative—another suicide, the death throes of an infant, the drowning of a child. The climax of the violence is Giorgio's leap; the culmination of the horror a series of vivid pictures of lepers and other mendicant monstrosities. These macabre tableaux are set next to scenes of the most refined sensuality. Thus, shortly before she is murdered, the heroine is allowed to enjoy a luxurious meal of peaches and amber and pink *loukoumes,* and to recall with pleasure the thick flakes of the iced champagne at Danieli's.[25]

The constant shifting between sensual delight and physical horror is a projection of Giorgio's feelings about his mistress Ippolita. She is tasteful but also on occasion coarse; aristocratic in manners but of plebeian origins; beautiful but barren; voluptuous but epileptic. For Giorgio her "impurities" increase her attractiveness, and at the same time provide excuses for his love-murder. Her lack of total refinement (she might some day take a vulgar lover) and her "malady" (she will doubtless lose her beauty) are reasons for helping her to find consummation in death while she is in the full bloom of her beauty. Above all it is her barrenness that represents for Giorgio both the pointlessness of her beauty and the hopelessness of his obsession.[26] But his explanations of the source of his misery are unconvincing. Suicidal before he met Ippolita, he chose obsessive love as his roundabout road to self-destruction. Like Tristan and Isolde, he is totally given over to a grand passion because he has devoted himself to death. His love has therefore been hopeless from the start, and although Ippolita's barrenness may be neatly symbolic of this hopelessness, it can scarcely be considered one of the causes of it.

Giorgio is musically hyperaesthetic. His soul had been "fed only on music and exalting books"; once the repetition of a phrase in a Beethoven sonata had exalted him "almost to a state of madness." When his favorite uncle played violin and piano music with him "the fascination of a single melody held them prisoners an entire afternoon." For uncle Demetrius (who was also a suicide) music had been a private cult,[27] and Giorgio was resolved to imitate him in this respect as well as in the manner of his death.* A taste for mixing music with the occult had brought the death-devoted hero to the bizarre concert where he first met Ippolita. This was a private performance of "a mass by Bach," arranged by a Buddhist who had published two volumes of essays on Schopenhauer, and performed in a mysterious chapel before an audience of music-mad savants whose daughters sing in the chorus. Among the audience are a botanist-priest, a Helmholtzian physicist of acoustics, a Jewish pianist, and a Pre-Raphaelite painter. In addition to the music, incense and the atmosphere of self-indulgent refinement (on the altar there is actually a bouquet of faded violets!) prepare the future lover for his fatal meeting.[28]

The last days of Giorgio's ill-starred idyll begin with the arrival of a hired piano and a box of music. Although the lovers have not practiced at all during the months of travel, they are able to perform Schumann, Grieg, and Chopin, their "new ecstasy" and "quasi-delirious fever" undisturbed by the difficult fingering of scale passages.† But their favorite piece is the *Tristan* Prelude, for in it

---

* In Giorgio's mind the cult of music and the wish to die begin to merge into one vague set of notions, out of which may be extracted a glossary of Tristanism: "Without doubt [Giorgio thought] it is music that initiated him [the uncle] into the mystery of Death, that showed him, beyond this life, a *nocturnal empire* of marvels. *Harmony*, an element superior to time and space, had given him, like a beatitude, a glimpse of the possibility of freeing himself from space and time, of *detaching himself from the individual will* that confined him in the prison of a personality enclosed in a restricted place, that kept him perpetually subject to the *brutish matter of corporeal substance.* How he had a thousand times felt in himself, in the moments of inspiration, the awakening of the *universal will.* . . . He believed that death would be a means for prolonging his existence in the infinite, that he would become *dissolved in the continuous harmony of the Great All* and would participate in the *endless Voluptuousness of the Eternal.* Why should I, too, not have the same initiator into the same mystery?" One of the "exalting books" on which Giorgio fed his soul was obviously *The World as Will and Idea.* (Italics in the quoted passage are mine.—E.Z.)

† In a greater story in which murder is associated with music—Tolstoy's *Kreutzer Sonata*—the narrator's wife, only an amateur, can play the piano part of Beethoven's virtuoso work, including, presumably, the broken thirds and sixths in the development section of the first movement.

"the leap of love toward death" is "unchained with inconceivable violence"; and their piano performance is presumably as efficient as a phonograph in "transporting them to the marvelous Empire."[29] Before Giorgio finally resolves upon turning his metaphorical leap of love into fact, he is reminded of his first religious pilgrimage to the Ideal Theater of Bayreuth, and the fifteen-page description of *Tristan* begins. D'Annunzio's rendering of the Prelude in prose seems to have been influenced by Wagner's 1860 program notes. The groupings of related verbs are especially decorative in Italian.[30] The invisible Bayreuth orchestra is transformed into a *Golfo Mistico*, which is by turns inflamed, irradiated, and transfigured. Out of it variously arise sighs, flames, waves, and fatal motifs. In between these irruptions of the music the story of *Tristan* is told in an interpretation that is designed to recapitulate Giorgio's ideas of passion and death. Isolde is from the start intent on destroying Tristan because she cannot possess him: "Passion aroused in her a homicidal mania, awakened in the roots of her being a need of dissolution, of annihilation."[31] And to the mystical yearning of Wagner's lovers Giorgio adds a touch of aesthetic thrill seeking:

Nothing could extinguish or soften that fatal ardor; nothing, except death. They had vainly tried every caress; they had vainly summoned all their strength to unite in a supreme embrace, . . . to become one and the same being. Their sighs of voluptuousness were transformed into agonizing sobs.[32]

Ippolita is temporarily seduced by the music, and the description of it, into thinking of herself as Isolde:

In the vertiginous heights of their love-dream they believed they equalled the personages in the drama. Did it not seem to them that they, too, had drunk a philter? Were they not also linked together by an indissoluble bond, and did they not often feel in voluptuousness the horrors of the death-agony?[33]

But the seduction had been funereal. What hitherto might still have been construed by the reader as eccentric self-indulgence is suddenly revealed as a homicidal mania. Sadistic visions pass through Giorgio's brain, and he imagines the sensual murder of Ippolita, as in this Senecan scene: "On the marble threshold of a door, full of shadow and expectation, the woman who was about to die appeared, extending her naked arms; and at the extremities of the arms, from the slashed veins, spouted and palpitated two red fountains."[34] At first Ippolita counters with easy practicality what she thinks of as Giorgio's idle fancies:

"Wouldn't you like to die such a death as Isolde's?" asked Giorgio, with a smile.

"I would," she answered. "But, on earth, people don't die like that." . . .

"Why die," she said, "if I love you, if you love me, if nothing henceforth prevents us from living for ourselves alone?"[35]

Later she tries to disarm him by making love; but her own lasciviousness, repulsed, is converted into a hysterical fit which increases Giorgio's determination to kill her. Her violent death is the opposite of Isolde's calm transfiguration, and the lovers' leap a caricature of the *Liebestod*:

"Are you mad?" she cried, choked by anger. "Are you mad?"

But when she saw him come after her without speaking a word, when she felt herself seized with more brutal violence and dragged again toward the precipice, she understood all, and a great, sinister flash of light struck terror to her soul. . . .

Insane with terror, she supplicated him, writhing. She hoped to stop him, to move him to pity.

"One minute! Listen! I love you! Forgive me! Forgive me!"

She stammered incoherent words desperately, feeling herself becoming weaker, losing her ground, seeing death before her.

"Assassin!" she then shrieked, as she was seized by the hair, thrown to the ground on the edge of the precipice, lost.

The dog barked at the tragic group.

It was a brief and fierce struggle, like the sudden outburst of supreme hate which, up to then, had been smouldering, unsuspected, in the hearts of implacable enemies.

And they both crashed down to death, clasped in each other's arms.[36]

Not long before the melodramatic murder Ippolita had gone to the piano, shut the cover over the keyboard, locked it, and hidden the key. "The music excites you too much," she told Giorgio. "We must have no more for a week."[37] She had hit upon the chief source of the danger to her, without recognizing its magnitude. The music of *Tristan* did not simply increase Giorgio's excitability; his extreme sensitivity to it led him to mythicize his obsession. His delusions are an extreme and perverted form of the Tristanizing Wagner himself engaged in when he idealized his relationship with Mathilde Wesendonk. D'Annunzio's case study of Tristanism is in part autobiographical, and it is possible that during his affair with Barbara Leoni his eccentricities matched Giorgio's (and Wagner's). But D'Annunzio, like Wagner, had work to do. Giorgio, on the other hand, is unemployed; and, as Gottfried von Strassburg had long ago observed, "when a man of leisure is overwhelmed by love's torment, leisure redoubles that torment."[38] Giorgio is a self-portrait of D'Annunzio up to a point, beyond which the tendencies that he represents are extended to an absurd termination. His love-death is the comedy of the Perfect Tristanite.

The City of Music

When Wagner died in Venice the young D'Annunzio may have helped to carry the coffin (which was bound for Bayreuth) from the Palazzo Vendramin-Calergi to the funeral boat.[39] D'Annunzio describes the event in his novel *Il Fuoco*. The subject of the novel is the poet's famous affair with Eleonora Duse, but it is also Venice; and the façades of the city are described with guidebookish completeness and in Ruskinian detail. Wagner's cortege provides the novel with an appropriately solemn and sentimental coda. According to D'Annunzio's account, the boatman's eyes were burnt with tears; and the "splendor" of Cosima's countenance seems to have been indelibly impressed on the memories of the devoted pall-bearers. The great silence of the procession was, we are told, worthy of a capitalized Him, who had "transformed the forces of the Universe for man's worship into infinite song."[40] At the end of the ceremony the Italian youths covered the hero's coffin with laurels evocative of Garibaldi.

Italian laurels buried at Bayreuth symbolize the close association

of Wagner and Venice. Liszt was perhaps alluding to that association in the piano piece he wrote while staying at the Palazzo Vendramin, just before Wagner's death: it is called *Le Lugubre Gondole*.* As early as 1858 Wagner had heard the bands in the Piazza
San Marco play selections from *Tannhäuser* and *Lohengrin;* by the
1890s even *Parsifal* contributed to their standard repertory.[41] The
pigeons remained as undisturbed by the *Tannhäuser* March as by
the *Gazza Ladra* Overture—just as German was accepted as the
standard language on the streets leading to the Lido beachfront.
Geographical convenience, Venetian Gothic, and Hapsburg politics conspired to make Venice the favorite resort of Central Europeans.

In the greatest of his novellas, Thomas Mann succeeds in portraying all that is strange and unhealthy about this attractiveness of
the Byzantine city for Teutonic tourists. Gustav Aschenbach is
fatefully drawn to the city which is a museum of splendid façades
that mask decay and corruption and a port which exposes Europe
to a plague-ridden East. At the time of his visit Venice is especially
dangerous; and the reader who brings to *Death in Venice* a
familiarity with Mann's earlier stories—in which decay and perversion are associated with music—may be forgiven if he expects
Aschenbach to be hearing strains of *Die Götterdämmerung* sung
by a distant gondolier.

For, in addition to using musical allusions to represent perilous
attractiveness, Mann followed Nietzsche in thinking of Venice as
the City of Music. "If I seek another word for music," Nietzsche
wrote in *Ecce Homo*, "I always find only one word, Venice."[42] But
Nietzsche had chosen Venice as un-Wagnerian; Mann, on the
other hand, thought of it as "the city of *Tristan*."[43] The author
of *Buddenbrooks* admired the Goncourts' *Renée Mauperin*, in
which the heroine breaks off playing the piano to exclaim that
Venice is the city "où tous les musiciens seraient enterrés."[44]
Wagner had done a service for Mann's symbolism as well as for

* The last musical performance of any kind Liszt ever attended was a *Tristan*
at Bayreuth. "Tristan," according to some accounts, was the last word he spoke
before he died.

d'Annunzio's national pride by dying in the city where he had orchestrated the Love Duet.

Although neither *Tristan* nor Wagner is mentioned by name in *Death in Venice,* Mann subsequently admitted that at the time when he wrote the novella Wagner was his "strongest and most decisive artistic experience."[45] And the motifs of the music-drama are interwoven into the story in Mann's best Wagnerian manner. In Mann's own phrase, the novella is constructed "according to the logic of music" and it is written in his most richly "chromatic" prose.[46] The hero of the tale—whose maternal grandfather was a musical conductor—shares the Christian name and some of the physical features of Gustav Mahler. Aschenbach's musical ancestry may show in his tendency to respond more immediately to the sounds than to the sights of his surroundings: the visual details are usually blurred for him—as in his first view of Venice, which is enveloped in haze and rain: the city of Monet rather than Canaletto.

The narrative is constructed so that Aschenbach may approach Venice from the sea, to which (according to R. H. Thomas, who uses the apt Nietzschean phrase) "Mann has attributed the same *dangerous fascination* as to music."[47] Aschenbach's love of the ocean has its source in a "yearning . . . for the unorganized, the immeasurable, the eternal—in short, for nothingness"—the Nirvana-urge which Wagner described as one of the sources of the *Tristan* music.[48] The beloved Tadzio is characteristically depicted as bathing in the sea, or lapped by the waves, or dripping wet; and it is the sea, of course, which carries the fatal plague from the Near Eastern ports into the Venetian canals.

The two people responsible for Aschenbach's love-death—the boy with whom he falls in love and the street singer from whom he probably contracts the plague—are introduced into the story through aural details. Aschenbach first hears Tadzio's name as "Adgio," or more accurately as "Adjiu"—with the "u" sound at the end drawn out like a call.[49] Perhaps the name contains a reference to the "incredibly old-fashioned adagio" which Nietzsche once heard on the Rialto Bridge, "just as if an adagio had never before existed."[50] At any rate, the musical name recurs in the story like the Desire motif in *Tristan* (which is heard most often in what may be described as the prolonged "u" sound of the woodwinds); and the name is heard in a *stretto* climax when it is yelled by the beardless youths in Aschenbach's Bacchanalian nightmare: "It would ring through the air like the bellow of a challenging stag, and be given back many-tongued; or they would use it to goad each other on to dance with wild excess of tossing limbs."[51]

Aschenbach hears Tadzio's uncomprehended Polish as "absolute music": to the infatuated listener the words are "mingled harmonies," a kind of love music. In contrast, a concert of death music is bizarrely performed on mandolin, guitar, harmonica, and reedy violin, led by the strange street musician who stinks of ineffectual disinfectant and mockingly warns Aschenbach of the plague. This weird program includes a "love-duet"—sung by a young woman with a "high shrill voice" and a "sweetly falsettoing tenor."[52] Perhaps the tenor mocks the singing of an operatic Tristan, just as the aging Aschenbach's preoccupation with a youth is a grotesque caricature of Tristan's obsession with Isolde.

In the fiction that preceded *Death in Venice*, and in much that came after, Mann similarly but less subtly associated sensual music with perverted sexuality. In "The Blood of the Walsungs," written in 1905, Mann had taken up d'Annunzio's device of combining a description of one of Wagner's music-dramas with a parody of it. The hero and heroine of this lubricous tale are the elegant nineteen-year-old twin children of wealthy, assimilated North-German Jews. The adolescents are snobbish, spoiled, and sensuous, and display a perverse interest in each other that is, one would assume, partly the result of their having been named Siegmund and Sieglinde. Like Wagner's Volsungs, Mann's twins belong to a "separate race," the "marks" of which keep appearing in their faces. Siegmund, like all of Mann's decadent and ill-fated characters, is sensitive and "artistic": that is to say, he paints a bit, and likes to have his favorite books expensively bound. Once he attended a course of lectures on the history of art, but "he had to leave off because his sense of smell indicated that the rest of the class did not wash often enough."[53]

Sieglinde is engaged to marry an undistinguished government official (whose prosaic parents neglected to name him Hunding). A week before the wedding day the twins go off to the opera together, leaving family and fiancé behind. The opera that evening is *Die Walküre*. After the performance they come home to find the house conveniently deserted. Siegmund eats a caviar sandwich and then commits incest with Sieglinde on a bearskin rug.

As in the case of *The Triumph of Death*, a critic inclined to moralizing may find in this story a lesson about the dangers of idleness. What concerns us here, however, is the connection made in the story between Wagner's music and unnatural passion. The performance that the twins go to see is, according to Mann's description of it, second-rate. The singers are heavy and rosy-skinned, and the orchestra is given to dragging the tempo—a habit which the twins criticize as "sentimental." But despite the inadequate performance, the "profound enchantment" of the music comes across strongly enough to arouse Siegmund's half-suppressed passion. He contemplates the orchestra—where simple folk are absurdly puffing and fingering to "bring to utterance the work of a master who suffered and created"—and his thoughts move on to the subject of creativity itself:

How did one create? Pain gnawed and burned in Siegmund's breast, a drawing anguish which yet was somehow sweet, a yearning—whither, for what? It was all so dark, so shamefully unclear! Two thoughts, two words he had: creation, passion. His temples glowed and throbbed, and it came to him as in a yearning vision that creation was born of passion and was reshaped anew as passion. He saw the pale, spent woman hanging on the breast of the fugitive to whom she gave herself, he saw her love and her destiny and knew that so life must be to be creative.[54]

Once again a character moves from music appreciation to madness. Siegmund progresses from contemplating the orchestra to committing incest, connecting the experiences by means of a few maudlin reflections on the kinship between those two Wagnerian activities, creating and suffering, and between the artistic and the unnatural. The theme which happens here to be treated ironically is nonetheless wearisomely familiar in Mann's other works, where the artist is perpetually being contrasted with the blond bourgeois, and the sensitive characters inevitably have dark shadows under their eyes. In its various permutations, it is Mann's most obtrusively recurrent leitmotif. All the notes of it are sounded as early as "Little Herr Friedemann" (1897), in which it is at a performance of *Lohengrin* that the crippled and "artistic" hero first feels the full impact of his suicidal love for Gerda—herself a lover of music and marked with the telltale "bluish shadows." Between this early story and *Doctor Faustus* Mann scarcely misses an opportunity to suggest that music is a sinister force, an idea which is at last symbolized grandly and obviously—in the Wagnerian manner—by Adrian Leverkühn's discovery that in order to write great music he must enter into a pact with the devil and contract a fatal syphilis.[55] It is disappointing to discover that Mann never tired of compounding the clichés left over from the Nordau Nineties.

"Tristan" in the Sanatorium

In his autobiographical sketch Mann tells of his adolescence in the early nineties. The most precious days were spent in the company of two friends, a painter and his musician brother:

The younger, Paul, . . . was a capital violinist as well. My liking for him had originally something of my former feelings for my blond schoolmate; but, thanks to our having much more in common mentally and spiritually, the relationship was happier. . . . While Paul painted my portrait, Karl in his admirably sustained and harmonious style would play to us both out of *Tristan*.[56]

Thus the music of *Tristan* is already linked with the sentimental homosexuality which, in *Tonio Kröger*, is represented by the attractiveness of "Nordic health" for the artist—and which becomes the central symbol in *Death in Venice*.

Mann's early intoxication with the metaphysics of Schopenhauer was, according to the autobiographical sketch, similarly "related to a late and violent outbreak of sexuality." His immediate enthusiasm was happily parallel to that of Wagner and Nietzsche: reading *The World as Will and Idea* was a "spiritual experience of absolutely first rank. . . , less philosophical than passionate and mystical." At twenty he read the work day and night, "as perhaps one reads only once in his life." What especially enraptured him was that "this intellectual and moral denial of life . . . was couched in a system of thought whose symphonic music* reached to my very depths."[57]

"It was a happy chance," Mann goes on to say, "that these suprabourgeois experiences of mine came at a time [when] I could weave them into the close of my bourgeois novel, where they serve to prepare Thomas Buddenbrook for death."[58] Hypersensitivity to music was a sign of the Buddenbrook decline. On his eighth birthday Hanno Buddenbrook—whose "blue shadows" already indicate that he has inherited the decadent musicality of his mother —performs for the family a fantasy he has composed, in a style which is precociously Tristanesque. The little performer strains to underline an effect that is "more harmonic than rhythmic," striving by the use of both pedals "to give each new harmony an emotional value."[59] As though he were parodying Wagner as a conductor, he stresses the significance of every harmonic change by means of retardation and accentuation. He exaggerates with Wagnerian tremolos and suddenly introduced pianissimos. There is something pathetically overripe, even obscene, about the way this child is determined to achieve an *espressivo* at any cost. Hanno dwells on a dissonance, denying himself and his audience the reso-

---

* The description of Schopenhauer's system as "symphonic music" naturally leads to another mention of *Tristan*—the work which gave musical expression to a similar "metaphysical intoxication," and in which Nietzsche also found the depths of Schopenhauer most thoroughly sounded: "What did concern me, and that in a sensual and supra-sensual way, was the element of eroticism and mystic unity in this philosophy—an element that also had influenced the not in the least ascetic music of *Tristan*—and if in those days I was emotionally close to suicide, it was just because I had grasped the thought that it would be by no means an act of 'wisdom.' Ah, youth, with its sacred pangs, its urgency, its disorders!"

lution, holding back the moment of "satisfying absorption into the B major chord"—the chord, it is pertinent to recall, on which *Tristan* ends and the Desire motif is at last resolved: "The kingdom of Heaven: only not yet—not yet! A moment more of striving, hesitation, suspense, that must become well-nigh intolerable in order to heighten the ultimate moment of joy." The child at last allows himself the orgiastic resolution of the dissonance:

The whole upper part of Hanno's little body straightened, his eyes grew larger, his closed lips trembled, he breathed short, spasmodic breaths through his nose. At last, at last, joy would no longer be denied. It came, it poured over him; he resisted no more. His muscles relaxed, his head sank weakly on his shoulder, his eyes closed, and a pathetic, almost an anguished smile of speechless rapture hovered about his mouth. . . .[60]

Thus the hard burgherliness of the older Buddenbrooks has disintegrated into musical hypersensitivity. The organist Pfühl had the right impulse when he initially wished to protect the little boy from Wagner, as from an emotional trauma. If Hanno had been taken to hear *Tristan*, he might have behaved indecently in the opera house. Indeed, he trembles, sobs, and shudders at a performance of *Lohengrin*.[61]

In the final section of the family saga Hanno plays again, this time improvising music of "wild and irresistible longing." The opening motif, which constantly returns in variant forms, represents "one single process of dissolution [*Auflösung*], a yearning and painful sinking [*Hinsinken*] from one key into the next."* Mann observes that "there was a sort of cynical despair" in the way Hanno reveled in the music, "a longing for joy, a yielding to

---

* Other details can be referred to passages of the Prelude, the Love-Duet, and the Love-Death: "A *fermate* followed, a silence. And then, quite softly, in a timbre of dull silver, there came the first *motif* again. . ." ". . .the original *motif* wound through it all, the pitiful phrase with its notes melting into one another!" ". . .an irresistible mounting, a chromatic upward struggle, a wild relentless longing, abruptly broken by startling, arresting pianissimi which gave a sensation as if the ground were disappearing from beneath one's feet, or like a sudden abandonment and sinking into a gulf of desire." "The resolution, the redemption, the complete fulfillment. . .and the harmony, in sweet *ritardando*, at once sank into another. It was the *motif*, the *first motif*."

desire, in the way the last drop of sweetness was, as it were, extracted from the melody, till exhaustion, disgust and satiety supervened."[62] The last of the Buddenbrooks has succumbed to music before he catches the physical fever which kills him. Immediately after this evocation of Hanno's yearning chromaticism the next chapter begins with the famous clinical account of the course of typhoid. The symbolism of the juxtaposition need not be underlined. Hanno has been playing the swan song of the family—which turns out to be the *Liebestod*.

"It is difficult," as one of Mann's critics has observed, "to imagine Bach and Mozart having the effect on the listener that Mann ascribes to music in general"; but the descriptions of musical drowning make sense if the composer is supposed to be Wagner.[63] "At such moments," Mann wrote of a passage in Siegfried's Funeral Music, "one scarcely knows whether it is Wagner's own peculiar and personal art, or *music itself*, that one so loves, that so charms one."[64] When Mann does describe "music itself" it is invariably music, like Hanno's, which expresses a yearning for surrender and unconsciousness. It is the sort of music that reached its peak in the work of Wagner that Mann considered to be his "deepest musical experience."*

In the sardonic story "Tristan" (1902) that work is definitely identified—not only in the story's title but by means of a "spectacular *tour de force*" in which Mann evokes in prose the essence of the legend and even the sound of the music itself.[65] Detlev Spinell, the "artistic" inmate of a magic-mountain sanatorium, seduces another patient, the fragile Frau Klöterjahn, into playing for him from the score of *Tristan*. Listening together, they achieve a symbolic union, which is followed by the quick decline and death of the delicate lady.

Her performance is nevertheless remarkable. Like D'Annunzio's

---

* "My passion for the Wagnerian enchantments began with me as soon as I knew it," Mann tells us, in a passage that seems to be intentionally reminiscent of the parallel confession in Nietzsche's autobiography. "All that I owe to him, of enjoyment and instruction, I can never forget: the hours of deep and single bliss in the midst of theater crowds, hours of nervous and intellectual transport and rapture, of insights of great and moving import such as only this art vouchsafes."

amateurs, she is able to play not only movingly but with professional accuracy, even though she had stopped practicing long before she came to the sanatorium. The violin runs of the great climax of the Prelude ring out with brilliant precision. In playing the second act she expertly conveys what Mann calls the "chromatic upward surge of metaphysical perception." And in the *Liebestod* her "flying fingers" build the music to another "unbelievable climax"—after which the music is "resolved in that ruthless, sudden *pianissimo* which is like having the ground glide from beneath one's feet, yet like a sinking too into the very deeps of desire."[66] For ladies like Frau Klöterjahn piano playing is something more than an "accomplishment." She can flawlessly execute the accompaniment to her own love-death.

Greatness and Suffering

Frau Klöterjahn's talent for playing the piano is identified with her tuberculosis, and it is because she allows herself to be persuaded to play (against doctor's orders) that she is so quickly conquered by the disease. The composer Adrian Leverkühn also bargains for music at the cost of health. His story is told in a grander style, for his Faust-pact is intended to symbolize the tragedy of Germany. It is the most musical nation that is also the most demonic, whose history best exemplifies the inseparability of creativity and disease, greatness and suffering.[67]

This last pairing of the characteristics of genius finds its way into the title of one of Mann's major essays on cultural history: "Leiden und Grösse Richard Wagners." The tradition which considers Wagner the most intense and yet many-faceted—one is tempted to say the "largest"—of geniuses, reaches its culmination in this essay, delivered as a speech at the University of Munich on the fiftieth anniversary of Wagner's death, in 1933.[68]

As Mann describes Wagner's comprehensive genius, it is compounded of qualities that might have been gathered from the corners of the continent. His naturalism is akin to Zola's; his symbolism to Ibsen's. His amplitude and "splendid long-windedness"

remind Mann of Tolstoy. Wagner has a Freudian intuition into the
erotic and a Dostoievskian sense of the misery of sin.[69] At the same
time he is the most German of geniuses—and this not simply in
the *Ring:*

The birth of drama from music, as it is consummated . . . at the height
of Wagner's creative powers, in the *Tristan,* could only spring out of
German life; and as German in the highest sense of the word we may
also characterize its tremendous sense-appeal, its mythological and
metaphysical tendencies.[70]

But the nationalism Wagner's art derives from is so soaked in the
currents of European art as to defy all efforts to simplify it. Its
intent is not so much national as it is democratic and cosmopolitan,
for "it is calculated to make Germany interesting to a foreigner
even of the meanest intelligence."[71] By "German in the highest
sense" Mann apparently means, among other things, *European;*
and since the borders between the adjectives have been broken
away, *nineteenth-century* may be included as well, for that century, like its representative composer, was Great, and Suffered.
Indeed, Mann confesses that he can scarcely distinguish between
two loves: his love of Wagner's work—"as magnificently equivo-
cal, suspect and compelling a phenomenon as any in the world of
art"—and his love of the century of which this work was the most
complete expression.[72]

Wagner, Germany, Europe, the nineteenth century: in the
fuzzy equation of all good things Mann would seem to include
himself. He thought of his novels as modeled on the music-dramas.
They were symphonic poems: "There are the themes, first presented in simple form. These are the characters. The themes are
then woven together and developed contrapuntally in ever-increas-
ing complexity."[73] All novelists do something of this sort, but
Mann insisted on the Wagnerian analogy. The critical literature on
Mann—which has itself reached Wagnerian proportions—has
completed the analogy. "It is almost impossible," one admirer has
noted, "to overstate Mann's feeling of kinship with Wagner."[74]
The verbal leitmotifs are traced and charted. The well-known

digressions are Wotan-like; Valhallan too is Mann's ability to combine tremendous scope with attention to the most minute details.[75] Only the famous Irony is accepted as un-Wagnerian.

Mann finds particular praise for Wagner as a psychologist, and as the recreator of epic myths. The talents are related—witness the profound transformation, in *Tristan*, of the legendary idea of a magic potion.[76] At the time of the anniversary speech, Mann had already launched his own psychological embellishment of a great legend. "Only the exhaustive," he once told his readers, "can be truly interesting."[77] It is this feeling, no doubt, that accounts for the growth of the Joseph story from a novella into a *Ring*-size tetralogy (with a "musical prelude"). *Joseph* expanded heroically, like *Siegfrieds Tod*. Works of epic size and depth were required for admission into the German pantheon, in whose ranks Mann placed himself. This assumption of the role of greatness was Mann's most unequivocally Wagnerian trait. Just as Wagner had numbered among his forerunners no one of lesser stature than Aeschylus, Shakespeare, and Beethoven, so Mann considered himself the accepted heir of Goethe, Nietzsche, and Wagner.

With Nietzsche in the pantheon, it may be expected that Mann's admiration for Wagner is "not without misgivings."[78] In *The Magic Mountain* Settembrini had paraphrased the later Nietzsche when, in crisp Mediterranean fashion, he warned Hans Castorp, who sat for hours at the gramophone, against the power of music as a sea of forgetfulness, soothing but immoral, dangerous, and death-bound.* In the anniversary speech—where Mann seems to have been determined to make every point that had ever been made about the most many-faceted genius, regardless of consistency— the listeners are reminded of all the evidence in the case of Nietzsche contra Wagner. Wagner's theories were mechanistic; he was theatrical and inartistically given to the grandiose; his luxuriance —"heavily upholstered"—is still disconcertingly appealing to the educated Philistine. Too often, Mann admits, quoting Nietzsche

* Castorp was listening not to Wagner but to his favorite *Aida* and *Carmen*— stories, like *Tristan*, of love-death and the struggle between honor and forbidden love.

almost directly, the music "has no dancing appeal to the muscles; it struggles, urges and drives most laboriously, most unsouthernly."[79]

But these are merely passing discords that add piquancy to the harmonies of hero worship. When Mann puts to himself the choice between the composer and the critic, he chooses the former. Nietzsche, after all, "in his paralytic night, used to listen to the sound of [Wagner's] name and say 'I love him very much.' " In fact the famous critique has always seemed to Mann "like a panegyric with the wrong label, . . . another kind of glorification." Rather than laming one's enthusiasm for the composer, it ought to prick it on.[80] That, at any rate, is what it had done for Mann himself: his passion for Wagner had gone through the fire of Nietzsche's critique and emerged the stronger.[81] Now Mann could explain the eccentricities of that critique as comic old-maidishness and arch-moralizing:

Nietzsche said he would not touch the *Tristan* score with tongs. "Who will dare," he cries, "to utter the word, the right word, for the *ardeurs* of the *Tristan* music?" I am more open to the rather comic old-maidishness of this question than when I was twenty-five years old. For what is there so venturesome about it? Sensuality, enormous sensuality, mounting into the mythical, spiritualized, depicted with the extreme of naturalism, sensuality unquenchable by any amount of gratification —that is the "word." And one asks whence comes the violent bitterness against sex that expresses itself . . . in the question of Nietzsche, the "free, very free spirit." Is not this Nietzsche the archmoralist and clergyman's son?[82]

Mann grants that Wagner's *unconscious* sensuality can irritate those people who feel the need, as Nietzsche did, for clear thinking.[83] But Mann speaks of feeling the need for clear thinking as though it were merely a matter of casual preference. And in the presence of Wagnerian grandeur one should, apparently, prefer not to think at all: "The sort of lashing to fury or drugging to calm which are among Wagner's effects—the ocean too can show the same, and nobody thinks of dragging its psychology to the light of day. What is allowed to great nature should be allowed to great art."[84] The final implication of Mann's praise seems to be this: that since the works of Wagner, like the German soul and the nineteenth century itself, are oceanic enough to survive criticism, they ought not to be criticized at all.* Nietzsche's danger-warnings are discounted as hyperbolic, and then dismissed as futile.

In his fiction, however, Mann had described the dangers. Strange children are weakened by music that is "sublimely morbid." Ailing ladies seem unable to survive their Wagnerian swim. Old artists die in Venice. These are the ironical facts. And Settembrini's civilized warnings only serve to give an extra thrill to gramophone listening.

---

* The German soul, of course, soon came up for criticism; but as late as 1940 Wagner's "natural" powers still rendered criticism of him insignificant. In a letter to the editor of the magazine *Common Sense*, written in reply to an article of January, 1940, on "Hitler and Richard Wagner," by Peter Viereck, Mann admits that there is "an element of Nazism in Wagner's music as well as in his literature— though in a loftier sense." But Mann hastens to add that "even today I am deeply stirred whenever a few bars of Wagner's music . . . impinge on my ear. The enthusiasm it engenders, the sense of grandeur that so often seizes us in its presence, can be compared only to the feelings excited in us by Nature at her noblest, by evening sunshine on mountain peaks, by the turmoil of the sea."

chapter VI

TO THE FINAL PERFORMANCE

"Tristan" Electrified

Between the last years of the nineties, when Mann wrote his first Wagnerian stories, and 1911, when *Death in Venice* appeared, lay the decade of Wagner's greatest posthumous influence. Many of the earliest Wagnerites were still at work, while the composers and writers who grew up during the vigorous years of the adolescence of Bayreuth had reached maturity. In 1901, when *Buddenbrooks* was published, the second of Richard Strauss's early music-dramas was performed—*Feuersnot*, with a libretto by the brother of Hans von Wolzogen, the unchallenged champion of *Bayreuthliteratur*.[1] Mann's "Tristan" followed in 1903, the year which saw the production of Chausson's *King Arthur* and d'Indy's *Stranger*. In 1905, when "The Blood of the Walsungs" was written, Dresden heard the premier of *Salome*, the work which made it clear to the followers of the new music that there was still life in the post-Wagnerian tradition.

That observation was confirmed by *Elektra* in 1907. The tragedy by Strauss and Hofmannsthal was, like *Tristan*, the psychoanalysis of mythical figures, written in a shocking orchestral language, above which only the bravest and most advanced singers could be heard. The harmonic coloration of late Wagner this time tinted the frenzies of an incestuous love-duet. In the third act of *Tristan* Wagner had discovered how his hero could musically uncover old wounds. Both the technique and the activity had been formulized,

and listeners familiar with the new psychology could now inter-
pret recurrent leitmotifs as the musical representation of repetition-
compulsions. The hysterical young ladies' return to traumatic
experiences was musically symbolized when the orchestra ham-
mered out the terrifying names of Jokanaan and Agamemnon.

Wagner's influence was discerned not only in German opera
and the school of Franck, but in remote and rival schools as well
—in Italian and French *verismo*, and in the Spanish nationalist
revival. *La Celestina* (1904), composed by Felipe Pedrell, the
teacher of Albéniz, Granados, and de Falla, was known as the
Spanish *Tristan*. Listeners detected the Wagnerian construction
in the Parisian realism of Charpentier's *Louise* (1900), and heard
the harmonies of *Tristan* in *Manon Lescaut*. "Fevered—with its
rising sequences, its yearning chromatic figures and imploring
sevenths"[2]—this is a description of the love-duet of Manon and
Des Grieux, which took place nearer to the dark garden in Cornwall
than did the brighter duets of *Butterfly* and *Bohème*. But the serious
composers who unavoidably apprenticed themselves to Wagner
were outnumbered by lifeless imitators. Academic operas, composed according to various codifications of the System, crowded
the programs of the opera houses on both sides of the Atlantic—
the works of the pianist Eugen d'Albert, for example, whom Shaw
described as "having sacrificed his individuality . . . at the Bayreuth
shrine"; or of Wagner's son Siegfried; or of Engelbert Humperdinck, who twice during the decade tried to repeat the success he
had won in the 1880's by dressing up a children's story in Wagnerian velvets.[3]

The sevenths and ninths—be they imploring or commiserating
—which, even in Puccini, are traceable to *Tristan*, were apotheo-
sized in Schoenberg's *Verklärte Nacht*, written (as a string quartet)
when the composer was twenty-five and "had heard the operas of
Wagner between twenty and thirty times each."[4] First performed
in 1903, the rather weary tone-poem stands at the midpoint of the
Viennese musical line which runs from the Wagnerized symphony
to the transmutation of post-Romantic chromaticism into the twelve-

tone row—midway, let us say, between the wonderful adagio on the death of Wagner in Bruckner's *Seventh* (1883) and the citation of the opening notes of *Tristan* in Alban Berg's *Lyric Suite* (1927). Schoenberg's symphonic poem *Pelléas and Mélisande*—another "peak of post-*Tristan* romanticism"—followed the *Transfigured Night*; and the construction of the Fafnirian *Gurrelieder* spanned the decade, from 1900 to 1911. Themes in the *Gurrelieder* echo *Tristan* and the *Ring*, while its legendary Norse subject matter includes a pair of star-crossed lovers who "doubtless could not have existed . . . without Tristan and Isolde."[5]

The major opera houses kept the original *Tristan* before the public. Berlin performed the work for the hundreth time in 1907, by which year even Paris had heard three performances (in French).[6] Between 1899 and 1910 *Tristan* was premiered in fifty cities, including Cairo, Buenos Aires, and Rio de Janeiro (half a century after Dom Pedro's withdrawn commission). It was performed in Italian,* Russian, and Hungarian, and translated into French and English verse that was intended for home reading. In 1904 and 1906 two different versions of *Tristan* were published in Catalan.[7]

At the Metropolitan Opera House in New York *Tristan* was performed thirty-five times during the first ten seasons of the century. There was a decade of great performances between 1899, when Lilli Lehmann sang in what she has called the ideal *Tristan* of her life, and the remarkable seasons of 1909, when New York heard both the farewell *Tristan* of Gustav Mahler in March and, in November, the American debut of Arturo Toscanini—conducting the same work. Lehmann's Tristan was Jean de Reszke, who in February, 1901, caught the grippe while singing the third act; but this Tristan recovered.[8] "I have never known a performance of *Tristan* to equal this," Mahler said of his farewell, which began at five in the afternoon and included an intermission for dinner.[9] The Isolde was Olive Fremstad, one of the trio of legendary dra-

* *Tristan* was translated into Italian by Arrigo Boito, the librettist of Verdi's final Shakespearean operas.

matic sopranos who replaced Lehmann. The other two were Ternina and Nordica; and Brangaene was often sung by Schumann-Heink.

Mahler had come to New York in 1907, after ten years as director of the Vienna Opera. There he had staged *Tristan* with the monochromatic settings and functional lighting which bespoke the influence of Adolphe Appia's *Die Musik und die Inscenierung.*[10] Coincidentally Toscanini had acknowledged the principles of Appia in the lighting for the first performances of *Tristan* at La Scala in 1900. When Toscanini returned to Milan for the season of 1923-24, he imported Appia himself to produce *Tristan*, according to the ideas that had been announced in the nineties and had not lost their novelty.

It was perhaps through Appia that Wagner had his most far-reaching effect on the theater. Wagner's music had inspired Appia's innovations.[11] The work on music and stage design appeared in 1899, with a dedication to Houston Stewart Chamberlain and an epigraph from Schopenhauer—about music expressing the "inner essence" of phenomena. From the first, Appia had selected the mature music-dramas to be the classical vehicles of his new visual ideas, and in an Appendix on "the Staging of *Tristan and Isolde*" he illustrated in detail how electric light, with its capacity for mobility—a kind of visible crescendo and diminuendo—could reflect the spiritual drama of the characters on stage. Appia describes that spiritual drama in the best Tritanite tradition: "What burns in their hearts appears to us, as to them, superior to their visible forms, and the fictitious existence of the music carries us deeper and deeper into the mysterious world where their union is consummated forever."[12] There is only one jarring effect in this secret world: we can still see the corporeal presences of the singing lovers. Indeed, although "we close our eyes in order not to see the gross inadequacies of the stage . . . the *presence* of the characters obliges us to open them again."[13] The problem set for the stage designer is to contrive some way for the listener to go on being carried away without having to rationalize—as a spectator—what he sees: without, as Appia puts it, "resorting to conscious thought." Blurs and shadows are the solution, and light that is progressively dimmed as the audience gets used to it and begins to discern clear outlines.

The light must also underscore the symbolism of Night and Day, and do so with a fluidity that matches that of the music: "As long as light is only a source of Tristan's suffering, it must not fall on him directly. But as soon as he really sees it and associates it with blissful visions, it comes and illuminates his face."[14] Light and shadow, in short, follow the drama as the musical motives do; and the visual leitmotifs, like the musical, can be developed and varied.

Now that lighting has been added to the arsenal of effects, the ideal of the *Gesamtkunstwerk* has been completed; and Appia is sure that Wagner would have welcomed the innovation. No doubt he would—for use in the second and third acts of *Tristan*, where the music has taken over more than its share in the synthesis, and the light cues seem to have been written into the score. But for the total-art-works it may be doubted whether Wagner would have wanted to give up the Makart literalness he required of the scene painter. Appia himself was disturbed by the apparent necessity for scenic realism in the first act of *Die Walküre*, and he attempted to find ways of simplifying the setting of Hunding's hut in the service of the "inner drama."[15] Our taste today welcomes the Appianized and oversimplified settings of the *Ring* at Bayreuth, and we are relieved to be rid of papier-mâché toads and Rhine-maidens hanging from ropes. The stark rocks and blank screens allow us to listen to the music without distraction. But the early theories of Wagner required that all the stage mechanisms be in full working order, with every detail visible: *Rheingold* and *Die Walküre* were written with *Opera and Drama* in mind.

So, too, was the first act of *Tristan*. Indeed, no commentary on *Tristan* illustrates better than Appia's the difference between the first act and the other two. Act I is "comparable to a last glimpse of the material and tangible world."[16] The illumination is to be for the most part constant and uniform, and although Appia always allotted to scene painting a minor role, certain details of the setting must be drawn in detail. Each of the later acts has its all-pervasive musical mood that can be reexpressed in a particular quality of light. After Isolde extinguishes her symbolic torch, the darkness of passion takes over the stage, until the intrusion of glaring daylight. The cold brightness of the third-act seacoast emphasizes Tristan's emptiness. Appia tries to find an equally "musical" function for the lighting in Act I, and complains about the invariable custom of cluttering the stage with maritime paraphernalia. But the fact remains that the first act belongs to an illustrated world, lighted realistically. There is no quality of light that can aid in suggesting the atmosphere of anger and tense waiting aboard ship in Act I. There the scene painter has one of his last chances in Wagner to rig imitation sails and letter the labels on bottles of potion.

The Wagnerian Decade

Attending performances, with or without mobile lighting, was apparently a minor course in the education of Wagnerites. It was necessary to instruct oneself in the varied ideas of the only composer who had always asserted that his music did not mean music alone. Not every kind of music, as Nietzsche noted, has been in need of literature; and the first decade of the new century confirmed his sardonic observation when it contrasted the most "cultured" of composers with, say, the still "childlike" Mozart.[17] There was always the danger that Wagner would not be understood with sufficient difficulty. Therefore the most diligent generation of orthodox Wagnerites was keeping the presses busy, to turn the decade into the classic age of Wagner-Lexicons and Bayreuth Encyclopedias.

In 1899 Carl Friedrich Glasenapp, the historian of Art and Culture in the Light of the Master's Views,[18] published the third volume of his monumental official biography—the volume which deals with the *Tristan* period. The remaining installments followed at three-year intervals, the sixth and final appearing in 1911. By

1903 Asthon Ellis had translated the first two volumes of Glasenapp into the quaint and special sort of English which he had already used for acquainting English devotees with the prose of the Master himself. Ellis then continued the biography as his own work.[19] In 1906 three important studies of Wagner as an aesthetician appeared.[20] Hans von Wolzogen kept up the unending *melos* of monographs he had been composing for decades, now writing about Wagner's relationship to Religion, the Church, the Greek Tragedians, the German Romantics, the Spiritual World, and the Animal World. Most of these studies were published in the dependable and familiar house organ of Bayreuth, of which Wolzogen was the editor.[21] Towards the end of the decade the most talented and notorious of the Bayreuth brethren, Houston Stewart Chamberlain, married Cosima's "Meistersinger" daughter, Eva Wagner, and settled permanently in the Festival City. His biography of his father-in-law was reissued in 1911—and by 1913 his strange study of Wagnerian drama, which he had written in 1892, had gone through five expensive editions.[22]

The prose works of Wagner himself were reprinted and reissued. The fourth edition of the Collected Works appeared in 1907, and in the same year the French translation of the prose was begun, eventually to be completed in thirteen volumes. The popular sets of letters, such as the Wesendonk correspondence, were issued in *art nouveau* editions, with frontispieces of the Madonna-like Mathilde, etchings of the Asyl, and presumably flattering photographs of Wagner, characteristically seated in a tasseled *fauteuil* and wearing a velvet beret.[23] The more obscure letters and fugitive articles of the composer were unearthed, along with the early Weber-ridden overtures and the young Wagner's Parisian potboilers for piano and voice. In this way editors and admirers marked time before the long-awaited release of *Mein Leben* in 1911. The elite of the national and international Wagner societies could also supplement their reading with the memoirs of Bayreuth conductors and retired Brünnhildes, or the latest study of Wagner's medieval sources, or a new multivolume analysis of the character of Lud-

wig II, or an eclectic outpouring such as that from the pen of
Washington Gladden, who, in a set of lectures at Harvard later
published as *Witnesses of the Light*, classed Wagner as a herald of
Christian and democratic enlightenment, along with Dante, Michelangelo, Fichte, Hugo, and Ruskin.[24] While Wagnerites were enjoying any number of romances and "fantasias" on Wagnerian
subjects, such as the novels about *Tristan* by Toni Schwabe and
Emil Ludwig, and the Hamlet-at-Wittenberg *Tantris der Narr*,
by Ernst Hardt, the less specialized reading public found the
operas discussed and the cult described in the works of Mann and
George Moore, Romain Rolland and Arnold Bennett, not to mention authors now no longer read. And readers of Albert Schweitzer's
respectable study of Bach could find the latest Master reverently
compared with the Greatest.[25]

"Omniscience" only knew, according to Shaw, what Wagnerism
committed a man to:

Vegetarianism, the higher Buddhism, Christianity divested of its alle-
gorical trappings (I suspect this is a heterodox variety), belief in a Fall
of Man brought about by some cataclysm which starved him into
eating flesh, negation of the Will-to-Live and consequent Redemption
through compassion excited by suffering (this is the Wagner-Schopen-
hauer article of faith); all these are but samples of what Wagnerism
involves nowadays. The average enthusiast accepts them all unhesita-
tingly—bar vegetarianism. Buddhism he can stand; he is not particular
as to what variety of Christianity he owns to; Schopenhauer is his
favorite philosopher; but get through Parsifal without a beefsteak
between the second and third acts he will not.[26]

The "Baedeker" of the French and English Wagnerians does not
mention beefsteaks, but it does include sausages (with sauerkraut)
among the dishes obtainable at the "fine and famous restaurants,"
along with *Pfannkuchen, omelette aux confitures*, and "SPICED
BREAD of an exquisite flavour, highly recommended to all visitors to
the Festivals." The Bread could be purchased in "a very pretty box,
decorated with scenes from the operas." Alternative souvenirs were
"CUFF BUTTONS and SCARF PINS, with the portrait of our great
Master, RICHARD WAGNER." Shirt fronts embroidered with leitmotifs

had recently gone out of fashion.[27] The standard guidebook, called *Voyage Artistique à Bayreuth*, had been written in 1897 by Albert Lavignac, Professor of Harmony at the Paris Conservatory and author of a history of the piano pedal. Lavignac included a sketch of "Life in Bayreuth"[28] and analyses of the poems and the music, replete with the dotted charts of characters and leitmotifs. The guidebook was translated immediately into English, under the more prosaic title *The Music Dramas of Richard Wagner*.

English and American readers who preferred a less schematic, though still respectful, introduction to the Master might have read the new biography by W. J. Henderson, the music critic of the New York *Times*, or the early books of Ernest Newman, who wrote the first two of his series of Wagnerian studies while he was still a businessman in Liverpool.[29] Newman was engaged in researches that later helped to set the record straight about such matters as Wagner's parentage* and the veracity of *Mein Leben*.[30] He laid down the standard whereby Wagner the Man was to be separated from Wagner the Artist—a distinction which, during the Master's lifetime, the more sensitive disciples had found it necessary to draw sharply, in self-protection. With absolute fairness Newman set forth all the evidence of Wagner's carelessness about other people. But not for a moment did he suggest that an unpleasant egoism may be reflected in the Artist. The music-dramas provide the evidence of Wagner's admirable qualities—indeed, apart from outbursts of sentimental friendship, a respect for dead geniuses, and kindness to animals, they are the only source of such evidence. Wagner's noblest traits are revealed in the very size and completeness of his compositions. Only with a unique self-confidence and an enviable patience could a man stake out a claim to greatness on the basis of works still in his head. "What belief in himself, in his strength, in his destiny, in his ability to wait! What a sublime confidence that Time would wait for him!"[31] And to these qualities

---

* The question—raised by Nietzsche and investigated by every biographer until Newman supplied the answer—of whether Wagner thought Ludwig Geyer was his real father (he probably did think so) seemed less compelling after the family tree of the "Jewish" Geyer had been traced to Protestant church organists in the eighteenth century.

there was added the unrelaxing energy which enabled Wagner to build his Empire and at the same time complete every work he had seriously projected—to the last detail of staging in the religious drama which had been conceived almost thirty years before it was completed.

According to Newman's separation of the two Wagners, the Artist transcended the nationality which the Man may have insisted upon. If the works were German they were so only in the aggrandized sense in which Thomas Mann was to use the word— that is to say, they were European. And they also had come to be considered the most representative expression of their century. Two years before that century had completed its course, Shaw had pronounced the *Ring of the Nibelungen* (or at any rate three fourths of it) correct according to the canons of a supranational socialism; and from the works of Wagner and Ibsen he had drawn up the case for the Sanity of European Art.[32] In the same year, at the other end of Europe, Tolstoy was ridiculing the *Ring* as an example of aesthetic counterfeiting, and as the largest illustration of how the art of the age had prostituted its moral purpose.[33] In the eighties of the *Revue wagnérienne* and the Aesthetic Movement the benefits and dangers of Wagner's influence had been argued mainly within the arenas of national schools of music and literature. The question was whether he could be admitted into a national culture from the outside. After the doors had been thrown open, Wagnerism helped to obscure the national differences. By the time the new century had begun, it was the habit to accept Wagner as the savior of a culture that was international; or to condemn him—in accord with a famous case study of *fin de siècle* degeneration—as the decadent emperor who had presided over the the Decline of the West.[34]

The Perfect Tristanite in America

Malwida von Meysenbug, who survived her century to die in 1903, at the age of eighty-seven, discovered that Wagner could be as "misunderstood" by critics of culture as he had been by the critics of music when she had first met him, unknown by the wider world, in London and Paris. She had, in fact, personally faced the earliest and greatest of the attacks on the larger Wagner, written by her friend Nietzsche. In 1888 she received *Der Fall Wagner* in the mail, with a note from Nietzsche asking her advice about the French translation.[35] It is hard to believe that Nietzsche did not realize the essay would offend her. He had attacked Malwida's favorite pieties—serious music and soft Christianity—both of which Wagner had flattered in the religious music-drama she revered; and what wit there was in Nietzsche's attack must have entirely misfired for the humorless devotee. Malwida replied with what she called a "Declaration of War" against Nietzsche, who in turn wrote back harsh words to his friend. "These are not matters in which I tolerate contradiction," he told her:

In questions of *decadence* I am the highest court of appeal existing now on earth. . . . That Wagner knew how to create the belief in himself (as you express it with adorable innocence) as the "last expression of creative nature," as it were its "epilogue," that requires, indeed, *genius*, but a genius of the lie. . . . I myself have the honor of being the reverse of it,—a genius of truth—.[36]

To another correspondent he described the exchange of letters:

Spoiled all her life she is perched at last on her sofa like a funny little Pythia and says: "You are in error about Wagner! I know better! Exactly the same as *Michelangelo*. . . ."

Thereupon I wrote her that Zarathustra wanted to do away with the good and just because they always *lie*.[37]

Within a year, however, Malwida had found consolation in the last of her artistic friendships, which was unreservedly Wagnerian. She became the guiding spirit in the early intellectual life of Romain Rolland. Rolland has described his first visit to Malwida's d'Annunziesque drawing room in Rome. In a corner, dramatically set against a purple background, stood a white bust of Wagner, beneath a silver vase filled with anemones. The young man in his early twenties and the lady more than fifty years his senior left behind a volume of correspondence—idealistic, Wagnerian, crowded with musical and artistic reflections. Malwida still enjoys talking of Renunciation. In 1889 they went together to Wahnfried and the Festival. In 1890 Rolland writes to her of the "Wagnerian" impression made on him by Rembrandt's *Night Watch*; and they discuss Michelangelo. In a last letter, written from Bayreuth in the summer of 1891, Malwida wishes he had been with her, for she has just seen *Tristan*.[38]

"I love *Tristan*," Rolland wrote later, in one of his musical essays: "for me and for others of my time it has long been an intoxicating draught."[39] The work has its faults: it is uneven and lacks balance—the cold light of Mark's lamentation, for example, is ineffectual after the glowing fire of the love-duet. Nevertheless the music-drama "towers like a mountain above all other love poems"; and this superiority is immediately announced in the Prelude, "that expression of eternal desire that is like a restless sea forever moaning and beating itself upon the shore."[40] Having paid the usual maritime compliment to the music, Rolland goes on to praise it for qualities that have seldom been discovered in it. Here Rolland seems to be arguing not only against the assertions of the later Nietzsche but against those of *The Birth of Tragedy* as well:

The quality that touches me most deeply in *Tristan* is the evidence of honesty and sincerity in a man who was treated by his enemies as a charlatan that used superficial and grossly material means to arrest and amaze the public eye. What drama is more sober or more disdainful of exterior effect than *Tristan?* Its restraint is almost carried to excess.[41]

Rolland's description of a sober and restrained *Tristan* may be unique. It is reassuring that most of the time he found the work intoxicating.

Americans of the high-Wagnerian decade learned of Rolland's devotion to music from the long volumes of that favorite novel, *Jean-Christophe;* but they did not know Rolland's essays.[42] The presses of New York and Philadelphia had their own impressionistic critic, who surpassed any European in versatility and extravagance. James Gibbons Huneker made a career of enthusiasms. For most of his life he was the reviewer of music, drama, and literature for major newspapers in the eastern cities.[43] In daily columns and annual books (including full-length studies of Liszt and Chopin, a novel, a two-volume autobiography, and more than a dozen collections of essays) there was scarcely a current genius he did not endorse. He introduced American readers to Maeterlinck and Strindberg. He corresponded with Huysmans, Conrad, and George Moore, and he matched wits with Shaw. He was an Ibsenite and one of the first American Nietzscheans. And chief among his imports was the most advanced European Wagnerism.

According to Huneker's friend and fellow critic, W. J. Henderson, "all that was most voluptuous in form and color filled him with a rapture which sought utterance in sonorous phrases."[44] But it was voluptuousness of *sound*—especially in the music of those composers who are still inaccurately called "late romantic"—that most frequently inspired Huneker's rhapsodies. His grab bag of essays for 1904, called *Overtones*, included pieces about Turgenev, George Moore, and Flaubert; but the first and longest essay is a panegyric of Richard Strauss, and the entire sheaf of essays is dedicated to that "supreme master of the orchestra" and "Anarch of Art."[45] Another article is about "Nietzsche the Rhapsodist." The closing essay is on Wagner; and here Huneker best displays his capacity for what his friend Henderson called "oratorical picturesqueness." The title of this florid article is "Isolde and Tristan," and the inversion of the names is intended to make a point.

In 1886 Huneker had pawned his overcoat to buy a ticket for the first *Tristan* at the Metropolitan. "I am Wagner mad," he wrote at the time, and claimed that he knew all the leitmotifs.[46] Ten years later he attended the Bayreuth festival. But Huneker was not an orthodox Wagnerite. He was, for example, given to telling bawdy stories about the relationship between Wagner and King Ludwig—and did so in the presence of Olive Fremstad when they were both touring Starnberg castle.[47] He found that relationship symbolized in *Parsifal*, in the characters of the hero and Amfortas, and he did not hesitate to suggest this discovery in his review of the first performance of the work outside of Bayreuth.[48] In 1903, over the objections of Frau Cosima, the Metropolitan Opera had

brought *Parsifal* to New York. A year later, Huneker included in
Overtones his long attack on the purloined stage-consecration-
festival drama. Quite apart from the aspects of the work which
Huneker liked to call "Parsiphallic," he found the last music-drama
laborious, undramatic, and boring:

It is a farrago of odds and ends, the very dust-bin of [Wagner's]
philosophies, beliefs, vegetarian, antivivisection, and other fads. You
see unfold before you a nightmare of characters and events. Without
simplicity, without lucidity, without naturalness . . . this book . . .
astounds one by its puerility, its vapidity.[49]

Uninspired and self-repetitious, Wagner had returned to the study
to write an Ideal Drama that turned out to be no more than "an old-
fashioned and very tedious opera." Ten years earlier, in *The Perfect Wagnerite*, Shaw had come to a similar conclusion about
Die Götterdämmerung.

Yet Wagner can make us accept this incredible medley. To
account for the fact, Huneker resorts to invoking the Magician
who hexed the scores of Debussy and Chausson:

It is an astounding feat of the old hypnotist—for hypnotist he is in
Parsifal as in no other composition. By sheer force of his musical will,
this Klingsor of Bayreuth hypnotizes his hearers with two or three
themes not of themselves remarkable, as Charcot controls his patients
with a shining mirror.[50]

Huneker shoots at the large Wagnerian target with Nietzsche's
bullets: Wagner's music is defiled by the footlights; it is rhetorical
and forever striving for effects. The actor Wagner is a danger for
young composers, who by following his example will never produce
the sort of music the Future needs: "intellectual music, music that
does not appeal merely to the feverish nerves of this generation."[51]

But when writing about *Tristan*, Huneker appears to have
closed his copy of *Nietzsche contra Wagner*. "The man whose
pulses do not quiver during the second act of *Tristan*," he once
wrote, "is as bloodless as a turnip, and we'll have none of him."[52]
The sly magician who hypnotized the public into accepting
Parsifal was, as the composer of *Tristan*, "the poet of passion, a

master of thrilling tones, a magician who everywhere finds willing thralls." The enemy of absolute music, who dangerously allowed the drama to take precedence, becomes, when Huneker writes about *Tristan*, "always the composer": "to the end his musical ruled his dramatic instincts."[53] And though the "morbid, . . . hysterical, and . . . sublimely erotic" music was what prompted Huneker to repeat Nietzsche's demand for "intellectual" music as a cure, he forgets to distinguish between poison and antidote in his search for new ways of praising the masterpiece: "And the music—how it searches the nerves. How it throws into the background, because of its intensity, all the love lays ever penned by mortal composer! How it *appeals to the intellect* with its exalted realism!"[54] The rest of the essay is an abstract of the Praise of *Tristan*, compiled with an enthusiastic disregard for orderliness of ideas. While *Tristan* expresses the pessimism of Schopenhauer and the spirit of Oriental mysticism, it is also epic and tragic in the manner of the Greek dramatists. At the same time it may be likened to the *Divine Comedy*, *Hamlet*, and *Faust*. This despite the fact that the music stifles the action and all the conventions of the drama have been set aside.[55] Wagner was so carried away by the music of *Tristan* that he abandoned all his previous theories; yet Huneker also credits the music with having faithfully reproduced every accent and nuance of human speech, according to the dictum of *Opera and Drama*. *Tristan* is the most complex of scores; nevertheless "it is built upon but one [*sic*] musical motif." Add to this that it is the most profound expression in art of Passion, Night, and the "eternal dualism" of Death and Love. And do not forget the ocean: the "weltering symphonic mass" is like "the surge and thunder of tropical seas."[56]

Isolde is the chief character:

Wagner's music-drama primarily concerns the woman; she is the protagonist, not Tristan. Even in Act III, where this lover of lovers lies awaiting Isolde and death, it is her psychology which most concerns the composer. So I call it Isolde and Tristan—the subjugation of man by woman.[57]

Perhaps Huneker's statement about the third act can be explained as an impression drawn from uneven performances. In most continental opera houses a weak tenor sang a cut role opposite a strong soprano who would not tolerate cuts; and in the days of Lehmann and Fremstad Isolde had already begun to dominate the performances of *Tristan* in New York. Since then there have been few Tristans who could rival the celebrity of such Isoldes as Gadski, Florence Easton, Frieda Leider, and the full-throated Flagstad—and who could be credited, during the love-duet, with singing something more than an accompaniment to Isolde's solo. Perhaps the fatal zeal of Ludwig Schnorr served as a warning for future Tristans. As Tristan's beard grew shorter (the beard began to go after 1885)[58] the power of his lungs proportionally diminished. It was left for the trimmest and most vigorous of recent Isoldes to enact on the stage of the Metropolitan the final "subjugation of man by woman"—and, incidentally, to bring Wagner, after many years of neglect, to the front page of the New York *Times*. In January, 1961, Mme. Birgit Nilsson appeared opposite three ailing Tristans in a single performance, and then sang the *Liebestod* as though she were ready to begin the opera again. With Huneker as her prophet, she enacted the triumph of Isolde.

The Secret of Form

"To praise moderately is always a sign of mediocrity." In the essay on Isolde, Huneker quotes this *mot* of the Marquis de Vauvenargues as an endorsement of the "absence of reserve" with which Swinburne adored both Wagner and the sea.[59] Vauvenargue's half-truth was apparently one of Huneker's critical maxims, and could serve as an epigraph to the collected essays of the enthusiastic impressionist.

"I can't soar; I can only indicate," complains a writer in one of the novels of E. M. Forster. "That's where the musicians have the pull, for music has wings, and when she says 'Tristan' and he says 'Isolde,' you are on the heights at once."[60] The impressionistic critic, with the musician as his model, tries to soar, and hopes, by repeating the words "Tristan" and "Isolde," at least to remind the reader of what it is like on the heights. He may indicate particular places as exquisite, but immoderate eulogizing does not require careful attention to details. There is, however, another method of praise which does require professional thoroughness. The technical analyst of music undertakes to uncover interrelationships of which the composer himself might have been unaware. Unlike the impressionistic critic who hovers overhead, the technical analyst burrows with ingenuity. They use different vocabularies. Yet— see any record jacket—the two encomiastic vocabularies are frequently combined. For the impressionist and the analyst want finally to say the same thing: that they are moved by the music. They are both, as Anatole France said of the former, describing the adventures of the soul among masterpieces.

The analytical scholars of *Tristan* inherited a set of musical "problems" for which it was obligatory to provide solutions. It was necessary to take a stand on classifying the notorious "first chord"—which is as ambiguous as the corresponding chord in *Meistersinger* (a tonic triad in any language) is not. Did the analyst agree with Tovey and the other "G-sharp appoggiaturists" that the chord was a variation of the French sixth? Or with Dyson, in Grove, that it implied a diminished seventh? Or with Ernst Kurth that it was another sort of modified subdominant?[61] Thomas Mann has written that at the piano he never tired of the *Tristan* chord.[62] Nor did the theorists tire of scrutinizing the spelling of the chord, which became one of the most widely discussed of all moments in music. Moreover, the analyst was bound to find in each subtlety of Wagner something more than musical craftsmanship. In Wagner every accidental had its dramatic and philosophical correlative, and each progression had to be related to the music-drama in particular and to the history of music in general.

The twin monsters of *Tristan*-analysis were Ernst Kurth's *Romantische Harmonik und ihre Krise in Wagners "Tristan"* and Alfred Lorenz's *Der Musikalische Aufbau von Richard Wagners "Tristan und Isolde,"* which is the second volume of an investigation into *Das Geheimnis der Form bei Richard Wagner*. Kurth announced the Crisis in 1920, and Lorenz uncovered the Secret in 1926.

Lorenz's secret about the form of the later music-dramas was that they *had* form. Indeed, every section, from the shortest phrase to the entire three-act opera, was demonstrably organized in a tripartite pattern—either an "arch" (*Bogen*: A B A) or a *bar* (A A B), the latter a characteristically "German" pattern which Wagner borrowed from medieval verse and has Hans Sachs explain to Walther in that most *bar*-ridden work, *Die Meistersinger*. Thus in *Tristan* fragments of, say, Brangaene's "Quieting Song" in Act I are analyzed as small *bars*, while the three acts of the music-drama turn out to be a vast *Bogen*.[63] In demonstrating the similarity in form between Act I and Act III Lorenz is nothing short of inspired in his ability to find parallels. Here is a sample:

Act I	*Act III*
The unaccompanied sailor's song opens the act.	The unaccompanied *alte Weise* opens the act.
Beginning: large ascending interval (6th).	Beginning: large ascending interval (5th).
Middle: numerous triplets.	Middle: numerous triplets.
Tritone effect next to folk-like intervals.	Tritone effect next to folk-like intervals.
It contains a main motive (*sea motive*) which is important only for this act.	It contains a main motive (*life's anguish*) which is important only for this act.
Brangaene looks over the sea.	The shepherd looks over the sea.
Isolde is awakened from her lethargy by the sailor's song. . . .	Tristan is awakened from his faint by the *alte Weise*. . . .
Not suspecting the true thoughts of the heroine, Brangaene sings a simple diatonic song. . . .	Not suspecting the true thoughts of the hero, Kurvenal sings a simple diatonic song. . . .
Second appearance of the sailor's song with a lonely tremolo on the basses. . . .	Second appearance of the *alte Weise* with a lonely tremolo on the strings. . . .
Isolde complains of her past sorrow in a long narrative. . . .	Tristan complains of his past sorrow in a long narrative. . . .

And so on down to the *Liebestod*, which (since there is no first-act parallel to it) must be considered "the Coda of the complete opera."[64]

After such clarity of form had been revealed, it was no longer possible to suggest—as Lorenz himself had heard music lovers do— that *Tristan* derived its expressive power from a kind of formlessness.[65] Indeed, Lorenz made his point so well that other Wagner theorists could disagree only about matters of emphasis; and those who wished to continue his technique had to carry their bows and bars to the uncharted lands of other composers.[66]

In *Opera and Drama* Wagner had described his method of composing in "poetic-musical" periods. In a single phrase—longer than a leitmotif but shorter than a "scene"—a complete musical statement was made to coincide exactly with a complete statement in the text. Such units of construction are discernible in the earlier parts of the *Ring*, and they probably entered as well into the construction of *Tristan*. In the later work, however, Wagner was particularly successful at disguising the joints between the periods in order to give the illusion of continuous texture and "endless melody." Hence Lorenz's first task was to redivide the work into coherent periods (which, in turn, could be shown to compose or be composed of *arches* and *bars*). The question was what criteria to use in deciding where the periods began and ended. Lorenz recognized the importance of metrical considerations, but he quite rightly laid the greatest stress on tonality.[67] Wagner often said that contrasting ideas might be expressed by modulations to contrasting keys; and it is clear that in *Tristan* changes of key coincide with important changes in the action and the mood of the characters. Lorenz was not among those theorists who exaggerated the tendency of Wagner's chromaticism to disintegrate tonality. His study serves to remind us that the effect of *Tristan* depends as much on the adherence to traditional tonal relationships as it does on the deviation from them.[68]

But Lorenz went far beyond the demonstration of Wagner's tonal craftsmanship. He devised a *mystique* of the tonalities of *Tristan*. Having discovered interesting correspondences between the dramatic action and the key relationships, he concludes that there is an elaborate tonal plan, grounded on the symbolism of the "inner drama." He hypothesizes, for example, that the main key of *Tristan* is E major, even though he can find only one substantial E-major tonic in the whole work (in Act III when Tristan envisions Isolde's arrival). Around E, which symbolizes the idea of love, he constructs a key-circle, each key symbolizing an idea or emotion. "In this diagram," as he describes it, "the parallel keys are arranged horizontally, the tonic-variants vertically; the sub-dominants overlook the tonic from the left, the dominants from the right." Moreover, everything radiates from the center to the sides, which mirror each other through relationships dictated by the dramatic development.[69] On contemplating the diagram, those of us who are properly "schooled in Schopenhauer" can observe that Suicide (in C minor) lies on the ladder of Assent (in C major), and that the Ability to Understand an Idea (in E major) is acquired only on the path of Sorrow (in E minor). Further examination will reveal such remarkable interrelationships as those between the two keys which are tonally most remote from E (because chromatically closest to it): E flat, the key of much of the music of Brangaene and the sailors, represents the Denial of Violent Death; and F minor, the key of the *alte Weise*, represents the Denial of Salvation in Death. At last, one might attain an ecstasy of neo-Pythagorean contemplation: "A MYSTIC SHUDDER runs through our soul, when we suddenly perceive that the bass notes of the four keys which build the circle, when read crosswise, give the FATE MOTIVE (A flat, A, C, B) in the tonality of the great Death motive."[70] The impressionistic critic may prefer to go directly to Bayreuth and listen to the sounds rising out of D'Annunzio's *golfo mistico*. But the magic of *Tristan* can penetrate to a one-page diagram based on the score; and a reader can also reach the Mystery through the circuitous route of formal arches and tonal circles.

World-Historical Music

Not structure but style is the subject of the other classic of *Tristan*-analysis, Ernst Kurth's *Romantische Harmonik*. In 600 pages of exhaustive and often profound attention to detail Kurth catalogues the devices of romantic harmony and discusses such significant changes in the musical language as the shift in emphasis from the fundamental to the leading tone.[71] Kurth's procedure is always to use *Tristan* as his starting place, from which he traces lines of development back, usually to Schubert and Schumann, and forward to Richard Strauss and Debussy. He starts where he does not simply because the style of *Tristan* is encyclopedic. When Wagner put aside the *Ring* and undertook to write in a fully chromatic idiom, Romantic Harmony had reached its Crisis. It was a crisis in all senses of the word. *Tristan* was the culmination of two centuries of musical development. It was also the source of all future development. Kurth placed *Tristan* at the most important turning point in the history of music since the time of Bach.[72]

No other aspect of music so easily fits into an evolutionary scheme as chromaticism. Gather together the right examples, and a chord can be shown somehow to have expanded in the course of decades. Diatonic intervals become augmented; they reach out through the extra half step to their resolution. Chromatic alterations, introduced experimentally, adapt, and are at some later time acceptable when presented without preparation. Ninth chords grow from sevenths, and elevenths from ninths. When the history of chromatic chords is being written it is almost inevitable that some kind of organic or evolutionary vocabulary be introduced. Indeed, a musical idiom, like an organism, can reach full ripeness and begin to die; a style, like a species, can develop into another, which replaces it. What Kurth described as a process of culmination could also be seen as a corrosion, which left nothing of the underlying material.[73] Whatever the analogy, *Tristan* seemed to present clear signs that the expressive—or overexpressive—possibilities of nineteenth-century harmony had reached a limit, and well before Kurth had documented the course of the crisis composers had recognized the symptoms of it in discomfort. Some had chosen to prolong it, by writing in some super-chromatic extension of the inherited idiom. Others attempted to cure the patient with injections of neoclassicism, or of modality, or of various concoctions of folk music and exotic scales. Still others accepted the patient as dead, and began afresh with the chromatic scale as the basis of a non-tonal music.

Something like the following statement can be found in its proper place in almost every history of music:

Tristan and Isolde, couched in a language of unprecedented expressivity, carried the chromatic idiom to the limit of its possibilities. . . . *Tristan*, the prime symbol of romantic yearning and unfulfillment, made it all too apparent that the classical system with its neatly defined key areas had begun to disintegrate.[74]

Expositors of atonalism are still more explicit about placing *Tristan* at the threshold of a new era. Here Rudolph Reti, in a book called *Tonality, Atonality, Pantonality*, describes the time of the Kurthian crisis:

In Germany Wagner's *Tristan* was given to the musical world. Whatever one's aesthetic attitude toward Wagner may be, the prophetic quality of his harmonic structure, particularly as realized in *Tristan*, cannot be questioned. Indeed, his harmonic vision reached farther into the future than that of his immediate successors. Here for the first time the enduring validity of the old harmonic "system" was not only challenged but, what in art is so much more effective, creatively disproved.[75]

No musical idiom can last forever and fondness for the old harmony should not lead us to regret that it has died. That is the worst form of artistic conservatism, a Burkean nostalgia for outmoded conventions. When Wagner "disproved" the enduring validity of tonality, he did so "creatively," which meant that Progress would follow. Indeed, by announcing the end of the old system, Wagner was a liberating hero; for he cleared the way for the next world-historical composer, whose mission it would be to invent the new system. The tyranny of the single tonic center would be overthrown, the restrictions of modulation thrown off, in favor of a music in which all the notes of the chromatic scale were to be given equal value. Between *Tristan* and the advent of this musical democracy tonality lingered on; but it was vestigial and without vigor, like the bourgeois state after the proletarian revolution.

The account may be paraphrased in Marxist language, for this is a theory in which a revolution is dictated by history. One of the foremost expositors of twelve-tone music, Egon Wellecz, states without qualification that "the abandoning of a single tonic center was a necessity at a certain historical moment in the development of music." The break with the past "freed us from the fetters of a routine which had become unbearable."[76] For Rudolph Reti the tonal system has already "practically withered away." At the same time he admits that "one cannot forget the riches, the wonders, unsurpassed in the whole history of music, that were produced within the system during the approximately three centuries of its domination." But at the end "even empires crumble; one age is replaced by another."[77] Karl Marx similarly acknowledged the achievements of the bourgeoisie.

The honor of discovering the logical and necessary consequence of the decline of tonality went, of course, to Arnold Schoenberg. At first he had tried to proceed in the same direction as Strauss and Mahler. According to the usual account of his expositors, when he found the way barren, "there seemed to be only one thing left—the very thing which he actually did—namely, to abandon tonality entirely and to assay patterns of music without any tonical relationship."[78] His discovery of the one thing left is an instance of genius having hit upon the inevitable.

The critics of Schoenberg give a different interpretation of the change in style. The young composer was "an unsuccessful imitator of Wagner, who, disappointed at his inability to write acceptable music in the post-romantic idiom, suddenly decided to make a name for himself by irresponsible innovation." This is how Dika Newlin, a disciple of Schoenberg, epitomizes what she considers "a popular misapprehension. . ., unfortunately fostered by far too many widely read books on music."[79] Whether it is a misapprehension or not, in a review of a concert of early Schoenberg Winthrop Sargeant typifies the unsympathetic view to which Miss Newlin refers. "I have heard quite a few 'Gurrelieder's,' " he writes, "and have always found the work moderately pleasing, despite a certain thinness of inspiration and the composer's tendency to trot out a lot of second-hand ideas derived from the quieter music of Richard Wagner." But uninspired and derivative as it is, the work nonetheless represents Schoenberg at his best—for it was written before the composer had "submerged himself [as Sargeant puts it in one of his less carefully chosen metaphors] in the dry mathematics of the atonal system." The early Schoenberg was "a restless, frustrated, often imitative composer, and . . . a distinctly minor one"; but his music is at least alive. Then came the submersion in dryness. The twelve-tone system marked "a withdrawal from competition with the masters of the past, and also a repudiation of musical meaning— in short, a sort of artistic suicide."[80]

Sargeant has outlined the biography of a Tristanite. The young composer is overinfluenced by the harmonies of *Tristan*. His music echoes the progressions of the *Liebesnacht*. Determined to be a composer of significance, he invents an arbitrary system—as cold and mathematical as *Tristan* is lush and organic—in order to exorcise the ghost of old Klingsor forever. Up to a point, the disciples of Schoenberg would agree with this sketch. They freely admit that the works written before 1908 are Tristanesque, for anyone's ear can recognize the typical chords and turns, not to mention the direct quotations of Wagner's music-drama. But the escape Schoenberg found was not, as Sargeant would have it, arbitrary. Atonalism was, on the contrary, the natural and inevitable consequence of the chromaticism of *Tristan*. It therefore follows that the twelve-tone way of writing evolved naturally and inevitably out of Schoenberg's early style.[81] According to one view, the oppressive influence of *Tristan* precipitated the invention of an arid system. According to the other, the exploration of the significance of *Tristan* gradually uncovered a new vein of musical expression. The difference lies in the evaluation of the music Schoenberg wrote after his break with the past. But there is no disagreement about why he had to break away.

When he was a schoolboy, Schoenberg and his friends used to play a game with *Tristan*:

Already over-familiar with its most celebrated strains—the "plums" which an intelligent listener might have for the picking—they delved deeper and deeper into the structure of the work, seeking for new melodies; and at every performance more and more such melodies came to light. . . . Richness of thematic material and interrelationships between the various themes became of paramount importance to him.[82]

Schoenberg was following the pattern later elaborated by Alfred Lorenz. One begins by responding to the deliciousness of the harmonies—the "plums"—and moves on to a deeper study of the structure of the work, until it is the richness of the thematic relationships that interests one most. (It was this same analytical habit of mind that required the young Schoenberg, enchanted as he was with Wagner, to declare himself a Brahmsian.) The early works of Schoenberg reflect his infatuation with the harmonies of *Tristan*. The atonal works reveal his Lorenzian study of the structure.

According to one interpretation of the social criticism of Nietzsche, the only hope he had for western art was in the repression of sensibility: "the ungovernable sense subdued, by an effort of will. The Superman was his remedy, arbitrary, unrelenting and authoritative."[83] If this interpretation is correct, then Schoenberg was Nietzsche's Superman. For not only was he schooled amidst the sensuousness he ultimately repudiated, but he managed to find in the greatest of the repudiated works a model for a new authoritative system. From weakly imitating the eroticism of *Tristan*, he progressed to the invention of a system that is neo-Wagnerian in almost every respect except that it does *not* admit sensuousness.

In a recent article on Wagner[84] Joseph Kerman has called attention to the many ways in which the twelve-tone doctrine was similar to the Wagnerian.* Both insisted upon a kind of "total organization," and provided a formula for achieving it: in one case the leitmotif, and in the other the row, guarantees unity. In both cases the music displays a characteristic "nervous intensity"; and one is supposed to discover in it some kind of "endless melody." Both doctrines have, in their time, influenced young composers whose true gifts seemed to lie elsewhere, and whose works were performed for audiences who thought it chic to subscribe. Nonsubscribers had

* To Kerman's list of similarities I have added some points of my own.

to be considered reactionary, for both doctrines were bound up with an interpretation of music history in which the new system represented Progress. Both composers made excursions into other arts —Schoenberg into painting as well as writing. And it should be added that just as Wagner in his best work did not follow all the prescriptions of his own system, so Schoenberg, in his unfinished opera *Moses and Aaron,* leaves the restrictions of his doctrine far behind.* Moreover, the typical criticisms of twelve-tone music still sound very much like the criticisms of Wagner that were standard a hundred years ago: the music is condemned as theoretical, labored, unsingable, unmelodic, rhythmically feeble, and dissonant beyond endurance.

For only two of the ingredients of Wagnerism is it difficult to find a correlative in the later doctrine. One is the egoism of the composer-inventor: it is not simply for reasons of euphony that the label "Schoenbergism" is never used. The other is the freedom to indulge in highly sensuous musical effects. But the new system had been invented precisely because the post-romantic idiom had begun to cloy. And the new theorists amply compensated for the rejection of Tristanesque harmony by enshrining the work itself. First, they elevated *Tristan* to the most prominent position in the history of music—at the threshold of the new era. Second, they derived from *Tristan*—or at least claimed to do so—the characteristic device of the new mode of composition: the use of a chromatic scale in which all the notes are equally significant. Analyses such as Kurth's tended to support this derivation, which was further supported by the chance anticipations of chromatic rows in the Wagnerian vocal line.† Lastly, the new theorists discovered in *Tristan,* as Lorenz did, the kind of schematic organization that was the ideal of the new system. In this sense *Tristan* could be the aesthetic model as well as the historical source. It did not matter

---

* Another masterpiece, Alban Berg's *Wozzeck,* is strictly serialistic only in a few passages, and at times Berg is unashamedly tonal.

† Particularly in the music of *Parsifal* that seems to represent a return to the idiom of *Tristan;* see, for example, the stammered music of Kundry at the beginning of Act II.

that the complex interrelationships of twelve-tone music, like many of those in the *Tristan* that Lorenz diagrammed, are not discernible in the listening. Heard melodies are not always the sweetest.

"*Tristan*" at Home

The masterpieces of music change with their audiences. A century ago Handel's *Messiah* had swollen to such enormous size that the Albert Hall had to be built around it. Today it is performed in recital rooms with the original orchestration. Shaw, in his days as a music critic, tried to persuade his contemporaries that *The Magic Flute* was not merely a collection of tunes written by "a sort of Papageno among composers."[85] Fifty years later he might have parodied those who considered it a solemn allegory about Temptation and Wisdom. And Mozart's *Don* has been in turn comic, didactic, and demonic.

Such works have an existence apart from the total achievement of their composers. The great works of Bach, in the view of Albert Schweitzer, "would have been the same even if his existence had run quite another course. Did we know more of his life than is now the case, and were we in possession of all the letters he had ever written, we should still be no better informed as to the inward sources of his works than we are now."[86] For Schweitzer, writing more than fifty years ago, Bach is the "objective" artist, Wagner the "subjective." This means that in the case of Wagner we must seek the roots of his art in the fortunes of his life, and that full enlightenment requires knowing as much as possible about the conditions of creation. Wagner obliged by telling the world all he could. As a consequence the masterpieces of Wagner have been slow in acquiring their independence. No composer was more successful in presenting *himself* before the public; and when an audience encountered Wagner in one of his works they were reminded that he was also on view in other mythical disguises. "*Tristan* is a miracle," wrote Thomas Mann as late as 1940, "—especially in its irksome affinity with the *Meistersinger*, which almost defies mental grasp. It is still more of a miracle when both of these are taken for what they really are, mere relief from the minute, gigantic thought structure of the *Ring*." The real miracle here, of course, is Wagner himself, who was capable of controlling so many different kinds of great structures. "Wagner's work," Mann goes on to say, "is a veritable eruption of talent and genius, the profoundly serious yet enchanting work of a sensuous sorcerer, drunk with his own wisdom."[87] But the sorcerer sometimes obstructed the view of his magic tricks. Indeed, his disciples sent up smoke screens of legend and theory that often hid the whole show. Not until the Bayreuth mists had begun to lift did it become clear that Wagner had not made the old opera disappear. He had simply joined the ranks of the great composers, having effected a greater change in music itself than in the musical theater or art in general.

The Bayreuth mists have blown away. Nazi Germany probably saw the last of the circles where the Wagnerian ideology "could flourish divested of any essential artistic import."[88] Wagner's political prose now seems irrelevant to any living issue, despite the rather impatient efforts, during and after the Second World War, to discover the roots of Nazism in his "metapolitics" and his "racial thinking."[89] The aesthetic theories are just as decidedly out of date. It is true that a discerning observer of our culture could recognize Wagnerian ideas and attitudes where they lie transformed or hidden away.[90] Aesthetic Wagnerism may have lingered as an insidious evil, but at least the dogmas about art-synthesis and folk art are no longer seriously announced in their original form. For between the Wagnerite decade of 1900-1910 and today the ratio between the interest in the Master and the interest in his masterpieces has been inverted. Hero worship has given way to the adoration of the work of art itself.

It is more than a century since a French poet first expounded Wagner's theories to the art-lovers of Paris. A hundred years after the appearance of Baudelaire's essay Joseph Kerman, addressing a wider and more varied audience, could conclude that there is no longer an artistic entity called "Wagner." There are "only four fantastic works of art . . . with their great beauties and their bêtises."[91] Elsewhere he speaks of not four but one:

The fervor of the original Wagnerians seems . . . remote, and the in-
cantations of the anti-Wagnerians seems less and less real with time,
less forceful and obligatory. . . . Many have set out to expose the
chicanery, while many more have declared the magic vision of
Bayreuth has simply faded away. But as high feelings and self-interest
abate, *Tristan and Isolde* remains.[92]

It remains in the histories of music, where *Tristan* has replaced
Wagner as a chapter heading. Even in those histories uncommitted
to atonalism one can read the safe assertion that *Tristan* has influenced more works than any other score extant.[93] An English
critic, when trying to account for the dearth of British music that
preceded the recent renaissance, adduces the fact that *Tristan* was
not performed in the Provinces.[94] An eminent Verdian can think
of no higher praise for *Otello* than to rank it with *Tristan* as one
of the two greatest tragic operas of the world.[95] *Tristan* has been
separated from its composer in the adjective "Tristanesque": there
are very few other works in the history of art that live a verbal
life of their own. In one of those rare histories of music that are not
simply surveys the adjective is used to refer to the harmonic coloration in the works of a dozen composers who were in no other way
pre- or post-Wagnerian—from the late mazurkas of Chopin to
Delius' *Song of the High Hill,* and including the "Tuba Mirum"
of the Dvořák *Requiem.* "*Tristan,*" Wilfred Mellers concludes,
echoing Ernst Kurth, "was an experience that became a historical
event."[96] And that event was not confined to the history of music.
One study of the modern theater sets out to demonstate that *Tristan* is *not* a tragedy.[97] In another, it is proved a masterpiece of the
"theater of passion," and honored with a separate chapter, in the
company of *Oedipus, Hamlet,* and Racine's *Bérénice.*[98]

Tristan also remains in the permanent repertory of the opera
houses, and there is no indication than any management would drop
it for more than a few years at a time. It is cheaper to produce than
any other Wagner opera: no ballet, no large chorus, no special
effects, no competing prima donnas—although the lone Isolde is
likely to be expensive. Even if the *Heldentenor* should become as
rare as the *castrato,* there would probably be some way devised

of having the favorite soprano sing opposite a dubbed voice. Recordings have made it possible for one to be overwhelmed at home by a tenor who may have sung his arduous role *pianissimo* into a microphone. Wagner could not have expected his work to be heard more than a few times in the life of any single Bayreuth-goer. Now it can be heard any evening, far from any opera house. Having learned that art is oracular, we look to it for the revelation of a truth in our living rooms. And because of our respect for the integrity of the work of art, there are fewer of us who would suggest, like M. Verdurin, that one listen to "just the *Liebestod*."

Perhaps this means that Tristanism, once the private problem of French composers and the heroes of autobiographical novels, has become a matter of public concern. The respectable participants in the Metropolitan Opera Quiz have, after all, openly announced to the nation that they enjoy being "mowed down" by *Tristan*.[99] Opera managements and record companies ought to be reminded of the Platonic injunction against arousing emotions to no purpose, and phonograph listeners directed to the seventh book of Aristotle's *Ethics*, on aesthetic self-indulgence. We all, in any event, ought to look forward to that time when we can find *Tristan* (as one American composer says he does) chaste and restrained—when we can admire the masterful dramaturgy of Act III without being carried away by the progressions.

Nietzsche thought Wagner threatened the public health, and numbered the seductiveness of *Tristan* first among the dangers. The music still confronts us, its virulence no longer diluted by doctrinaire Wagnerism. If Nietzsche was right in discerning a malady, it is useful to know its symptoms.

THE DATES OF THE FIRST PERFORMANCES
OF WAGNER'S MUSIC-DRAMAS IN THE
MAJOR OPERATIC CITIES

The dates are from Loewenberg's *Annals of Opera*. Unless it is otherwise noted the performances were in German. I have omitted the dates for the separate operas of the *Ring*, but they follow a pattern similar to that for the complete tetralogy. *Parsifal* is a special case, because it was restricted to Bayreuth until the Metropolitan Opera broke the monopoly in 1903. But New York and London heard concert performances of it in 1884 and 1886, respectively: it was not performed in Paris until 1914.

Tannhäuser
Dresden	1845
Berlin	1856
Vienna	1859
New York	1859
London	1882 (earlier in Italian and in English)
Paris	1861 (in French; revived 1895)

Lohengrin
Weimar	1850
Vienna	1858
Berlin	1859
New York	1871
London	1882
Paris	1887 (in French)
Paris	1891 (Opéra, in German)

Tristan

Munich	1865
Berlin	1876
London	1882
Vienna	1883
New York	1886
Paris	1884 (concert version in French)
Paris	1899 (Nouveau Théâtre, in French)
Paris	1914 (Opéra, in German)

Die Meistersinger

Munich	1868
Dresden	1869
Vienna	1870
Berlin	1870
London	1882
New York	1886
Paris	1897 (in French)
Paris	1914 (Champs Elysées, in German)

The Ring (complete)

Bayreuth	1876
Vienna	1879
Berlin	1881
London	1882
New York	1889
Paris	1911 (in French)
Paris	1929 (in German)

A NOTE ON SWINBURNE AND THE SEA

In 1907 William Morton Payne, the leading spirit of the Chicago *Dial*, privately printed a cycle of sonnets called *Richard Wagner*. There are thirteen poems, on as many pages—one sonnet for each of the eleven operas from *Rienzi* to *Parsifal*, plus an introductory sonnet about Wagner the man and a closing piece called "Bayreuth" (the "shrine" which, as far away as Chicago, commanded "the reverence due the sacred spots of earth").[1] Each of the opera-sonnets celebrates some central theme of the plot, announced with exclamation points and expanded with a good deal of uncomfortable inversion for the sake of rhyme.[2] For all that the tone and diction of the poems reveal, "The Master-Singers" must have sounded to Payne much like "The Rhine-Gold," and he must have found *Rienzi* as admirable as *Parsifal*. It was, apparently, sufficient endorsement for any of the operas that it was written by Wagner. There is no early Wagner or late, good Wagner or bad—only the Master, who from first to last had

> learned creation's secret, and laid bare
> The tragic striving of the Cosmic Will.[3]

Payne's cycle is an awkward, albino descendant of French Symbolism: remember the sonnet-catalogues of the music-dramas that appeared in the *Revue wagnérienne*. The English champion of French Symbolism, Arthur Symons, also composed poems with Wagnerian as well as Baudelairean titles to include in his tasteful collection.[4] So, indeed, did the Pre-Raphaelites and many of the practitioners of Tennysonian blank verse—not to mention the minor poets among the orthodox Wagnerites. The original works of *John* Payne—the polyglot

translator of Villon, Hafiz, and the *Arabian Nights*—are ridden with
allusions to the music-dramas; and he published his own inevitable cycle
of sonnets to Wagner in a work called *Vigil and Vision*.[5] John Payne
has, in fact, a claim to the honor of having started an English tradition
of Wagner poetry. As early as 1871—by which time he had played a
major role in establishing the vogue of Wagner in England—he published a sonnet called "Bride Night," which is a description of *Tristan*,
Act II, Scene II:

> Sweet summer, if thy roses knew the song
>   The linnet sang in that sweet dream of old,
>   Flooding the night with ripples of song-gold,
> The while two lovers did their bliss prolong . . .[6]

Payne's word painting of Wagnerian scenery antedates by fifteen years
the sonnets collected by Dujardin for the *Revue*.

If any of the operas had been significantly singled out for special
celebration in English poetry, it was not *Tristan* but *Tannhäuser*.
Wagner's "sin-satiate" poet-knight (the adjective is William Payne's)[7]
was tirelessly described, usually in the easy iambics of the *Idylls of the
King*. Thirty years after Wagner had converted *Rienzi* into bad
Meyerbeer, Lord Lytton's son translated the Venusberg Bacchanal into
bad Tennyson:

> . . . weird strains of magic, direful-sweet,
> That lap the wanton sense in blissful ease,
> While through the ear a reptile music creeps,
> And, blandly-busy, round about the soul
> Weaves its fell web of sounds.[8]

The "lascivious limbs" of Wagner's Venus, "languid in light," shim-
mered in English verse as the Lohengrin swan did in French; and
Dorian Gray read the tragedy of his soul into the music of *Tannhäuser*
just as King Ludwig had Lohengrinized his similar perversity.[9]

Although the best-known variation of the *Tannhäuser* theme, Swinburne's *Laus Veneris* (1866), was not directly influenced by Wagner's
opera, Swinburne probably knew Baudelaire's essay; and the poem's
free-flowing sensationalism is Wagnerian in spirit. In like manner, Swinburne's retelling of *Tristram of Lyonesse* (1882), though written before he had had a chance to hear Wagner's music-drama (it appeared
one month after the first performance of *Tristan* in England), may
fairly be called Tristanesque. There could be no better setting for the
second act of Wagner's *Tristan* than one of Swinburne's overgrown

and darkened gardens, and no better setting for the third act than that Forsaken Garden where the dead weeds had grown from the graves of the roses. Moreover, there is in English verse no closer approximation to Wagner's "infinite melody" than Swinburne's long nephelidian lines. A certain Ferdinand Wagner, who was an admirer of both the composer and the poet, has noticed another similarity: "The masterly hand with which [Swinburne] holds the threads that seem to float unconnectedly . . . and which he always succeeds in tying together when least expected seems to me exactly like Richard Wagner."[10]

This confused metaphor is taken from a passage in which the writer is describing the pleasure of having, as he puts it, "*dived* into the turbulent *waves* of Swinburne's gigantic mind."[11] Just as there were Wagnerian waters for the aesthetic drowning of music lovers, there was a Swinburnian sea of words. The sea was, in fact, an all-purpose image for Swinburne: swimming was the subject of some of his better poems, and "sea" seems to have been his favorite monosyllable. "Its salt," he once explained, "*must* have been in my blood before I was born":

I can remember no earlier enjoyment than being held up naked in my father's arms and brandished between his hands, then shot like a stone from a sling through the air, shouting and laughing with delight, held foremost into the coming wave. . . . But this is enough of my infancy; only it shows the *truth* of my endless passionate returns to the sea in all my verse.[12]

Swinburne's father was an admiral: his "Mother," according to the autobiographical poem "Thalassius," was "the sea" itself. In the five hundred lines of that poem alone the word "sea" appears more than forty times, sometimes rhymed with its homonym "see"; it is compounded with other Swinburnian leitmotif-words—sea-waves, sea-wind, sea-bird, sea-flowers, sea-pulses, and sea-things—and transformed into such words as "sere" and "seeing." The Sea pervades the poem, like the "Rhine" arpeggio in *Das Rheingold* and the "Desire" scale in *Tristan*. In the early *Poems and Ballads* the sea symbolizes both the passion and the weariness of erotic love. Thus the Queen of Evil who has trapped the Tannhäuser of *Laus Veneris* is "sea-born" and pictured amidst oceanic images; and Swinburne's *Tristram*, like Wagner's, begins aboard ship.

Swinburne wrote three poems about Wagner and his works: two roundels on the Preludes to *Lohengrin* and *Tristan*, and a triple roundel on "The Death of Richard Wagner."[13] The *Lohengrin* poem is sprinkled with water from a "dewfall" and some "watersprings"—

merely enough to float the expected swan ("sweet-souled as a dove") which turns up in a hiss of "s" sounds.[14] The other roundels, however, are sea poems.

> Fate, out of the deep sea's gloom . . .

is how the Tristan "Prelude" opens. It closes symmetrically:

> More deep than the wide sea's womb,
>   Fate.[15]

In the Wagner roundel Swinburne observes that the composer spoke "from the hollows of ocean": his music was like "seas that revolve and rivers that depart" and the "sound of tides in gulf and firth":

> Eye might not endure it, but ear and heart with a rapture of dark delight,
> With a terror and wonder whose core was joy, and a passion of thought
>   set free,
> Felt inly the rising of doom divine as a sundawn risen to sight
>   From the depths of the sea.[16]

Swinburne must himself have "felt inly" what it was like to be overwhelmed by sound—if not by the sound of Wagner's music (for it is probable that he was not acutely sensitive to it), then by the sound of his own words. For Swinburne's verbal excesses were like Wagner's musical excesses; and the criticism of Swinburne sounds like the criticism of Wagner. "You could not condense The Triumph of Time," T. S. Eliot has observed: "You could only leave out. And this would destroy the poem; though no one stanza is essential."[17] (Tristan, according to Eric Bentley, "seems overrepetitious and long however much you cut it.")[18] Swinburne's "emotion," Eliot goes on to say, "is never particular, never in a direct line of vision, never focussed"—"a fuzz of words," as Browning succinctly put it.* Matthew Arnold, in turn, was offended by what he called Swinburne's "fatal habit of using one hundred words where one would suffice." Change "words" to "notes" and you have Nietzsche contra Wagner.[19] Both Swinburne and Wagner, in short, lack sharpness, conciseness, and wit: Swinburne, despite his admiration for Mazzini, is as un-Mediterranean as Wagner.

The similarity between Swinburne and Wagner is a sign of affinity rather than influence. The lushness of Swinburne's verse resembles that of Tristan, but it is not the result of an attempt—like that of

---

* "The miaulings of a delirious cat" was what Carlyle called Swinburne's verse, and one is reminded of Berlioz' description of the Tristan Prelude as a "long moan."

D'Annunzio and Mann—to translate Wagner's chromaticism into words. Swinburne may be listed with the English poets who, like the French, wrote about Wagner because they thought his aesthetic doctrines resembled their own. Swinburne and John Payne are, in this respect, the literary progenitors of Symons and William Payne, who carried into the twentieth century the tradition of poetizing Wagner and his world but not his music.

A NOTE ON JOYCE AND ELIOT

To catch all the allusions in *Ulysses* one must know Wagner's epics as well as Homer's, and be as closely acquainted with Nibelheim and Valhalla as with the geography of Dante's *Comedy*. Stephen Dedalus, for example, exclaims "Nothung!" as he lifts up his ashplant to smash a chandelier in a Dublin brothel.[1] The name of the Volsung's sword is well known, but to notice the pun in "ashplant" one must remember that the tree in which Wotan had planted the sword was an ash. Just as other details in *Ulysses* were supposed to delight connoisseurs of Celtic lore, the parody of Siegmund's heroic moment was intended for well-informed Wagnerians.*

Ulysses is also a virtuoso display-piece of verbal leitmotif technique. The famous "Sirens" episode opens with an Overture of fragmentary phrases drawn from the narrative that follows. The opening fragment, for example, "Bronze by gold heard the hoofirons, steelyringing," is a string of motifs drawn from the first sentence of the narrative: "Bronze by gold, Miss Douce's head by Miss Kennedy's head, over the cross-blind of the Ormond bar heard the viceregal hoofs go by, ringing steel."[2] Joyce's verbal Overture is comparable to a Wagnerian Prelude. The two pages of motifs are an epitome of the succeeding thirty-page episode. Confusing on first reading, the Overture becomes intelligible when it is reread after the episode that follows has become familiar—just as the denotation of a Wagnerian Prelude is clear only after the significance of the leitmotifs has been learned from the context of the music-drama. Of course the opera Prelude is nevertheless musically satisfying as an independent piece, and displays a logic of form that does not depend upon the contextual significance of the motifs. Pre-

---

* See also, in *Ulysses*, the chanting of the bloodoath air from the *Dusk of the Gods*.

sumably Joyce intended his Overture to be equally satisfactory as a "musical" arrangement of verbal sounds.*

In *Finnegans Wake*, the puns, tropes, and anagrams allude to various simultaneous sub-narratives. The Tristram myth is mentioned on the first page, and provides one of the more important casts of characters for the perpetual interchange of identities.[3] H. C. Earwicker is King Mark; his son Shem, Tristan; his daughter Isabel, Isolde.[4] The myth in its Wagnerian form comes closest to the surface of the language in the section which begins "—Three quarks for Muster Mark!"[5] Here four old men who are named for the four gospels comment on the lovers who are aboard ship.[6] The leering foursome gossips about the liaison of Trustan and Usolde, Trisolanisans and Isolamisola, Tricks and Doelsy.[7] Other doublets—"luistening and listening," "kiddling and cuddling," "handsome and huntsem"—seem to parody the language of Wagner's lovers.[8] Even Wagner's personal life enters into the *Tristan* theme of *Finnegans Wake*: earlier in the book there is a reference to "a wagoner" and his "mudheeldy wheesindonk."[9]

T. S. Eliot, like Joyce, refers to the Wagnerian as well as the original tellings of the favorite medieval legends. Wagner, as much as Frazer or Jessie Weston, presides over the introduction of the Grail motif into *The Waste Land*: and in addition to Verlaine's sonnet on *Parsifal*, Eliot quotes the wailing of the Rhinemaidens as a refrain for the Song of the Thames-daughters, a trio who have been similarly violated.[10] But in *The Waste Land*, as in *Finnegans Wake*, *Tristan* provides the most prominent quotations, which frame one of the scenes in the first part of the poem:

> *Frisch weht der Wind*
> *Der Heimat zu*
> *Mein Irisch Kind*
> *Wo weilest du?*
> "You gave me hyacinths first a year ago:
> "They called me the hyacinth girl."
> —Yet when we came back, late, from the Hyacinth garden,
> Your arms full, and your hair wet, I could not
> Speak, and my eyes failed, I was neither
> Living nor dead, and I knew nothing,
> Looking into the heart of light, the silence.
> *Oed' und leer das Meer.*[11]

In the Notes to the poem, Eliot identifies the familiar quotations, but he

---

* The "Sirens" chapter may also be read as a verbal fugue, with the Overture as an Exposition in five (?) voices.

does not elucidate the obscurities of the passage between them. The first lines are from the Sailor's song which opens the opera and angers Isolde; the concluding line is spoken by the Shepherd at the beginning of the third act, and is associated with the desolation of that scene—evoked by the English horn and the empty thirds and fourths of the strings.[12] The context of the intervening passage is erotic, and the language that of a mystical experience: perhaps a kind of love-death is being described.[12] Whatever the full significance of the scene, certainly one of the gardens referred to must be that in the second act of *Tristan*: quotations from Acts I and III, that is, frame an allusion to Act II.[13]

The studies of *The Waste Land* point out the relevance of the second quotation to the sea-imagery of the poem, but they overlook the interesting reference to the sea in the first quotation. The Sailor sings these words to one of the few immediately memorable snatches of tune in the opera:

Any reader familiar with the opera will hear the music as he reads the lines, just as he would hear the tune that goes with the quoted words of a popular song. And he would recognize the music of these lines as the leitmotif that is unambiguously associated with the sea.* In this way a musical leitmotif may enter the pattern of a poem: in addition to the ordinary poetic suggestion of music by the sound of words, the post-Wagnerian poet can use words that remind the reader of music which in turn denotes a concept. Wagnerian leitmotif-hunters are given the opportunity to play their game in reverse.†

---

* Gottfried von Strassburg puns on the triple meaning of LAMEIR: Love, Bitter, Sea.

† Although Joyce, in *Finnegans Wake*, and Eliot, in *The Waste Land*, seem to have preferred *Tristan* to the other music-dramas as a source for reference, none of these examples—not even Eliot's suggestion of the tune—qualifies as Tristanism. Joyce and Eliot were interested in the relevance of the myth to Everyman; D'Annunzio and Mann, on the other hand, were interested in the effect of the music on a susceptible few.

NOTES

NOTES TO CHAPTER I: SCHOPENHAUER, THE MYTH, AND THE MUSIC

1. See for example *Mein Leben* (2 vols., Munich, F. Bruckmann, 1911), II, 603-5; the letter of December, 1854, to Liszt, in *Briefwechsel zwischen Wagner und Liszt*, ed. Erich Kloss (2 vols. in 1), which is vol. IX of *Richard Wagners Briefe in Originalausgaben* (17 vols. in 9, Leipzig, Breitkopf und Härtel, 1911-13), II, 42-44; and the letter of August 23, 1856, to Röckel, in *Briefe an August Röckel*, Vol. XI of *Wagners Briefe*, pp. 65-72. Thomas Mann has suggested that "probably never in the history of the mind has there been so wonderful an example of the artist, the dark and divine human being, finding spiritual support, self-justification and enlightenment in another's thought." "Sufferings and Greatness of Richard Wagner," in *Essays of Three Decades*, tr. H. T. Lowe-Porter (New York, Knopf, 1947), p. 331.

2. See Wagner's letter of June 28, 1857, to Liszt, in *Briefwechsel . . . Wagner. . . Liszt*, II, 172-73.

3. *The World as Will and Representation*, tr. E. F. J. Payne (2 vols., Indian Hills, Colorado, The Falcon's Wing Press, 1958), I, xxxv (Schopenhauer's preface to the second edition).

4. The article was by John Oxenford, drama critic of the *Times* and translator of Goethe. *The Westminster and Foreign Quarterly Review*, LIX (no. cxvi, April 1, 1853), 388-407. According to Wagner, Herwegh had learned of Schopenhauer from a pamphlet by "a certain Herr Frauenstadt"—probably Schopenhauer's friend and disciple, Julius (1813-74). *Mein Leben*, II, 603. Oxenford's article laid the foundation of Schopenhauer's fame. See Francis Hueffer, "Arthur Schopenhauer," in *The Fortnightly Review*, no. CXX, new series (December 1, 1876), pp. 773-92.

5. See V. J. McGill, *Schopenhauer: Pessimist and Pagan* (New York, Brentano's, 1931), p. 10; Charles Andler, *Nietzsche, sa vie et sa pensée* (3d. ed., 6 vols. in 3, Paris, Gallimard, 1958), I, 308-9; and A. G. Lehmann, *The Symbolist Aesthetic in France, 1885-1895* (Oxford, Basil Blackwell, 1950).

6. See Ernest Newman, *The Life of Richard Wagner* (4 vols., New York, Knopf, 1933-46), Vol. II, *1848-1860* (1937), pp. 291, 430.

7. See for example the letters to Liszt and to Röckel cited in note 1, and *Mein Leben*, II, 769.

8. *Mein Leben*, II, 603-5, and the letter to Röckel. See Bernard Shaw's discussion of this point in the *The Perfect Wagnerite* (2d. ed., New York, Brentano's, 1911), pp. 110-18.

9. Letter of December, 1854, in *Briefwechsel. . .Wagner. . .Liszt*, II, 42.

10. *Perfect Wagnerite*, p. 14.

11. *Oper und Drama*, in *Sämtliche Schriften und Dichtungen* (12 vols., Leipzig, Breitkopf and Härtel, 1911), III, 222-320, and IV, 1-102. Tr. by Edwin Evans as *Opera and Drama* (2 vols., New York, Scribner's, 1913).

12. See *World as Will*, I, 255-67 (Book III, sec. 52); and II, 447-57 (Supplement to Book III, chap. xxxix).

13. Letter of June 7, 1855, in *Briefwechsel. . .Wagner. . .Liszt*, II, 77.

14. "Zukunftsmusik," in *Schriften*, VII, 87-137. See Jack M. Stein, *Wagner and the Synthesis of the Arts* (Detroit, Wayne State University Press, 1960), p. 149.

15. *Schriften*, VII, 88. See Newman, *Life*, II, 236. On Nietzsche's involvement in the proofs of *Mein Leben* see Wagner's letter of December 3, 1869, in *Wagner und Nietzsche zur Zeit ihrer Freundschaft*, ed. Elisabeth Förster-Nietzsche (Munich, Georg Müller, 1915), p. 25; and William Wallace, *Richard Wagner: As He Lived* (London, Kegan Paul, Trench, Trübner, 1925), pp. 225-26.

16. *Schriften*, VII, 110-12; and see the paraphrase in Stein, *Synthesis*, pp. 152-53. Nietzsche recognized the shift in Wagner's aesthetic theory: "Consider. . .Schopenhauer's curious, and to some of us most fascinating, attitude to art. It was doubtless that which first converted Wagner to Schopenhauer. . .to such a degree that his later esthetic views completely contradict his earlier ones. As an example of the earlier view, we may take the treatise *Opera and Drama*, of the latter, his articles from 1870 onwards. What most impresses one is the radical change in his notion of the position of music itself. . . .It suddenly dawned on him that Schopenhauer's theory was much more favorable to the sovereignty of music: music seen as apart from all the other arts, the triumphant culmination of all art, not concerned like the others with images of the phenomenal world but, rather, speaking the language of the will directly from the deep source of Being, its most elementary manifestation." *Zur Genealogie der Moral*, Third Essay, sec. v, in *Werke in Drei Bänden* (Munich, Carl Hanser, 1956), II, 844-45; tr. by Francis Golffing,

in *The Birth of Tragedy and The Genealogy of Morals* (Garden City, New York, Doubleday [Anchor], 1956), p. 237.

17. *Schriften*, VII, 129; tr. from Stein, *Wagner and the Synthesis of the Arts*, p. 154.

18. *Schriften*, VII, 119.

19. Letter of January 30, 1844, to Karl Gaillard, in *Letters of Richard Wagner*, ed. Wilhelm Altmann, tr. M. M. Bozman (2 vols., New York, Dutton, 1927), I, 107.

20. See Ernest Newman, *The Wagner Operas* (New York, Knopf, 1949), p. 196.

21. Letter of December 19, 1856, quoted in Newman, *Wagner Operas*, p. 194. See also pp. 195-96.

22. Letter of December 22, 1856, in *Briefe Richard Wagners an Otto Wesendonk*, Vol. VI of *Wagners Briefe*, p. 44.

23. Letter of March 4, 1857, to Marie Wittgenstein, in *Letters of. . . Wagner*, I, 327.

24. *Wagner Operas*, p. 196.

25. Paul Bekker, *Richard Wagner, His Life in His Work*, tr. M. M. Bozman (London and Toronto, Dent, 1931), p. 292.

26. *Wagner Operas*, p. 202.

27. *World as Will*, II, 449 (Supplement to Book III, chap. xxxix).

28. *Ibid.*, I, 262 (Book III, sec. 52); and Wagner, "Zukunftsmusik," in *Schriften*, VII, 121-80.

29. Cecil Gray, *A Survey of Contemporary Music* (2d. ed., London, Oxford University Press, 1927), p. 42.

30. Sacheverell Sitwell, *Liszt* (Boston and New York, Houghton Mifflin, 1934), p. 178.

31. Letter of July 20, 1856, in *Briefwechsel . . . Wagner . . . Liszt*, II, 130.

32. Letter of October, 1859, in *Briefe an Hans von Bülow* (Jena, Eugen Diederich, 1916), pp. 125-26. See Bekker, *Wagner*, p. 294.

33. The quotations are from Stein, *Wagner and the Synthesis of the Arts*, p. 131; and Bekker, *Wagner*, p. 290. It has often been observed that among the many foreshadowings of *Tristan* in Liszt's music, a passage in his song "Ich möchte hingehen," written before 1845, anticipates the opening phrase of the Prelude. But this is probably a chance coincidence. See Gerald Abraham, *A Hundred Years of Music* (2d. ed., London, Duckworth, 1949), p. 114; and Humphrey Searle, *The Music of Liszt* (London, Williams and Norgate, 1954), p. 52.

34. Letter of April 15, 1859, to Mathilde Wesendonk, in *Richard*

Wagner an Mathilde Wesendonk: Tagebuchblätter und Briefe, 1853-1871, Vol. V of *Wagners Briefe*, p. 125.

35. See Stein, *Wagner and the Synthesis of the Arts*, pp. 131-48, for other examples of this point and those that follow.

36. *Den als Tantris unerkannt ich entlassen,/ als Tristan kehrt er kühn zurück...* (Bars 9-15 after the change to the signature of F major, in Isolde's Narrative).

37. Debussy draws a similar analogy to "a harmless lunatic, who, on presenting his visiting card, would declaim his name in song." Léon Vallas, *The Theories of Claude Debussy*, tr. Maire O'Brien (London, Oxford University Press, 1929), p. 190.

38. See the letter of June 28, 1857, to Liszt, in *Briefwechsel...Wagner...Liszt*, II, 171-73.

39. William Wallace observes that in only two works—*Tristan* and *Die Meistersinger*—was Wagner not at the mercy of the stage machinist (*Wagner*, p. 78).

40. Camille Saint-Saëns, *Harmonie et Mélodie* (Paris, Calmann Lévy, 1885), p. xi. "The original character of the theme attracts me," Wagner told his prospective publishers, "as opening a region of musical treatment wherein I have long desired to spread myself at large and luxuriantly." Letter of September 30, 1857, to Breitkopf and Härtel, in *Letters of Wagner*, I, 335.

41. The translator of the version Wagner read, Kurtz (the second edition was in 1847), added his own ending to the unfinished original, and noted that the legend contained the elements of a tragic drama. Gottfried's narrative, composed at the beginning of the thirteenth century, was based on the version of Thomas (*c.* 1160-70), supplemented by the slightly later German version of Eilhart d'Oberge (*c.* 1190-1200), a Saxon vassal of Henry the Lion, duke of Brunswick. Eilhart, in turn, probably used the same source as Béroul (*c.* 1180). Wagner also knew the discussion of the legend in the fourth volume of F. H. von der Hagen's *Minnesinger* (1838). See Newman, *Wagner Operas*, pp. 170, 188. The translation of Gottfried's version by A. T. Hatto includes the surviving fragments of the *Tristan* of Thomas.

42. Hatto translation, pp. 55, 212.

43. Letter of May 30, 1859, to Mathilde Wesendonk, in *Wagner an Mathilde*, p. 148.

44. See Helaine Newstead, "The Origin and Growth of the Tristan Legend," in *Arthurian Literature in the Middle Ages*, ed. Roger Sherman Loomis (Oxford, Clarendon Press, 1959), p. 123.

45. See Hatto's introduction to his translation of Gottfried, pp. 23, 27-28.

46. See W. T. H. Jackson, "Gottfried von Strassburg," in *Arthurian Literature*, pp. 145-56.

47. Eric Bentley observes that Wagner's "fantasy, controlled by realism, was fantasy mechanized and therefore partly spoiled." *The Playwright as Thinker* (2d. ed., New York, Noonday Press [Meridian], 1957), p. 106.

48. Letter of May 30, 1859, to Mathilde Wesendonk, in *Wagner an Mathilde*, p. 146.

49. *Love in the Western World*, tr. Montgomery Belgion (rev. ed., Garden City, New York, Doubleday [Anchor], 1957). This is a translation of *L'Amour et l'Occident* (rev. ed., Paris, Plon, 1956). The British edition is entitled *Passion and Society*.

50. *Ibid.*, pp. 14-27. The summary that follows is based on Book I, chaps. 4-7.

51. *Ibid.*, p. 224.

52. Indeed, the chord recurs, in one inversion or another, at almost every important place in the score. See Ernst Kurth, *Romantische Harmonik und ihre Krise in Wagners "Tristan"* (2d. ed., Berlin, Max Hesse, 1923), pp. 44-96.

53. *World as Will*, II, 455-56 (Supplement to Book III, chap. xxxix).

54. *Ibid.*, I, 259 (Book III, sec. 52). For an interesting schematization of Schopenhauer's musical metaphysics, see André Faucconet, *L'Esthétique de Schopenhauer* (Paris, Félix Alcan, 1913).

55. *World as Will*, I, 259.

56. Letter of October 29, 1859, to Mathilde Wesendonk, in *Wagner an Mathilde*, p. 189.

57. See *World as Will*, I, 261 (Book III, sec. 52).

58. "Ludwig Schnorr von Carolsfeld," in *Schriften*, VIII, 186.

59. *Ibid.*

60. Letter of January 19, 1859, to Mathilde Wesendonk, in *Wagner an Mathilde*, p. 96.

61. Letter of October 19, 1858, to Liszt, in *Briefwechsel . . . Wagner . . . Liszt*, II, 225.

62. Letter of October 6, 1858, to Mathilde Wesendonk, in *Wagner an Mathilde*, p. 60.

63. See Victor Zuckerkandl, *Sound and Symbol*, tr. Willard R. Trask (New York, Pantheon Books, 1956), pp. 50-51.

64. *World as Will*, II, 448 (Supplement to Book III, chap. xxxix).

65. *Love in the Western World*, p. 8.

66. Text and translation from Jackson, in *Arthurian Literature*, p. 148.

67. Hatto translation, p. 293.

68. *Ibid.*, p. 285.

69. *Ibid.*, p. 206.

70. *Ibid.*, p. 232.

71. *Ibid.*, p. 202.

72. See Mark's reference to Isolde in the middle of his lament: *Der mein Wille nie zu nahen wagte, / der mein Wunsch ehrfurchtschen entsagte. . . .*

73. D. H. Lawrence, in his essay on "Pornography and Obscenity," couples *Tristan* with *Jane Eyre*, as "much nearer to pornography than is Boccaccio. Wagner and Charlotte Brontë were both in a state where the strongest instincts have collapsed, and sex has become something slightly obscene, to be wallowed in, but despised." *Selected Literary Criticism*, ed. Anthony Beal (London, Heinemann, 1956), p. 39.

74. *Der Fall Wagner*, ix; in *Werke*, II, 922.

75. Herbert Marcuse observes that modern western civilization "admires the convergence of death instinct and Eros in the highly sublimated. . .creations of the *Liebestod*." *Eros and Civilization* (Boston, Beacon Press, 1955), p. 51.

76. See the classic discussions of Agape and Eros in Anders Nygren, *Agape and Eros*, tr. Philip S. Watson (Philadelphia, Westminster Press, 1953); and M. C. D'Arcy, S. J., *The Mind and Heart of Love* (London, Faber and Faber, 1945).

77. *Love in the Western World*, pp. 49 ff.

78. See Arthur Prüfer, "Novalis 'Hymnen an die Nacht' in ihren Beziehungen zu Wagners 'Tristan und Isolde,'" in Vol. I of *Richard Wagner-Jahrbuch*, ed. Ludwig Frankenstein (Leipzig, Deutsche Verlagsactiengesellschaft, 1906), pp. 290-303. A. T. Hatto concludes that "whatever other religious matter Gottfried has drawn on, the one consistent theme is that of twelfth-century mysticism. . . . It is not without interest that when Wagner was exploiting Gottfried's story for his music drama he had recourse to the quasi-mystical philosophy of Schopenhauer." Introduction to translation, p. 17 and n.

79. Letter of October 5, 1858, to Mathilde Wesendonk, in *Wagner an Mathilde*, pp. 56-60. See also the summary of *Die Sieger* in Newman, *Life*, II, 486-88.

80. Letter of March 3, 1860, to Mathilde Wesendonk, in *Wagner an Mathilde*, p. 217; translation borrowed from H. F. Redlich, *Alban Berg* (New York, Abelard-Schuman, 1957), p. 143.

81. Quoted in Newman, *Wagner Operas*, p. 662.

82. Letter of May 30, 1859, to Mathilde Wesendonk, in *Wagner an Mathilde*, p. 144.

83. *Ibid.;* see Bekker, *Wagner,* p. 478.

84. See the introduction by William Ashton Ellis to his translation of Wagner's letters to Mathilde: *Richard Wagner to Mathilde Wesendonck* (2d. ed., London, H. Grevel, 1905), p. lv.

85. *Der Fall Wagner,* iv; in *Werke,* II, 911.

86. *Mein Leben,* II, 682-86; Newman, *Life,* II, 558-70.

87. Letter of December 22, 1858, to Mathilde Wesendonk, in *Wagner an Mathilde,* p. 83.

88. *Mein Leben,* II, 717-19; Newman, *Life,* II, 460-61. See *Memoirs of Malwida von Meysenbug: Rebel in Bombazine,* ed. Mildred Adams from the trans. by Elsa von Meysenbug Lyons (New York, W. W. Norton, 1936), pp. 211-13, 294-95. The German title of Malwida's autobiography is *Memoiren einer Idealistin: Der Lebensabend einer Idealistin* (3 vols., Berlin, Schüster and Loeffler, 1900).

89. *Memoirs,* p. 212.

90. *Ibid.,* p. 294.

91. Quoted in E. H. Carr, *The Romantic Exiles* (Harmondsworth, Penguin Books, 1933), p. 215.

92. *Memoirs,* p. 301.

93. See *Mein Leben,* II, 719.

NOTES TO CHAPTER II: TO THE FIRST PERFORMANCE

1. *Baker's Biographical Dictionary of Musicians* (4th. ed., New York, G. Schirmer, 1940), p. 980, incorrectly lists the date of the death of Ludwig Schnorr von Carolsfeld as June 21, 1865. He died on *July 21.* See Newman, *The Life of Richard Wagner,* Vol. III, *1859-1866* (New York, Knopf, 1941), pp. 404-6.

2. Letter of the beginning of August, 1860, to Mathilde Wesendonk, in *Richard Wagner an Mathilde Wesendonk,* Vol. V of *Wagners Briefe in Originalausgaben* (Leipzig, Breitkopf and Härtel, 1911-13), pp. 242-3.

3. Letter of April, 1859, to Mathilde Wesendonk. *Ibid.,* p. 123.

4. Letter of December, 1854, to Liszt, in *Briefwechsel zwischen Wagner und Liszt,* Vol. IX of *Wagners Briefe,* II, 43.

5. Letter of August 21, 1858, to Mathilde Wesendonk, in *Wagner an Mathilde,* p. 33.

6. See *Johannes Brahms und Mathilde Wesendonk: ein Briefwechsel* (Vienna, Luckmann, 1943), pp. 109 ff.

7. See Newman, *The Life of Richard Wagner,* Vol. I, *1813-1848* (New York, Knopf, 1933), pp. 59-60.

8. Quoted in the introduction by William Ashton Ellis to *Richard*

Wagner to Mathilde Wesendonck (London, H. Grevel, 1905), p. xli. "Redemption through love," observes Cecil Gray, "is an idea which Wagner shares with all typical rakes." *Survey of Contemporary Music*, p. 154.

9. Letter of August 23, 1856, to Röckel, in *Briefe*, XI, 66.

10. Ernest Newman, *The Wagner Operas*, (New York, Knopf, 1949) p. 190.

11. *Life*, I, 418.

12. *Ibid.*, Vol. II, *1848-1860* (New York, Knopf, 1937), p. 390.

13. *Enemies of Promise* (2d. ed., Garden City, New York, Doubleday [Anchor], 1960), p. 144.

14. *The Women in Wagner's Life*, tr. Hannah Waller (London, Routledge, 1932), from *Richard Wagner und die Frauen: eine erotische Biographie* (Berlin, Schüster and Loeffler, 1912).

15. *Women in Wagner's Life*, p. 284.

16. *Ibid.*

17. *Ibid.*, pp. 281-82.

18. *Ibid.*, p. 9.

19. See Richard Count du Moulin Eckart, *Cosima Wagner*, tr. Catherine Alison Phillips (2 vols., New York, Knopf, 1930), II, 529.

20. Introduction to *Wagner to Mathilde*, p. xii.

21. *Ibid.*, p. xl.

22. The characterization of the affair as a "bourgeois drama" is Jacques Barzun's, in *Darwin, Marx, Wagner* (rev. ed., Garden City, New York, Doubleday [Anchor], 1958), p. 239.

23. "Gedenkblatt," in *Allgemeine Musik-Zeitung* (February, 1896).

24. Quoted in Newman, *Life*, II, 320.

25. *Mein Leben* (Munich, F. Bruckmann, 1911), II, 560.

26. *Ibid.*, p. 650.

27. Letter of July 9, 1857, to Liszt, in *Briefwechsel . . . Wagner . . . Liszt*, II, 174-75.

28. See the introduction to Wagner's *Briefe an Hans von Bülow*, (Jena, Eugen Diederich, 1916) p. iv.

29. *Briefe und Schriften*, ed. Marie von Bülow (3 vols., Leipzig, Breitkopf and Härtel, 1896), III, 114.

30. *Letters of Hans von Bülow, to Richard Wagner, et al.*, ed. Richard Count du Moulin Eckart, tr. Hannah Waller (New York and London, Knopf, 1931), pp. xix, xxvi.

31. Introduction to *Wagner to Mathilde*, p. lxi.

32. The dating here and in the following paragraphs follows Newman, *Life*, II, 530 ff., and the summary in *Wagner Operas*, pp. 169-278.

33. Newman, *Life*, II, 530.

34. Quoted in Ellis, *Wagner to Mathilde*, p. 17.

35. *Mein Leben*, II, 658.

36. *Briefe an Bülow*, p. 92; *Mein Leben*, II, 663.

37. *Mein Leben*, II, 705.

38. *Ibid.*, p. 666. The letter found its way to the Burrell Collection of Wagneriana. It was published for the first time, in German and English, in *Letters of Richard Wagner: The Burrell Collection*, ed. John N. Burk (London, Gollancz, 1951), pp. 509-12 and 369-72.

39. According to *Mein Leben*, II, 666.

40. See Newman, *Life*, II, 541.

41. *Ibid.*, p. 542.

42. *Memoirs of Malwida von Meysenbug* (New York, Norton, 1936), p. 303.

43. See E. H. Carr, *The Romantic Exiles* (Penguin Books, 1933).

44. Letter of August 20, 1858, to Clara Wolfram, in *Letters of Richard Wagner*, ed. Wilhelm Altmann (New York, Dutton, 1927), II, 6.

45. "The Sanity of Art," in *Major Critical Essays* (London, Constable, 1932), p. 288.

46. See *Letters of Bülow*, p. 209.

47. William Wallace thinks that even the Klindworth arrangements have been "the despair of many a lover of Wagner." *Richard Wagner* (London, Kegan Paul, Trench, Trübner, 1925), p. 175.

48. The quotations in the footnote on page 46 are from Bülow's *Briefe*, III, 27; the *Letters of Bülow*, p. 210; and Wagner's *Briefe an Bülow*, p. 101. See also Newman, *Life*, II, 574; and *Wagner Operas*, p. 210.

49. Quoted in Newman, *Life*, II, 587.

50. See Gerald Abraham, "The Influence of Berlioz on Wagner," in *Music and Letters*, V (no. 3, July, 1924), 239-46; and Jacques Barzun, *Berlioz and the Romantic Century* (2 vols., London, Gollancz, 1951), I, 336-38.

51. *Mein Leben*, II, 755.

52. See the letters of January 28, March 3, and April 10, 1860, to Mathilde Wesendonk, in *Wagner an Mathilde*, pp. 206-31; and *Briefwechsel . . . Wagner . . . Liszt*, II, 263.

53. See Newman, *Life*, II, 519-21, 546, 587, 590.

54. As late as 1881 Wagner confessed to the impresario Angelo Neumann that "I ought to have made *Tristan* at least humanly possible for a theater evening, etc., only I never found time to do it. As it is,

far too much is expected and in every respect the impossible is aimed at." *Letters*, ed. Altmann, II, 300.

55. See Newman, *Life*, III, 137-39, 147-48, 150, 153.

56. *Ibid.*, pp. 153, 185-86, 196.

57. The Prelude to *Tristan* alone had already been received with hostility by papers not only in Vienna but in Karlsruhe and Cologne (though not in the musical city of Prague). See Rosemary Park, *Das Bild von Richard Wagners Tristan und Isolde in der deutschen Literatur* (Jena, Eugen Diederich, 1935), pp. 32, 34.

58. See Newman, *Life*, III, 197-200, 202; and, on the number of Vienna rehearsals, 208n.

59. See, for example, Otto Zarek, *The Tragic Idealist, Ludwig II of Bavaria*, tr. Ella Goodman and Paul Sudley (New York and London, Harper, 1939); Werner Richter, *The Mad Monarch: The Life and Times of Ludwig II of Bavaria*, tr. William S. Schlamm (Chicago, Regnery, 1954)—the German title is simply *Ludwig II, König von Bayern* (Erlenbach-Zurich and Leipzig, Rentsch, 1937); Guy de Pourtalès, *Louis II de Bavière; ou, Hamlet-roi* (Paris, Gallimard, 1928); and Desmond Chapman-Huston, *Bavarian Fantasy: The Story of Ludwig II*, ed. Osyth Leeston (London, Murray, 1955).

60. *König Ludwig II und Richard Wagner: Briefwechsel*, ed. Otto Strobel (5 vols., Karlsruhe, G. Braun, 1936-39).

61. Letter of December 11, 1864. *Ibid.*, I, 40-41.

62. See the standard biography by Gottfried von Böhm, *Ludwig II, König von Bayern* (2d. ed., Berlin, Bondi, 1924); and du Moulin Eckart, *Cosima*, I, 157.

63. *Briefwechsel*, I, 105.

64. See Alfred Einstein, "Wagner and Ludwig II," in *Essays on Music*, ed. Paul Henry Lang (New York, Norton, 1962), pp. 257-65. Einstein's opinion is that Ludwig was "utterly unmusical. It is not *Tristan* or *Meistersinger*, or *The Ring*, or *Parsifal* that represents Wagner's true musical relation to the King, but the bombastic and jejune *Huldigungsmarsch* for military band" (p. 330).

65. *Life*, III, 265n.

66. See Newman, *Life*, III, 216-21, 234-35; and Eduard Stemplinger, *Richard Wagner in München (1864-1870): Legende und Wirklichkeit* (Munich, Knorr und Hirth, 1933), pp. 46-60, 116 ff.

67. *Ausgewählte Schriften und Briefe*, ed. Paul Egert (Berlin, Bernhard Hahnefeld, 1938), pp. 312-13. Nevertheless the influence of *Tristan* has been observed in parts of Act II of *The Cid*. Despite a number of rifts, Cornelius remained faithful.

68. See the German original of du Moulin Eckart's biography of Cosima (2 vols., Munich and Berlin, Drei Masken, 1929-31), I, 813.

69. Du Moulin Eckart, *Cosima* (English tr.), I, 153 ff.

70. In *Wagner to Mathilde*, p. 363.

71. See Newman, *Life*, III, chap. xxiv.

72. Quoted in Newman, *Life*, III, 329.

73. *Ibid.*, pp. 63, 329-30, 366 and n., 367, 381.

74. At the time of the first attempt Malvina refused to sing Isolde, apparently because she wanted to save her then ailing fiancé from the strain of singing Tristan. *Ibid.*, p. 133.

75. *Ibid.*, II, 491; III, 133n., 134-35, 249n. See the description of Schnorr in Edouard Schuré, *Souvenir sur Richard Wagner: La première de "Tristan et Iseult"* (Paris, Perrin, 1900), p. 44. For a good photograph of Schnorr, see C. H. N. Garrigues, *Ein Ideales Sängerpaar* (Copenhagen, Levin and Munksgaard, 1937; Berlin, Hermann Wendt, 1937), p. 263.

76. Newman, *Life*, III, 193-94, 363.

77. *Ibid.*, p. 369.

78. Quoted in Newman, *Life*, III, 368.

79. *Ibid.*, pp. 369-73. The playwright Grillparzer was among those who urged Ludwig to let Wagner go. See du Moulin Eckart, *Cosima*, I, 194-95. The 1859 letter of Wagner to Bülow quoted in the footnote on page 55 is in *Letters*, ed. Altmann, II, 73-74.

80. Newman, *Life*, III, 383, 375. The Porges guide was published in 1906. Peter Cornelius and Liszt were not at the Munich *Tristan*: Cornelius was in Weimar, looking after a production of *Der Cid*; and Liszt, who had just taken minor orders, was in Rome.

81. *Ibid.*, p. 376.

82. *Ibid.*, pp. 377-79.

83. See H. F. Redlich, *Bruckner and Mahler* (London, Dent [Master Musicians], 1955), pp. 13-14.

84. Newman, *Life*, III, 469.

85. Quoted in Newman, *Life*, III, 449.

86. In *Sämtliche Schriften*, (Leipzig: Breitkopf and Härtel, 1911), VIII, 222-41. For an account of the cause of Schnorr's death see Schuré, *Souvenirs*, pp. 73-74.

87. August 24, 1865; quoted in Newman, *The Life of Richard Wagner*, Vol. IV, *1866-1883* (New York, Knopf, 1946), p. 19.

88. Letter of July 22, 1866, to Ludwig, in *Ludwig . . . Wagner . . . Briefwechsel*, I, 132.

89. *Ibid.*, pp. 134-35.

90. Newman goes so far as to see *Tristan* as "the root cause of all the trouble." *Life*, IV, 16.

91. The misrepresentation of the facts of the Malvina Schnorr episode was continued by Cosima-inspired biographers. Cosima's son-in-law Houston Stewart Chamberlain ignores Malvina in his account of the 1865 performances—see *Richard Wagner*, tr. G. Ainslee Hight (rev. ed., London, Dent, 1897), pp. 90-91—and Carl Glasenapp goes so far as to disparage her singing, in *Das Leben Richard Wagners* (4th ed., 6 vols., Leipzig, Breitkopf und Härtel, 1904-11), IV, 91 ff. All this despite the evidence that in 1865 Wagner considered his "unforgettable Isolde," beyond comparison. But Malvina is not even mentioned in Wagner's memoir of Schnorr. On the traditional neglect of Malvina Schnorr see Garrigues, *Ideales Sängerpaar*, pp. 433 ff; and for the whole story, expertly unraveled, see Newman, *Life*, IV, chapters i and ii.

92. "One had to give up everything to Wagner," Liszt once said, "even one's happiness. . . . Von Bülow and I were his first admirers and his first slaves. . . . Von Bülow did it heroically." Juliette Lamber Adams, *Mes Premières Armes politiques et littéraires*, quoted in Barzun, *Darwin, Marx, Wagner*, p. 268.

93. *Letters of Bülow*, pp. 243-48.

94. *Cosima*, I, 363.

NOTES TO CHAPTER III: NIETZSCHE PRO TRISTAN

1. See Kurt Hildebrandt, *Wagner und Nietzsche: Ihr Kampf gegen das Neunzehnte Jahrhundert* (Breslau, Ferdinand Hirt, 1924); and Walter Kaufmann's discussion of Ernest Newman on Nietzsche and Bayreuth, in *Nietzsche: Philosopher, Psychologist, Antichrist* (rev. ed., New York, Noonday Press [Meridian Books], 1956), pp. 41-45 and notes.

2. Elisabeth Förster-Nietzsche, *Wagner und Nietzsche zur Zeit ihrer Freundschaft;* English trans., *The Nietzsche-Wagner Correspondence*, by Caroline V. Kerr (New York, Boni and Liveright, 1921), p. 280. Page references in this chapter will refer to the English edition.

3. *Ibid.*, p. x.

4. Among these critics have been Ernest Newman, in *The Life of Richard Wagner*, Vol. IV, *1866-1883*, (New York, Knopf, 1946), chaps. xv, xvi, xxv, and xxx; and, most recently, Paul Arthur Loos, in *Richard Wagner: Vollendung und Tragik der deutschen Romantik* (Munich, Leo Lehnen, 1952).

5. From the Inaugural Lecture delivered at Oxford in June, 1956,

entitled "Making, Knowing and Judging," printed in *The Dyer's Hand and Other Essays* (New York, Random House, 1962), p. 48. Auden goes on to say that it was *The Wagner Case* "which first taught me to listen to Wagner, about whom I had previously held silly preconceived notions."

6. Kaufmann, *Nietzsche*, pp. 37-38; Hildebrandt, *Wagner und Nietzsche*, p. 183.

7. *Ecce Homo*, ii, 6 (*Werke*, ed. Karl Schlechta [Munich, Manser, 1956], II, 1091-92). Most of the translation is from Kaufmann, *Nietzsche*, p. 38.

8. *Nietzsche-Wagner*, p. 3.

9. *Ibid.*

10. Letter of October 28, 1868, in *Briefe* (3 vols., Munich, C. H. Beck, 1938), Vol. II, *Briefe der Leipziger und Ersten Basler Zeit*, ed. Wilhelm Hoppe, pp. 258-60. Hildebrandt, *Wagner und Nietzsche*, p. 183. See Charles Andler, *Nietzsche, sa vie et sa pensée* (Paris, Gallimard, 1958), I, 322.

11. *Briefe*, II, 245.

12. *Ibid.*, Vol. III, *Briefe der Basler Zeit*, ed. Wilhelm Hoppe, pp. 85-86.

13. Letter of December 21, 1871. *Ibid.*, pp. 177-79.

14. An earlier Preface, never used, was written in February, 1871.

15. See Kaufmann, *Nietzsche*, p. 38.

16. See *The Birth of Tragedy*, chaps. ii and xxiv. Page references will be to the translation by Francis Golffing, in *The Birth of Tragedy and The Genealogy of Morals* (Garden City, New York, Doubleday [Anchor], 1956). Quotations in this paragraph are from pp. 27 and 143. See also George Allen Morgan, *What Nietzsche Means* (Cambridge, Mass., Harvard University Press, 1943), pp. 209-13.

17. *Birth of Tragedy*, chap. xvii; p. 105.

18. *Ibid.*, chap. xvi; pp. 96-102. In chap. xvi Nietzsche quotes verbatim the passage from *The World as Will and Idea* which became the classic exposition of how music expresses the will directly. The question of whether Wagner's *Beethoven* was influenced by Nietzsche's formulation of Schopenhauer is still being discussed—see T. Moody Campbell, "Nietzsche's *Die Geburt der Tragödie* and Richard Wagner," in *The Germanic Review*, XVI (1941), 185-200—but we know that Wagner had already adapted Schopenhauer's thesis to fit his own in the 1850s, having read the philosopher a decade before Nietzsche did. The recognition of the deeper and more direct expressiveness of music may be found as far back as Aristotle (in the *Politics*, VIII, v-vii,

music is considered the best reflection of moral character), and indeed the idea has probably occurred in one form or another to everyone who has been more than a casual music-lover.

19. *Birth of Tragedy*, chap. xvi; p. 98.

20. *Ibid.*, chap. xxi; pp. 124-31.

21. See the beginning of the note on *The Birth of Tragedy* in *Ecce Homo* (*Werke*, II, 1108).

22. *Birth of Tragedy*, chap. xix; pp. 113-18.

23. Quoted in Alfred Einstein, *Gluck*, tr. Eric Blom, (London, Dent, [Master Musicians], 1936), pp. 98-100.

24. *Birth of Tragedy*, chap. xvii; pp. 106-7.

25. *Ibid.*, chap. xix; pp. 113-18.

26. *Ibid.*, pp. 119-20; and chap. xxiii; p. 138.

27. *Ibid.*, chap. xix; p. 120; and chap. xiv; p. 90; chap. xv; pp. 95-96; chap. xvii; p. 105.

28. *Ibid.*, chap xxi; pp. 126-27.

29. *Ibid.*, p. 127. "The direct answer to Nietzsche's rhetorical question," according to Francis Fergusson (who apparently saw his music-dramas in New York City) "would be that, when the curtain falls on Act III, one does in fact catch the subway toward one's un-primitive home, such as it is—unutterably feeble and discouraged perhaps, but a wretched human individual still." *The Idea of a Theater* (Princeton University Press, 1949), pp. 96-97.

30. *Birth of Tragedy*, "A Critical Backward Glance," chap. iii; p. 6.

31. *Ibid.*, chap. xxi, pp. 127-28.

32. *Ibid.*, p. 128.

33. *Ibid.*, p. 131; and chap. xxii; p. 132.

34. I have substituted the correct text of Isolde's final lines for the slightly incorrect (misremembered?) version given in *Werke*, I, 121.

35. *Birth of Tragedy*, chap. xxi; p. 131.

36. See Kaufmann, *Nietzsche*, pp. 245, 350-51.

37. *The Disinherited Mind* (New York, Noonday Press [Meridian Books], 1959), p. 136.

38. Daniel Halévy, in his biography of Nietzsche—*The Life of Friedrich Nietzsche*, tr. J. M. Hone (New York, Macmillan, 1911) —neglects to observe that Nietzsche did not see *Tristan* before 1872; Hildebrandt doesn't mention it; and Andler, despite his attention to detail, does not point it out, but merely reports the facts that imply that the performances which Nietzsche did attend in 1872 were his first. *Nietzsche*, I, 444. The letters referred to in the footnote on pages 73-74 may be found in *Briefe*, Vol. I, *Briefe der Schüler- und Bonner Stu-*

dentenzeit, ed. Wilhelm Hoppe and Karl Schlechta, pp. 317-22, 322-25, 325-27, 327-29; and II, 325-27, 327-30, 331-32. See also Andler, *Nietzsche,* I, 330.

39. See Halévy, *Life,* p. 132; and Andler, *Nietzsche,* I, 444. The *Annals of Opera, 1597-1940,* ed. Alfred Loewenberg (2d ed. rev., Geneva, Societas Bibliographica, 1955), incorrectly lists the 1872 performances as having been in October.

40. Letter of June 25, 1872, in *Wagner und Nietzsche,* ed. Förster-Nietzsche, p. 122.

41. Letter of June 24/25, 1872, in *Briefe,* III, 253-54.

42. *Ibid.,* p. 257; and the letter of July 24, 1872, to Krug, pp. 267-69. In his own music, we are told, Nietzsche reveled in Wagnerian harmonies. See Newman, *Life,* IV, 323-24. Bülow, who saw some of the scores in 1872, thought *Tristan* was responsible for Nietzsche's musical sins. Nietzsche denied it: "Such music as I wrote," he told Bülow, "I would surely have been unable to compose *after* hearing *Tristan.*" Letter of October, 1872, in *Unpublished Letters,* tr. and ed. Kurt F. Leidecker (New York, Philosophical Library, 1959), p. 61.

43. An *Index to Nietzsche,* ed. Robert Guppy (vol. XVIII of *The Complete Works of Friedrich Nietzsche,* ed. Oscar Levy [New York, Macmillan, 1924]) lists, for example, only four specific references to *Tristan* in Nietzsche's later essays.

44. T. M. Campbell has pointed out that Nietzsche's criticisms of Wagner might have begun even before *The Birth of Tragedy* was finally revised. See the article cited above in note 18, and "Nietzsche-Wagner, to January, 1872," in *PMLA,* LVI (1941), 544-77. Campbell believes that the long *Tristan* section was inserted merely out of loyalty to Wagner, and that by the time Nietzsche had completed his essay he no longer saw Wagner as the hope for a renaissance of tragedy. But even if *Tristan* now seemed to Nietzsche to be a sentimental search for Nirvana rather than the achievement of heroic Dionysian tragedy, the description of *Tristan* indicates that he was nonetheless affected by the music, a fact which is substantiated by his comments on the performances seen after *The Birth of Tragedy* was in print.

45. In *Werke,* II, 1043; tr. by Walter Kaufmann in *The Portable Nietzsche* (New York, Viking Press, 1954), p. 666.

46. See Barzun, *Berlioz and the Romantic Century* (London, Gollancz, 1951), II, 176-202; and André Gide, *Notes on Chopin,* tr. Bernard Frechtman (New York, Philosophical Library, 1949).

47. *Ecce Homo,* chap. ii, 7; in *Werke,* II, 1092.

48. Robert Schumann, *Music and Musicians,* ed. and tr. Fanny

Raymond Ritter (First Series, 8th ed., London, William Reeves, n. d.), p. 178.

49. See Ernest Newman, *Wagner as Man and Artist* (rev. ed., London, John Lane, 1925), p. 178.

50. Noted in William Wallace, *Richard Wagner: As He Lived* (London, Kegan Paul, Trench, Trübner, 1925), p. 99.

51. The quotations in the footnote on page 77 are from Finck, *Wagner* (2 vols., 3d ed., New York, Scribner's, 1896), II, 159-60; and Shaw, *The Perfect Wagnerite* (New York, Brentano's, 1911), p. 130.

52. *The History of Music* (2d ed., New York, Knopf, 1931), p. 238.

53. *Der Fall Wagner*, chap. x; in *Werke*, II, 925.

54. See, for example, Curt Sachs, "The Road to Major," in *The Musical Quarterly*, XXIX (1943), 381-404.

55. *Ecce Homo*, chap. ii, 7; in *Werke*, II, 1092.

56. *Contra Wagner*, in *Werke*, II, 1043 (*Portable Nietzsche*, p. 667).

57. See particularly *Der Fall Wagner*, chap. vii and viii; in *Werke*, II, 916-21.

58. *Jenseits von Gut und Böse*, aphorism 229; in *Werke*, II, 694.

59. *Der Fall Wagner*, chap. vi; in *Werke*, II, 914.

60. *Ibid.*, chaps. vii and viii; in *Werke*, II, 918-19.

61. Morgan, *What Nietzsche Means*, p. 224; *Contra Wagner*, in *Werke*, II, 1041.

62. *Der Fall Wagner*, chap. v; in *Werke*, II, 912.

63. Morgan, *What Nietzsche Means*, p. 224.

64. *Ecce Homo*, chap. ii, 6; in *Werke*, II, 1092.

65. See *Contra Wagner*, in *Werke*, II, 1054-55.

66. *Der Fall Wagner*, Preface; in *Werke*, II, 903-4. The letters quoted in the footnote on page 81 are from *Unpublished Letters*, pp. 154, 152

67. *Der Fall Wagner*, Preface; in *Werke*, II, 904.

68. *Life*, IV, 538.

69. *Ibid.*, p. 539.

70. See Roger Hollinrake, "Nietzsche, Wagner and Ernest Newman," in *Music and Letters*, XLI (no. 3, July, 1960), 245-55.

NOTES TO CHAPTER IV: WAGNER AND TRISTAN IN PARIS

1. See, for example, *Jenseits von Gut und Böse*, aphorism 254, in Nietzsche's *Werke* (Munich, Hanser, 1956), II, 721-23.

2. See Roger Stengel, *Guillaume Lekeu (1870-1894)* (Brussels, Editions de la Nouvelle Revue Belgique, n. d.), p. 58.

3. *Ibid.*, p. 55; O. G. Sonneck, "Guillaume Lekeu," *The Musical*

Quarterly, V (no. 1, January, 1919), 124. See also Paul Prist, *L'Enfant de génie de la musique contemporaine: Guillaume Lekeu* (Brussels, J. Lebèque, 1946).

4. Letter of October 2, 1893, to Chausson, quoted in Edward Lockspeiser, *Debussy* (London, Dent [Master Musicians], 1936), p. 52.

5. Lockspeiser, *Debussy*, (Master Musicians), p. 39.

6. See John Rewald, *Paul Cézanne*, tr. Margaret H. Liebman (London, Spring Books, n. d.), p. 41.

7. See Louis Reynaud, *L'Influence allemande en France au XVIIIe et au XIXe siècle* (Paris, Hachette, 1922), p. 263. It is of course also true that during the seventies the popular press associated Wagner with Prussia.

8. See Gustave Kahn, *Fantin-Latour*, tr. Wilfrid Jackson (London, John Lane, 1927).

9. Quoted in Léon Vallas, *The Theories of Debussy* (Oxford University Press, 1929), p. 80.

10. See Lockspeiser, *Debussy*, (Master Musicians) pp. 54-55.

11. See Raynaud, *L'Influence allemande*, pp. 274-76.

12. Quoted (in French) in Grange Woolley, *Richard Wagner et le Symbolisme Français* (Paris, Presses universitaires de France, 1931), p. 108.

13. *Revue wagnérienne*, I (no. vi, July 8, 1885), 168. See Jacques Barzun, *Darwin, Marx, Wagner* (Garden City, New York, Doubleday [Anchor], 1958), pp. 290-91.

14. *Devant la Douleur* (2d series, Paris, Nouvelle Librairie Nationale, 1915), p. 209.

15. See *Revue wagnérienne*, I (no. xii, January 8, 1886), and II (no. xii, January 15, 1887).

16. See "Richard Wagner et Tannhäuser à Paris," pp. 199-252, in *L'Art Romantique*, ed. Jacques Crépet (Paris, Louis Conard, 1925), Vol. II of *Oeuvres Complètes de Charles Baudelaire*, p. 211.

17. Ferdinand Hiller, *Musikalisches und Persönliches* (Leipzig, Breitkopf and Härtel, 1876), p. 281.

18. Georges Servières, *Richard Wagner jugé en France* (Paris, Henry du Parc, 1887), p. 19. For a review of the chief Wagnerian propagandists in France, see also Kurt Jäckel, *Richard Wagner in der französischen Literatur* (2 vols., Breslau, Priebatsch, 1931), I, 10-46.

19. September 9, 1850, and September 29, 1857; Servières, *Wagner en France*, p. 22. Gérard's article was included in his *Souvenirs de Thuringe* and may be found in the Pléiades edition of his *Oeuvres*, ed. Albert Béguin and Jean Richer (Paris, Gallimard, 1956), II, 794-96.

20. See Woolley, *Wagner et Symbolisme*, pp. 30-36.

21. The articles appeared in June, July, and August; see Servières, *Wagner en France*, pp. 20-26.

22. See Ernest Newman, *The Life of Richard Wagner*, Vol. III, *1859-1866* (New York, Knopf, 1941), p. 3.

23. *Richard Wagner an Mathilde Wesendonk*, Vol. V of *Wagners Briefe* (Leipzig, Breitkopf and Härtel, 1911-13), p. 210.

24. *La Nouvelle Allemagne musicale, Richard Wagner* (Paris, 1866).

25. See Servières, *Wagner en France*, pp. 128-31; and Woolley, *Wagner et Symbolisme*, p. 56.

26. *Grandes figures* was published in Paris in 1860. The other essays in the book are on Balzac and Gérard de Nerval. Champfleury's brochure—*Richard Wagner à Paris*—was published shortly after the January concerts, and within the year was issued in a German translation. See Servières, *Wagner en France*, p. 57.

27. *Wagner an Mathilde*, p. 210.

28. See Servières, *Wagner en France*, pp. 45-54, and, for the quotation of Challemel-Lacour in the footnote on page 91, Newman, *Life*, III, 54.

29. February 9, 1860. Reprinted in *A Travers chants: Etudes musicales, adorations, boutades et critiques* (Paris, Michel Lévy Frères, 1862), p. 297.

30. "Sans autre thème qu'une sort de gémissement chromatique, mais rempli d'accords dissonants dont de longues appoggiatures, remplaçant la note réelle de l'harmonie, augmentent encore la cruauté." *Ibid.*

31. Wagner's letter was published in the *Débats* of February 22. Ernest Newman finds the "friendly letter" a "model of dignity and restraint"; Jacques Barzun considers it "a master stroke for putting Berlioz in the wrong." See Newman, *Life*, III, 17-21, and Barzun, *Berlioz and the Romantic Century* (London, Gollancz, 1951), II, 172-77.

32. *Wagner an Mathilde*, p. 206.

33. Here is an exerpt. The story of *Tristan* is one of "endless yearning, longing, the bliss and the wretchedness of love; world, power, fame, honor, chivalry, loyalty, and friendship all blown away like an insubstantial dream; one thing alone left living—longing, longing unquenchable, a yearning, a hunger, a languishing forever renewing itself; one sole redemption—death, surcease, a sleep without awakening. . . . In one long succession of linked phrases" the composer "let that insatiable longing swell forth from the timidest avowal to sweetest protraction, through anxious sighs, through hopes and fears, laments and desires, bliss and torment, to the mightiest forward-pressing, the most

powerful effort to find the breach that will open out to the infinitely craving heart the path into the sea of love's endless delight. In vain! The exhausted heart sinks back, to pine away in a longing that can never attain its end, since each attainment brings in its wake only renewed desire, till in final exhaustion the breaking eye catches a glimpse of the attainment of the highest bliss—the bliss of dying, of ceasing to be, of final redemption into that wondrous realm from which we only stray the further the more we struggle to enter it by force. Shall we call it Death? Or is it not the wonder-world of Night?" Quoted in Ernest Newman, *The Wagner Operas* (New York, Knopf, 1949), p. 206.

34. *Wagner an Mathilde*, p. 217.

35. Newman, *Life*, III, 21-22. See also Wagner's *Mein Leben* (Munich, Bruckmann, 1911), II, 730.

36. *Mein Leben*, II, 770.

37. See, for example, Paul Bekker, *Richard Wagner* (London and Toronto, Dent, 1931), p. 331.

38. See Newman, *Life*, III, 25-27.

39. The three performances were on March 13, 18, and 24.

40. See Barzun, *Berlioz*, II, 180-81.

41. Servières, *Wagner en France*, pp. 80-113.

42. *Memoirs of Malwida von Meysenbug* (New York, Norton, 1936), p. 306.

43. Letter of February 13, 1860; see Enid Starkie, *Baudelaire* (New York, Putnam's, 1933), pp. 331-32.

44. "Les Phares," *Les Fleurs de Mal*, VI.

45. *Jenseits von Gut und Böse*, aphorism 256, in *Werke*, II, 725.

46. See Starkie, *Baudelaire*, pp. 336-38.

47. *Ibid.*, pp. 184, 189-90, 221. See also André Ferran, *L'Esthétique de Baudelaire* (Paris, Hachette, 1933), Part II; and Margaret Gilman, *Baudelaire the Critic* (New York, Columbia University Press, 1943), pp. 113-14.

48. In *L'Art Romantique*, p. 208. The *Tannhäuser* essay first appeared in *La Revue Européenne* of April 1, 1861, and then in *La Presse Théâtrale et Musicale* of April 14 and 21, and May 5, 1861. It was issued as a pamphlet in 1861 (with some additional remarks dated April 8) and collected in *L'Art Romantique* of 1868.

49. See A. G. Lehmann, *The Symbolist Aesthetic in France* (Oxford, Blackwell, 1950), pp. 213 ff.

50. In *L'Art Romantique*, p. 206.

51. See Isabelle Wyzewska, *La Revue wagnérienne, essai sur l'interpretation esthétique de Wagner en France* (Paris, Librairie Académique

Perrin, 1934), pp. 46, 59; and Ferran, *Esthétique de Baudelaire*, pp. 356-61.

52. *L'Art Romantique*, p. 219.

53. See Gilman, *Baudelaire the Critic*, pp. 174 ff.

54. *L'Art Romantique*, p. 209.

55. Quoted in Starkie, *Baudelaire*, p. 334.

56. "La Musique," *Fleurs de Mal*, LXIX.

57. See Appendix B.

58. *Tannhäuser* essay, in *L'Art Romantique*, p. 239.

59. *Ibid.*, p. 221.

60. See Servières, *Wagner en France*, pp. 116, 228-30, 297. There exists a monograph that lists all the performances of Wagner in France between 1850 and 1914: *L'Oeuvre de Richard Wagner à Paris* (Paris, Maurice Sénart, 1920).

61. See Romain Rolland, *Musicians of Today*, tr. Mary Blaiklock (New York, Holt, 1915), pp. 273-83.

62. See Servières, *Wagner en France*, pp. 121-22, 126-28. The count of Frenchmen at the Munich *Tristan* excludes embassy personnel. Leroy's article was in the *Nain Jaune* of June 19, 1865.

63. *Le Rêve d'une vie* (Paris, Perrin, 1928), p. 8.

64. *Le Drame musicale: Richard Wagner, son oeuvre et son idée* (2d ed., Paris, Perrin, 1895).

65. See Newman, *The Life of Richard Wagner*, Vol. IV, *1866-1883* (New York, Knopf, 1946), pp. 277-78n.

66. Edouard Dujardin, " 'La Revue wagnérienne,' " *Revue Musicale*, October, 1923, pp. 237-56. The essay is reprinted in Dujardin's *Mallarmé, par un des siens* (Paris, Albert Messein, 1936), pp. 195-234.

67. Curiously enough, in one of Schuré's later books, *The Mystical Idea in Wagner*, tr. Fred Rothwell (Hampstead, Priory Press, 1910), *Tristan* is not mentioned at all. The book is divided into three sections: The Revolutionary Period (*Tannhäuser* and *Lohengrin*); The Period of Pessimism (the *Ring*); and The Christian Period (*Parsifal*). Schuré considers Wagner chiefly as an esoteric poet and the restorer of tragedy.

68. See Servières, *Wagner en France*, pp. 138-39; Newman, *Life*, III, 124; and Martin Cooper, *French Music, from the Death of Berlioz to the Death of Fauré* (London, Oxford University Press, 1951), p. 56.

69. See *Die Briefe Richard Wagners an Judith Gautier* (with an introduction on "Die Freundschaft Richard Wagners mit Judith Gautier"), ed. Willi Schuh (Zurich and Leipzig, Rotapfel, n. d.). Mendès and Judith separated in 1874. For a satirical portrait of Mendès in his later years, written by Jean Cocteau, see Edward Lockspeiser, *Debussy: His Life and Mind* (Vol. I, London, Cassell, 1962), p. 98.

70. See Newman, *Life*, IV, 271-72, 277. Dujardin says that Mendès remembered Wagner's insult to France only after the Wagners took Judith's part at the time the couple separated (*Mallarmé*, p. 203).

71. See the summaries of the novel in Newman, *Life*, IV, 57-58n; and Jäckel, *Wagner in französischen Literatur*, II, 24-30.

72. *Revue wagnérienne*, I (no. 5, June 8, 1885), 131-51.

73. Translation quoted in Cooper, *French Music*, pp. 56-57. See Cooper's intelligent account of French theoretical Wagnerism, pp. 55-60.

74. Quoted in Victor I. Seroff, *Debussy: Musician of France* (New York, Putnam's, 1956), p. 101.

75. See Lehmann, *Symbolist Aesthetic*, p. 194.

76. Quoted in Seroff, *Debussy*, p. 201.

77. *Wagner at Home*, tr. Effie Dunreith Massie (New York, John Lane, 1911), p. 2

78. *Ibid.*, p. 3.

79. *Briefe Wagners an Judith*, p. 145.

80. *Life*, IV, 606.

81. See Servières, *Wagner en France*, p. 227n.

82. *Richard Wagner and His Poetical Work*, tr. L. S. J. (Boston, A. Williams, 1883), pp. 5-6.

83. See Servières, *Wagner en France*, pp. 139-47. *Rienzi* was the first of a projected series of productions of all of Wagner's works.

84. *Ibid.*, pp. 140-41, 151-52.

85. *Deutsche Kunst und deutsche Politik*, in *Schriften*, vol. VIII. See Newman, *Life*, IV, 94-96.

86. Quoted in Newman, *Life*, IV, 278n.

87. Quoted in Winton Dean, *Bizet* (London, Dent [Master Musicians], 1948), p. 91.

88. See Servières, *Wagner en France*, pp. 169-88.

89. *Ibid.*, pp. 206-15.

90. *Ibid.*, pp. 229-30, 248-49, 263, 265, 273 ff.; Dujardin, *Mallarmé*, p. 198.

91. *Wagner en France*, p. xi.

92. Issue of May 1, 1887.

93. *Musicians of Today*, p. 253.

94. "Les Premiers Amis Français de Wagner," *Revue Musicale*, October, 1923, pp. 115-38; quoted in Woolley, *Wagner et Symbolisme*, p. 96.

95. See Woolley, *Wagner et Symbolisme*, pp. 144-46, 150-52; and Malcolm Brown, *George Moore: A Reconsideration* (Seattle, University of Washington Press, 1955), p. 142.

96. Other contributors were Alfred Ernst, René Ghil, Louis de Fourcaud, Victor Wilder, Georges Nouffland, Edouard Rod, Emile Hennequin, Pierre Bonnier, Charles Morice, Charles Vignier, and Jules de Brayer. The last-named was supposed to have made the journey from Paris to Bayreuth on foot. See Dujardin, *Mallarmé*, pp. 213-14.

97. *Ibid.*, p. 197.

98. *Ibid.*, pp. 199-200.

99. *Ibid.*, p. 200.

100. *Ibid.*, pp. 205-6.

101. Quoted in Lehmann, *Symbolist Aesthetic*, p. 194.

102. *Ibid.*

103. *Ibid.*, pp. 194 ff., for an account of Wyzewa's contradictions. According to Romain Rolland, Wyzewa did not study "the literature that commented on and the paintings that illustrated Wagner's works, but the literature and painting that were inspired by Wagner's principles—from Egyptian statuary to Degas's paintings, from Homer's writings to those of Villiers de l'Isle Adam" (*Musicians of Today*, p. 253).

104. In I (no. 11, December 8, 1885), 314-29.

105. *Ibid.*, p. 329. See Barzun, *Darwin, Marx, Wagner*, p. 201.

106. See *The Music Dramas of Richard Wagner*, tr. Esther Singleton (New York, Dodd, Mead, 1898).

107. In I (no. 7, August 8, 1885), 195-200. It was reprinted in *Pages* (1891) and *Divagations* (1897), and in the Pléiades edition of *Oeuvres complètes*, ed. Henri Mondor and G. Jean-Aubry (Paris, Gallimard, 1945), pp. 541-46. There is an English translation in *Mallarmé: Selected Prose Poems, Essays and Letters*, tr. Bradford Cook (Baltimore, Johns Hopkins Press, 1956), pp. 72-73.

108. See *Oeuvres*, p. 1586.

109. See Lehmann, *Symbolist Aesthetic*, p. 150; and Joseph Chiari, *Symbolisme from Poe to Mallarmé* (London, Rockliff, 1956), pp. 131-32.

110. *Oeuvres*, p. 1585; tr. by Cook in *Prose Poems*, p. 146.

111. See E. Carcassonne, "Wagner et Mallarmé," *Revue de Littérature Comparée*, XVI (no. 2, April-June, 1936), 347-66.

112. See Lehmann, *Symbolist Aesthetic*, p. 230.

113. "Est-ce qu'un fait spirituel, l'épanouissement de symboles, ou leur préparation, nécessite endroit, pour s'y développer, autre que le fictif foyer de vision dardé par le regard d'une foule! Saint de Saints, mais mental. . . ." The translation is by Cook, in *Prose Poems*, p. 77.

114. See Chiari, *Symbolisme*, pp. 127-45; and Hasye Cooperman,

The Aesthetics of Stephane Mallarmé (New York, Hasye Cooperman, 1933). Bradford Cook observes that Mallarmé came to feel "the inapplicability, to his own genius and to the essential quietness and abstractness of Symbolism, of the highly colored, openly sensuous, and somewhat noisy art of Wagner. . . . He quickly returns to the claims of the written word as though in fear of drowning in the musical sea." See introduction to *Prose Poems*, p. 77.

115. Wilson, *Axel's Castle* (New York and London, Scribner's, 1948), p. 21; Symons, *The Symbolist Movement in Literature* (rev. ed., New York. Dutton, 1919), p. 8.

116. Symons, *Symbolist Movement*, p. 6.

117. Quoted in Wilson, *Axel's Castle*, p. 20.

118. *Ibid.*, p. 18.

119. See Appendix C.

120. Quoted in *The Poem Itself*, ed. Stanley Burnshaw (New York, Rinehart and Winston, 1960, p. 58.

121. *Mallarmé*, pp. 207-8.

122. See Jean-Pierre Barricelli and Leo Weinstein, *Ernst Chausson* (Norman, University of Oklahoma Press, 1955), pp. 34-35; and, for a list of the items in Chabrier's art collection, Joseph Desnayard, *Emmanuel Chabrier, d'après ses lettres* (Paris, Fernand Roches, 1943), pp. 352-54.

123. See Charles Oulmont, *Musique de l'amour* (2 vols., Paris, Desclée de Brouwer, 1935), Vol. II (on Duparc).

124. Cooper, *French Music*, p. 67. See also Sydney Northcote, *The Songs of Henri Duparc* (London, Dennis Dobson, 1949), p. 99.

125. The quotations of Duparc and Lekeu are from Cooper, *French Music*, p. 3 and p. 67.

126. *Ibid.*, p. 38.

127. *Le Roi malgré lui* (1887). See Eric Blom, "The Tragedy of a Comic Opera," in *Stepchildren of Music* (New York, Dial Press, 1926), pp. 173-79.

128. Chabrier is usually described as having been "chorus master"— as though *Tristan* had a chorus as large as that in *Lohengrin*. Chabrier "rehearsed the chorus for the production of the first two acts of *Tristan*," according to Martin Cooper, who forgot for a moment that in the second act there is no chorus at all (*French Music*, p. 39). The *Souvenirs de Munich* contain a *Galop* that is based on a tune which it is difficult at first to identify, but which turns out to be the music of the chorus of sailors in Act I. The score of the *Souvenirs* ("pour piano à quatre mains, sur les thèmes favoris de *Tristan et Iseult*") was printed

in the Chabrier issue of *S. I. M., Revue musicale mensuelle*, April 15, 1911, pp. 33 ff.

129. *A Hundred Years of Music* (London, Duckworth, 1949), p. 201. The statement is also inaccurate. Chabrier heard *Tristan* at *Munich* in 1879. It was not performed at Bayreuth until 1886. He heard it again (and wept) in 1889, this time at Bayreuth. On the effect of the 1879 *Tristan* on Chabrier, see Desnayard, *Chabrier*, p. 34.

130. See Cooper, *French Music*, p. 40.

131. Quoted in Edward Burlingame Hill, *Modern French Music* (Boston and New York, Houghton Mifflin, 1924), p. 63.

132. Letter of December 1, 1887, in Desnayard, *Chabrier*, pp. 140-41.

133. Vocal score, arr. André Messager (Paris, Enoch Frères et Costallat, n. d.), pp. 164, 136, 263, 265-68.

134. *Ibid.*, pp. 247, 261; see also the contralto of the chorus, p. 43.

135. Quoted in Léon Vallas, *Vincent d'Indy* (2 vols., Paris, Albin Michel, 1946), II, 297.

136. *Richard Wagner* (Paris, Delagrave, 1930).

137. Vocal score, arr. d'Indy (Paris, A. Durand et Fils, 1895). See also Vallas, *d'Indy*, II, 283-308.

138. See for example the love scene in Act I, and vocal score, pp. 124, 137.

139. Vocal score (Paris, A. Durand et Fils, 1902), pp. 29 ff. See also pp. 94-96; and Woolley, *Wagner et Symbolisme*, p. 158.

140. See Vallas, *d'Indy*, II, 308-26; and Cooper, *French Music*, pp. 118-19.

141. See Abraham, *Hundred Years*, p. 202. A list of French "Wagnerian" operas written in the last fifteen years of the century would include Lalo's *Roi d'Ys* (1888), Reyer's *Salammbô* (1890), Bruneau's *Le Rêve* (1891) and *L'Attaque du Moulin* (1893), Bourgault-Ducoudray's *Thamara* (1891), and Camille Erlanger's *Julien l'Hospitalier* (1891).

142. Quoted in Abraham, *Hundred Years*, pp. 203-4.

143. Barricelli and Weinstein, *Chausson*, pp. 11, 27-28.

144. *Ibid.*, pp. 72, 38, 67, 27. For one of the most obvious imprints of *Tristan* on *Le Roi Arthus*, see the rhythm at the height of the love duet, in the vocal score (Paris, Choudens, 1920), p. 154.

145. Quoted in Lockspeiser, *Debussy* (Master Musicians), p. 225.

146. *Ibid.*, pp. 26, 115, 117, 49; Vallas, *Theories of Debussy*, pp. 112-13.

147. According to Edward Lockspeiser, "recently published correspondence reveals that the Wagnerian conflict preoccupied Debussy

throughout his career." "We recently had a very serious conversation on the subject of Richard Wagner," Debussy once wrote to Pierre Louÿs. "I merely stated that Wagner was the greatest man who had ever existed, and I went no further. I didn't say that he was God himself, though indeed I may have thought something of the sort." Quoted in "The Mind of Debussy," *The Listener*, LXVII (no. 1729, May 17, 1962), 853-54. In his recent full biography of Debussy, Lockspeiser concludes that the composer both admired and feared Wagner (*Debussy: Life and Mind*, p. 91). "It is certain that Debussy's attitude to Wagner was complex, compounded of love and fear, displaying many contradictions and compelling him to lash out with ironic jibes at the object of his admiration" (*Ibid.*, p. 96).

148. Joseph Kerman, in *Opera and Drama* (New York, Knopf, 1956), has aptly characterized *Pelléas* as a Sung Play, while *Tristan* is a Symphonic Poem. The famous Interludes between the scenes of *Pelléas* derive, needless to say, from *Parsifal*. "That's the whole of *Parsifal*," Richard Strauss announced about a passage in *Pelléas*, when he heard it for the first time. Quoted in Lockspeiser, *Debussy: Life and Mind*, p. 96n.

149. Gray, *A Survey of Contemporary Music* (London, Oxford University Press, 1927), p. 99.

NOTES TO CHAPTER V: LOVE AND DEATH IN VENICE

1. Marcel Proust, *Swann's Way*, tr. C. K. Scott-Moncrieff (New York, Random House [Modern Library], 1928), p. 270.

2. *Ibid.*, pp. 294-95.

3. *Axel's Castle* (New York and London, Scribner's, 1948), p. 259.

4. See Harry T. Moore, *The Life and Works of D. H. Lawrence* (New York, Twayne, 1951), p. 82.

5. *The Trespasser* (London, Heinemann, 1912), p. 35.

6. *Ibid.*, p. 138.

7. *Ibid.*, pp. 24, 51, 284, 26-27.

8. *Ibid.*, pp. 290, 37, 92, 110.

9. *Ibid.*, pp. 117, 128, 189, 260.

10. *Ibid.*, pp. 76, 87, 31-32.

11. *Ibid.*, pp. 29-30.

12. See, for example, Morgan's *Sparkenbroke* (New York, Macmillan, 1936), in which the hero is writing a book about *Tristan*.

13. *The Dark Sun: A Study of D. H. Lawrence* (New York, Macmillan, 1957), p. 41.

14. Walter Hamilton, *The Aesthetic Movement in England* (2d ed., London, Reeves and Turner, 1882), pp. 32-34.

15. *The Picture of Dorian Gray*, in *The Works of Oscar Wilde*, ed. G. F. Maine (London and Glasgow, Collins, 1948), p. 107.

16. See *Evelyn Innes* (1898; New York and London, Appleton, 1927), pp. 173 ff. *Sister Teresa* (1901) is its sequel.

17. See *The Lake* (London, Heinemann, 1905), pp. 168-72.

18. Quoted in Joseph Hone, *The Life of George Moore* (New York, Macmillan, 1936), p. 213.

19. *Ibid.*, p. 132.

20. *Ibid.*, p. 131.

21. *Ibid.*

22. See Alfredo Casella, *et al.*, *Gabriele D'Annunzio e La Musica* (Milan, Fratelli Bocca, 1939); and G. Donati-Petteni, *D'Annunzio e Wagner* (Florence, Felice le Monnier, 1923).

23. Letter of November 27, 1916, quoted in Harry T. Moore, *The Intelligent Heart: The Story of D. H. Lawrence* (New York, Farrar, Straus and Young, 1954), p. 219.

24. *Trionfo della Morte* (6th ed., Milan, Fratelli Treves, 1896); English trans., *The Triumph of Death*, by Arthur Hornblow (Boston, L. C. Page, 1896). References, with one exception, will be to the Hornblow translation (which is also available as a Modern Library edition), but I have retained the Italian forms of the names of the characters. The novel first appeared in 1889 in the *Tribuna Illustrata*, under the title *L'Invincibile*. It is one of the series "I Romanza della Rosa."

25. *Triumph of Death*, pp. 393-95.

26. *Ibid.*, pp. 307-8.

27. *Ibid.*, pp. 35-36, 144, 330. The passage quoted in the footnote on page 132 is from p. 311.

28. *Ibid.*, pp. 38-39.

29. *Ibid.*, p. 363.

30. "Con una divorante furia, come un incendio all' improvviso erotto da un abisso ignorato, il desiderio si dilatava, s'agitava, fiammeggiava sempre più alto, sempre più alto, alimentato dalla più pura essenza di una duplice vita. . . . Ma contro un invisibile ostacolo quel gran getto vitale si frangeva d'improvviso, ricadeva, s'estingueva, non risorgeva più." *Trionfo della Morte*, pp. 438-39. Compare with Wagner's program notes, quoted in n. 33 to chap. IV. above. At the turn of the century D'Annunzio's description of *Tristan* was well enough admired to be printed separately as a set piece. See "Tristan and Isolde," tr.

Mrs. V. M. Crawford, in *Studies in Music* (by various authors), re-printed from *The Musician*, ed. Robin Grey (London, Simpkin, Mar-shall, Hamilton, Kent, 1901), pp. 137-51.

31. *Triumph of Death*, p. 366.

32. *Ibid.*, pp. 370-71.

33. *Ibid.*, p. 379.

34. *Ibid.*, p. 398.

35. *Ibid.*, p. 380.

36. *Ibid.*, p. 412.

37. *Ibid.*, p. 384.

38. Hatto translation (Baltimore, Penguin Books, 1960) p. 42.

39. This is according to Tom Antongini, *D'Annunzio* (London, Heinemann, 1938), p. 218. The fact (or poetic surmise) is not men-tioned in any of the later biographies of D'Annunzio, or in the standard biographies of Wagner. In 1911 D'Annunzio *was* chosen to compose the inscription on the monument commemorating Wagner's death at the Venetian palazzo. *Ibid.*, pp. 217-20.

40. *The Flame of Life*, tr. Kassandra Vivaria (Boston, L. C. Page, 1900), pp. 399-401.

41. See *Richard Wagner an Mathilde Wesendonk*, Vol. V of *Wag-ners Briefe* (Leipzig, Breitkopf and Härtel, 1911-13), pp. 48-49; and Finck, *Wagner and His Works* (New York, Scribner's, 1896), II, 442.

42. *Ecce Homo*, ii, 7; in *Werke* (Munich, Hanser, 1956), II, 1092-93. See also Ernst Bertram, *Nietzsche, Versuch einer Mythologie* (Berlin, Bondi, 1920), p. 290.

43. See "Sufferings and Greatness of Richard Wagner," in *Essays of Three Decades*, tr. H. T. Lowe-Porter (New York, Knopf, 1947), p. 351.

44. Quoted in R. Hinton Thomas, *Thomas Mann: The Mediation of Art* (Oxford University Press, 1956), p. 36. Thomas, carried away by the neatness of the coincidences, refers to Venice as "the place where Wagner's *Tristan* was born and where Wagner died" (p. 36). The first part of this statement is of course inaccurate.

45. Letter of May 25, 1926, to Ernst Fischer, in "Letters of Thomas Mann," tr. Ralph Mannheim, in *Encounter*, no. 111 (December, 1962), p. 8. Mann wrote an essay on Wagner in the year in which *Death in Venice* appeared: "Wie Stehen Wir Heute zu Richard Wagner?" in *Reden und Aufsätze*, Vol. II, which is Vol. X of *Gesammelte Werke* (12 vols., Frankfurt a. M., S. Fischer, 1960), pp. 893-96.

46. See R. H. Thomas, *Mann*, pp. 75-77.

47. *Ibid.*, p. 79. My italics.

48. In *Stories of Three Decades*, tr. H. T. Lowe-Porter (New York, Knopf, 1936), p. 401.

49. *Ibid.*, pp. 401-2.

50. See Bertram, *Nietzsche*, p. 293; and R. H. Thomas, *Mann*, p. 77.

51. *Stories of Three Decades*, p. 431.

52. *Ibid.*, pp. 411, 413, 423.

53. *Stories of Three Decades*, p. 307.

54. *Ibid.*, p. 314.

55. Music, Mann's daughter Monika has observed, was for her father "necessarily somehow linked with sin. For all that, it may be a divine sin, and no small stimulus to his own art." Quoted in Ethel E. Caro, "Music and Thomas Mann." (Stanford University Press, 1959), p. 3.

56. *A Sketch of My Life*, tr. H. T. Lowe-Porter (New York, Knopf, 1960), pp. 18-19.

57. *Ibid.*, pp. 24-25. The quotation in the footnote on page 141 is from pp. 25-26.

58. *Ibid.*, p. 27.

59. *Buddenbrooks*, tr. H. T. Lowe-Porter (New York, Knopf, 1946), p. 413.

60. *Ibid.*

61. See Frank Donald Hirschbach, *The Arrow and the Lyre: A Study of Love in the Works of Thomas Mann* (The Hague, Martinus Nijhoft, 1955), p. 178.

62. *Buddenbrooks*, pp. 595, 597. The quotations in the footnote on page 142 are from pp. 596-97. See R. H. Thomas, *Mann*, p. 51.

63. J. M. Lindsay, *Thomas Mann* (Oxford, Basil Blackwell, 1954), p. 41.

64. "Sufferings and Greatness," in *Essays of Three Decades*, p. 321. The passage quoted in the footnote on page 143 is from p. 314.

65. So I am told by, among others, the German tutor at an American women's college, who plays recordings of *Tristan* excerpts before her students study Mann's story, to demonstrate the remarkable "translation" of Wagner's music in Mann's prose. See Henry Hatfield, *Thomas Mann* (Norfolk, Conn., New Directions, 1951), p. 25.

66. *Stories of Three Decades*, p. 155.

67. In his account of the genesis of *Doctor Faustus*, Mann often mentions the talks he had with Theodor Adorno and Hans Eisler, both of whom had strongly ambivalent attitudes to Wagner. Adorno's book on Wagner, with its critical dichotomies, reminded Mann of his own Wagner essay. Eisler's talk about Wagner was compounded of "enthusiasm and malice." *The Story of a Novel: The Genesis of*

Doctor Faustus, tr. Richard and Clara Winston (New York, Knopf, 1961), pp. 94-95, 103, 226. See Theodor W. Adorno, *Versuch über Wagner* (Berlin and Frankfurt a. M., Suhrkamp, 1952).

68. On February 10. Later in 1933 the speech was repeated at Amsterdam, Brussels, and Paris. In 1937 Mann used an abridged version of the essay as a lecture, in German, at the New School for Social Research in New York. The essay was included in the volume to which it contributed part of the title, *Leiden und Grösse der Meister* (1935), and it appeared in English in *Past Masters and Other Papers* (1933). It was also issued in 1937 together with the essays on Freud and Goethe.

69. *Essays of Three Decades*, pp. 308-11.

70. *Ibid.*, p. 349.

71. *Ibid.*, p. 350.

72. *Ibid.*, p. 307.

73. Quoted in *Thomas Mann's World*, ed. Joseph Gerard Brennan (New York, Columbia University Press, 1942), p. 104.

74. Lindsay, *Mann*, p. 76.

75. See, for example, Ronald Peacock, *Das Leitmotif bei Thomas Mann* (Bern, P. Haupt, 1934); Hatfield, *Mann*; and Lindsay, *Mann*.

76. *Essays of Three Decades*, p. 311.

77. In the introduction to *The Magic Mountain*, tr. H. T. Lowe-Porter (New York, Knopf, 1951), p. vi.

78. *Essays of Three Decades*, p. 314.

79. *Ibid.*, p. 321.

80. *Ibid.*, p. 314.

81. See also *Story of a Novel*, p. 228.

82. *Essays of Three Decades*, p. 337.

83. *Ibid.*, p. 338

84. *Ibid.* The letter quoted in the footnote on page 148 is printed in the revised edition of Viereck's *Metapolitics: The Roots of the Nazi Mind*, (New York, Knopf [Capricorn Books], 1961), pp. 356-63.

NOTES TO CHAPTER VI: TO THE FINAL PERFORMANCE

1. On the echoing of *Tristan*—done "in a way which is so brazen as to be amusing"—in Strauss's earlier opera *Guntram* (1894), see Norman Del Mar, *Richard Strauss* (Vol. I, London, Barrie and Rockliff, 1962), pp. 119, 99, 107. Later, according to Willi Schuh (quoted by Del Mar, p. 354), the love-duet is parodied by Octavian in the first act of *Der Rosenkavalier*.

2. Richard Specht, *Giacomo Puccini*, tr. Catherine Alison Philips (New York, Knopf, 1933), p. 200.

3. Shaw, *How to Become a Musical Critic*, ed. Dan H. Laurence

(New York, Hill and Wang, 1961), p. 82. The Humperdinck works referred to are *Dornröschen* (1902) and *Die Heirat wider Willen* (1905).

4. Dika Newlin, *Bruckner, Mahler, Schoenberg* (New York, King's Crown Press, 1947), p. 3.

5. *Ibid.*, p. 254.

6. At the Nouveau Théâtre in 1899, at the Chateau d'Eau in 1902, and at the Opéra, for the first time, in 1914.

7. Later *Tristan* was performed in Czech, Danish, Flemish, Dutch, Norwegian, Rumanian, Croatian, and Lettish.

8. See Irving Kolodin, *The Story of the Metropolitan Opera: 1883-1950* (New York, Knopf, 1953).

9. Alma Mahler, *Gustav Mahler: Erinnerungen und Briefe* (Amsterdam, Albert de Lange, 1940), p. 119.

10. See Newlin, *Bruckner, Mahler, Schoenberg*, pp. 138-39. *Die Musik und die Inscenierung* (Munich, F. Bruckmann, 1899) was a German translation of Appia's French text. Until recently only the appendix on *Tristan* was available in English: "The Staging of *Tristan and Isolde*," tr. Lee Simonson, in *Theatre Workshop*, I (no. 3, April-July, 1937), 61-72. Recently the entire work has appeared, as number 3 in the Books of the Theatre Series, ed. by H. D. Albright: *Music and the Art of the Theatre*, tr. Robert W. Corrigan and Mary Douglas Dirks (Coral Gables, University of Miami Press, 1962). In this edition the appendix on the staging of *Tristan* is translated by Walter R. Volbach.

11. *Music and the Art of the Theatre*, p. 9.

12. *Ibid.*, p. 200.

13. *Ibid.*, p. 198.

14. *Ibid.*, p. 204.

15. *Ibid.*, pp. 217-18.

16. *Ibid.*, p. 120.

17. For a late and mild example of the view of Wagner as the most cultured composer, see Ernest Newman, *More Essays from the World of Music*, ed. Felix Aprahamian (New York, Coward-McCann, 1958), p. 37.

18. See *Haupterscheinung der Kunst- und Kulturgeschichte in Lichte der Anschauung Richard Wagners* (2 vols., Leipzig, Breitkopf and Härtel, 1891).

19. *Life of Richard Wagner* (6 vols., London, Kegan Paul, Trench, Trübner, 1900-8).

20. They are: Paul Moos, *Richard Wagner als Aesthetiker* (Berlin

and Leipzig, Schuster and Loeffler, 1906); Arthur Symons, "The Ideas of Richard Wagner," in *Studies in the Seven Arts* (New York, Dutton, 1906); and Raoul Richter, *Kunst und Philosophie bei Richard Wagner* (Leipzig, Quelle and Meyer, 1906).

21. *Bayreuther Blätter: Monatsschrift des Bayreuther Patronatvereines, unter Mitwirkung Richard Wagners,* I (1878)–LXI (no. 6, November/December, 1938). The subtitle varies.

22. *Das Drama Richard Wagners* (5th ed., Leipzig, Breitkopf and Härtel, 1913).

23. Ellis' *Richard Wagner to Mathilde Wesendonck* (London, H. Grevel, 1905) is a good example.

24. The book was published in Boston and New York by Houghton Mifflin (1903).

25. See *J. S. Bach*, tr. Ernest Newman (2 vols., Leipzig and New York, Breitkopf and Härtel, 1911), I, 1.

26. "Bayreuth and Back," from *The Hawk*, August 13, 1889; in *Musical Critic*, p. 147.

27. Lavignac, *The Music Dramas of Richard Wagner* (New York, Dodd, Mead, 1898), pp. 13-14.

28. Lavignac was also the editor of the *Encyclopédie de la Musique et Dictionnaire du Conservatoire*. He taught theory to the student Debussy, and introduced to him the music of Wagner. See Edward Lockspeiser, *Debussy: His Life and Mind* (London, Cassell, 1962), p. 31.

29. Henderson, *Richard Wagner: His Life and His Dramas* (New York, Putnam's, 1901); Newman, *A Study of Wagner* (London, B. Dobell, 1899); and *Wagner* (London, P. Wellby, 1904).

30. See *Wagner as Man and Artist* (London, John Lane, 1925), Appendix A; and *The Life of Richard Wagner*, Vol. I, *1813-1848* (New York, Knopf, 1933), pp. 14 ff.

31. *Man and Artist*, p. 153.

32. See *The Perfect Wagnerite* (New York, Brentano's, 1911); and "The Sanity of Art," in *Major Critical Essays* (London, Constable, 1932).

33. See *What is Art?*, tr. Aylmer Maude (London, Oxford University Press [World's Classics], 1930).

34. See Max Nordau, *Degeneration* (tr. from 2d ed., New York, Appleton, 1895), Book II, chaps. iv, v; Book III, chap. iv.

35. See Nietzsche, *Unpublished Letters* (New York, Philosophical Library, 1959), p. 145.

36. Letter of October 18, 1888, *ibid.*, pp. 143-44.

37. Letter to Meta von Salis, *ibid.*, p. 145.

38. *Letters of Romain Rolland and Malwida von Meysenbug, 1890-1891,* tr. Thomas J. Wilson (New York, Holt, 1933), pp. 6, 4, 23-24, 88, 272.

39. *Musicians of Today* (New York, Holt, 1915), p. 95.

40. *Ibid.,* pp. 90-94.

41. *Ibid.,* p. 94.

42. *Musiciens d'Aujour d'hui* appeared in 1908, but it was not translated into English until 1915.

43. Beginning in 1891, Huneker was the music critic for the (new) New York *Evening Recorder.* In 1900 he moved to *The Sun,* for which he also wrote about art and literature. After 1917 he wrote music criticism for the Philadelphia *Press* and, later, until his death in 1921, for the New York *World.* The first and long-awaited full-length biography of Huneker has recently appeared: Arnold T. Schwab, *James Gibbons Huneker: Critic of the Seven Arts* (Stanford University Press, 1963).

44. "James Huneker," in the *Dictionary of American Biography.*

45. *Overtones: A Book of Temperaments* (London, Isbister, 1904), p. 2

46. Schwab, *Huneker,* pp. 38, 41.

47. *Ibid.,* p. 122.

48. *Overtones,* pp. 106-7

49. "Parsifal: A Mystic Melodrama," in *Overtones,* p. 93. An earlier version of this essay had appeared in *The Musical Courier.*

50. *Ibid.*

51. *Overtones,* pp. 134, 308.

52. Schwab, *Huneker,* p. 104.

53. *Overtones,* pp. 330, 134, 331.

54. *Ibid.,* p. 330. My italics.

55. "The action is psychologic rather than theatric." *Ibid.,* p. 329.

56. *Ibid.,* pp. 327-29.

57. *Ibid.,* p. 327.

58. See Newman, *The Life of Richard Wagner,* Vol. IV, *1866-1883* (New York, Knopf, 1946), p. 464.

59. *Overtones,* p. 330.

60. *The Longest Journey* (1907; Norfolk, Conn., New Directions [New Classics] 1922), p. 163.

61. See Abraham, *A Hundred Years of Music* (London, Duckworth, 1949), pp. 138-39.

62. See *The Story of a Novel* (New York, Knopf, 1961), p. 95.

63. *Geheimnis der Form* (4 vols., Berlin: Max Hesse, 1924-33), Vol.

I (on the *Ring*), pp. 44-48 and *passim*. For my account of Lorenz I am indebted to an unpublished paper by Bruce McKinney, "Alfred Lorenz and Form in Wagner's *Tristan*."

64. *Geheimnis der Form*, Vol. II (on Tristan, published in 1926), pp. 181-84. Lorenz had predecessors in the profession of investigating the structure of Wagner's music-dramas. Guido Adler, in 1904, had noted that "in *Tristan* one finds a series of passages, musically symmetrical, . . . which contribute more than a little to the holding together of the entire structure." Quoted in Abraham, *Hundred Years of Music*, p. 143.

65. Lorenz quotes Alois John, who talks about *Tristan* "obeying no law, singing its melodies like the storm wind or, transformed into a holy whisper, rustling the spring flowers. . . . Such an original autocratic power is the absolute music, a free being, a separation from all rule and school . . ." (*Geheimnis der Form*, II, 3).

66. See, for example, Siegmund Levarie, *Mozart's Le Nozze di Figaro: A Critical Analysis* (University of Chicago Press, 1952).

67. *Geheimnis der Form*, I, 19-21; II, 2.

68. See the conclusion of the chapter on Wagner in Adele T. Katz, *Challenge to Musical Tradition* (London, Putnam, 1945), pp. 246-47.

69. *Geheimnis der Form*, II, 177-79.

70. *Ibid.*, p. 179.

71. See *Romantische Harmonik und ihrer Krise in Wagners "Tristan"* (2d ed., Berlin, Max Hess, 1921), pp. 32, 76-77.

72. *Ibid.*, pp. 40-41.

73. *Ibid.*, pp. 305-13. Paul Hindemith concludes that in *Tristan* "beyond doubt, the diatonic was . . . replaced by the chromatic as the basis of all lines and chords" (*The Craft of Musical Composition*, Book I, tr. Arthur Mendel [New York, Associated Music Publishers, 1945], p. 49).

74. Joseph Machlis, *Introduction to Contemporary Music* (New York, Norton, 1961), p. 34.

75. *Tonality, Atonality, Pantonality: A Study of Some Trends in Twentieth Century Music* (New York, Macmillan, 1958), p. 21.

76. "The Origins of Schönberg's Twelve-Tone System," lecture delivered on January 10, 1957 (Washington, Library of Congress, 1958), p. 21. The author of *Doctor Faustus* was influenced by the atonalist view of Wagner: "This bold musical pioneer, who in *Tristan* stands with one foot already upon a-tonal ground—today he would probably be called a cultural Bolshevist!—this man of the people . . . whose dream of a theatre . . . was one set up to a classless community;

such a man no retrograde spirit can claim for its own; he belongs to that will which is directed toward the future." Mann, *Essays of Three Decades* (New York, Knopf, 1947), p. 352.

77. *Tonality, Atonality, Pantonality*, p. 13. It must be noted that Reti is not, in any strict sense of the word, an atonalist. Indeed, he is critical of much of the theory and practice of the atonal composers. He looks forward instead to a synthesis of tonality and atonality in a further development he calls Pantonality. But what is of interest for this study is his neat and classic description of the evolution of atonality from traditional harmony—the evolution in which *Tristan* is the turning point. For readers interested in Reti's synthesis of the two, his exposition has recently been republished under the less jingling title *Tonality in Modern Music* (New York, Collier Books, 1962).

78. *Ibid.*, p. 21.

79. *Bruckner, Mahler, Schoenberg*, p. 210.

80. "Musical Events: Schoenberg and After," in *The New Yorker*, March 18, 1961, pp. 164-65.

81. See Newlin, *Bruckner, Mahler, Schoenberg*, p. 210.

82. *Ibid.*

83. Edward Lockspeiser, "Schönberg, Nietzsche, and Debussy," in *The Listener*, LXV (no. 1667, March 9, 1961), 463.

84. "Wagner: Thoughts in Season," in *The Hudson Review*, XIII (no. 3, Autumn, 1960), 329-49.

85. *How to Become a Musical Critic*, p. 73.

86. *Bach*, I, 1.

87. The letter is quoted in Viereck, *Metapolitics* (New York, Knopf [reprinted, Capricorn Books, 1961]), p. 359.

88. Joseph Kerman, essay in *Hudson Review*, XIII, 330.

89. See Viereck, *Metapolitics;* Leon Stein, *The Racial Thinking of Richard Wagner* (New York, Philosophical Library, 1950); and for a recent summary of received ideas, William L. Shirer, *The Rise and Fall of the Third Reich* (New York, Simon and Schuster, 1960), pp. 101-3.

90. See Jacques Barzun, *Darwin, Marx, Wagner* (Garden City, New York, Doubleday [Anchor], 1958).

91. Essay in *Hudson Review*, XIII, 329.

92. *Opera as Drama* (New York, Knopf, 1956), pp. 192-93.

93. Marion Bauer, *Twentieth Century Music* (New York and London, Putnam's, 1933), p. 105. See also Donald Jay Grout, *A History of Western Music* (New York, Norton, 1960), p. 566; and Cecil Gray, *Survey of Contemporary Music* (London, Oxford University Press, 1927), pp. 112-13.

94. Gerald Abraham, *Hundred Years of Music*, p. 275.

95. Francis Toye, *Giuseppe Verdi* (New York, Random House [Vintage Books], 1959), p. 191.

96. *Romanticism and the Twentieth Century* (London, Rockliff, 1957), p. 160. See also the companion volume, *The Sonata Principle*.

97. Eric Bentley, *The Playwright as Thinker* (New York, Noonday Press [Meridian Books], 1957), pp. 87 ff.

98. Francis Fergusson, *The Idea of a Theater* (Princeton University Press, 1949), pp. 80-109.

99. Broadcast of February 13, 1960.

NOTES TO APPENDIX B: A NOTE ON SWINBURNE AND THE SEA

1. *Richard Wagner: A Cycle of Sonnets* (Chicago, Dial Press, 1907), p. 15.

2. The Sonnets are in the Italian form.

3. *Richard Wagner*, p. 3.

4. Such as *Knave of Hearts, 1894-1908* (New York and London, Heinemann, 1913).

5. *Vigil and Vision* (London, Villon Society, 1903).

6. *Intaglios: Sonnets* (London, Basil Montagu Pickering, 1871), p. 59. See Thomas Wright, *The Life of John Payne* (London, T. Fisher Unwin, 1919), p. 22.

7. William Payne, *Wagner*, p. 6.

8. Owen Meredith (Edward Robert Bulwer-Lytton) *Poems* (2 vols., Boston, Ticknor and Fields, 1866), Vol. I. See Max Moser, *Richard Wagner in der englischen Literatur des XIX Jahrhunderts* (Berne, Stämpfli, 1938), p. 25.

9. See Moser, *Wagner in englischen Literatur*, p. 55.

10. Quoted in Georges Lafourcade, *Swinburne: A Literary Biography* (London, Bell, 1932), p. 185. Lafourcade goes on to suggest that "there would indeed be, for a competent critic, an interesting parallel to attempt between the two masters who, about the same period, renovated music and poetry."

11. *Ibid.* My italics.

12. Letter of February 21, 1875, to E. C. Stedman, in *The Letters of Algernon Charles Swinburne*, ed. Edmund Gosse and Thomas James Wise (2 vols., New York, John Lane, 1919), I, 187.

13. In *Swinburne's Collected Poetical Works* (2 vols., London, Heinemann, 1927), II, 549-52.

14. *Ibid.*, p. 551.

15. *Ibid.*, pp. 551-52.

16. *Ibid.*, pp. 549-50.

17. *Selected Essays* (London, Faber and Faber, 1932), p. 324.

18. *The Playwright as Thinker* (New York, Noonday Press [Meridian Books], 1957), p. 88.

19. The quotations of Browning, Carlyle, and Arnold are from James Stephens, Edwin L. Beck and Royall H. Snow, eds., *Victorian and Later English Poets* (New York, American Book Co., 1934), p. 677.

NOTES TO APPENDIX C: A NOTE ON JOYCE AND ELIOT

1. *Ulysses* (New York, Random House [Modern Library], 1934), p. 567; and p. 547, for the reference in the footnote on page 186.

2. *Ibid*, pp. 252, 253.

3. *Finnegans Wake* (New York, Viking Press, 1947), p. 3.

4. See Adaline Glasheen, *A Census of Finnegans Wake* (Evanston, Illinois, Northwestern University Press, 1956).

5. *Finnegans Wake*, pp. 383-99.

6. Glasheen, *Census*, p. xxi; William York Tindall, *A Reader's Guide to James Joyce* (New York, Noonday Press, 1959), p. 287.

7. *Finnegans Wake*, pp. 383, 384.

8. *Ibid.*, p. 384.

9. *Ibid.*, p. 230.

10. Sec. III, ll. 202, 277-78, 290-91; and notes; in *Collected Poems, 1909-1935* (New York, Harcourt, Brace, 1936), pp. 79, 82, 83, 93.

11. Sec. I, ll. 31-42; *ibid.*, p. 70.

12. George Williamson, *A Reader's Guide to T. S. Eliot* (New York, Noonday Press, 1953), p. 132. Helen Gardner sees in the passage "the terror in the moment of ecstasy in love, when love passes beyond its object, and seems for a moment held in a kind of silence that seems outside time" (*The Art of T. S. Eliot* [New York, Dutton, 1950], p. 91).

13. See Grover Smith, Jr., *T. S. Eliot's Poetry and Plays* (University of Chicago Press, 1956), p. 76.

INDEX